HONOR:
THE LANGUAGE OF SONS

Restoring Heaven's Culture
of Value for God and All People

Christopher K. Turney

**COMPLETE WITH STUDY GUIDE
AFTER EACH CHAPTER**

Copyright Page

Honor: The Language of Sons
© 2025 Christopher K. Turney. All rights reserved.
Published by Kingdom Reign Ministries Publishing
Treasure Coast, Florida | Fort Wayne, Indiana

No part of this book may be reproduced, stored in a retrieval system, or transmitted in any form or by any means, electronic, mechanical, photocopying, recording, or otherwise, without prior written permission of the publisher, except for brief quotations used in reviews or educational materials.

Unless otherwise indicated, Scripture quotations are taken from the New King James Version® (NKJV). Copyright © 1982 by Thomas Nelson, Inc. Used by permission. All rights reserved.

ISBN: 979-8-218-94311-0
Printed in the United States of America.

DEDICATION

To every son and daughter learning Heaven's dialect, may your life speak fluently the language of honor.

To Jill, whose love exemplifies reverence, grace, and presence.

And to the sons and daughters of Kingdom Reign Ministries, who continually prove that honor is not a lesson to be taught but a culture to be lived.

ACKNOWLEDGMENTS

I honor the Father, who valued humanity enough to send His Son, and the Son, who valued the Father's will more than His own.

To the Holy Spirit, who is the living language of Heaven within us, thank You for teaching me the sound of honor.

Special gratitude to Bishop Gary and Pastor Lydia Clowers, whose example of humility and excellence showed me that Kingdom leadership begins and ends in honor.

To my parents, thank you for the love and support over all the years. I am so thankful for you!

To every leader, son, and daughter in the Kingdom Reign Ministries family, you are the living proof that a culture of value can transform lives, churches, and entire cities. Your pursuit of truth, your love for the Presence, and your hunger for the Kingdom make this message necessary.

And finally, to all who will read this book:

May the Spirit open your heart to see that honor isn't flattery or formality, it's the way Heaven breathes through humanity.

"Honor all men. Love the brotherhood. Fear God. Honor the king."
1 Peter 2:17 (KJV)

"Those who honor Me I will honor."
1 Samuel 2:30 (NKJV)

TABLE OF CONTENTS

Foreword 1
Preface 3
Introduction 5
   1. The Sound of Heaven's Culture 9
   2. The Language of Sons 21
   3. Honoring God: The Fountainhead of Value 33
   4. Honoring Authority: Receiving the Sent Ones 47
   5. Honor Among Men: The Culture of the Kingdom 65
   6. Honor in Adversity: Loving Those Who Wound You 83
   7. Honor vs. Respect: The Divine Distinction 101
   8. The Honor of Obedience: When Submission Becomes Strength 111
   9. Honor in Leadership: Serving from the Seat of Sonship 133
  10. The Ordered Life: The True Root of Honor 155
  11. Worth and the Gift: Why Honor Fueled the Cross 165
  12. The Honor of Unity: The Strength of One Sound 175
  13. Honoring Life Sources: The Wells That God Appoints . 197
  14. The Honor of Authority: Heaven's Government in Human Form 231
  15. The Honor of Correction: The Wisdom That Guards Growth 257
  16. The Honor of Glory: The Weight of Divine Recognition 281
  17. Honor: The Antidote to Shame and the Gateway to Glory 305

18. Honor: The Remedy for Global Chaos 313
19. Honor in Marriage, Family, and Generations
    Strengthening Covenant, Sustaining Legacy 321
Final Benediction of the Book Topic 335
Afterword 337
About the Author 339

FOREWORD

Once, maybe twice in your lifetime you will happen upon a literacy masterpiece on a particular subject. *"Honor The Language of Sons"* is one such time. I thought I knew about honor, until I read this book and realized just how much there was still to learn..!!

In Apostle Chris's opening chapter, he uses an interesting word, *"value."* This reiterates what we already know; that Honor is the currency of the Kingdom. He talks about honor in the environment of Heaven as being instinctive. Right from the onset this book he outlines the importance Kingdom places on Honor.

The constant thread of literacy excellence combined with wells of deep and profound revelation bring to life that Honor is a language born out of revelation from the Throne of Heaven. One of the many highlights for me in this book is Apostle Chris's use of the word, *"sound."* Bringing to mind that honor is sound, resonating within Kingdom people. Each chapter ends with a *"Review and Reflection"* section which makes this book not just a deeper revelation of Honor, but a powerful study guide that can be used by churches, cell groups and individuals. Littered with Scriptures underpinning Holy Spirit inspired insights these chapter reviews give you, the reader, the opportunity to reflect on your language of Honor and how you live this out in your everyday life and where Holy Spirit might be speaking to you.

Each chapter is a woven tapestry of life changing perspectives taking you on a journey of self-examination and deeper understanding of what the language of honor really means in a world full of disorder.

He writes books through his own personal lived experiences which are echoed through the pages of his books. *"Honor – The Language of Sons"* is one such book.

I have had the privilege to meet Apostle Chris and his beautiful wife Lady Jill and what I saw was profound. I saw and heard over the course of several days not just a lifestyle of honor but a life echoing the weightiness of honor. This is a man who KNOWS and understands the imperativeness of aligning our lives to the sound of honor. He exemplifies and embodies the true meaning of living the language of honor. His very presence carries the unmistakable fragrance and sound of honor.

"Honor gives love it's foundation" is another sentence that penetrated my Spirit deeply. Reinforcing the deeply insightful downloads The Holy Spirit has revealed to Apostle Chris through the pages of this book. I highly recommend this literacy masterpiece to everyone who is wanting a deeper understanding and revelation of how to embody the weightiness of honor in your lives.

Minister Lynn Hayter
Seeds For Wealth Ministries

PREFACE
THE LOST LANGUAGE OF HEAVEN

I did not set out to write another book on manners, leadership protocol, or cultural civility. Honor is not etiquette; it is essence. It is Heaven's original language, the dialect of a Kingdom where every being recognizes and values the divine in another. Before there was rebellion, there was reverence. Before there was sin, there was order. Before there was corruption, there was honor.

The language of Heaven was first broken when Lucifer ceased to value the One whose image he reflected. His dishonor fractured the symmetry of Heaven and infected creation with rebellion. From that moment forward, the language of Heaven was interrupted on earth. But when Christ, the express image of the Father, walked among men, He spoke the original dialect again. He honored the Father in all things, honored those who despised Him, and restored humanity's capacity to live from value instead of vanity.

We live in an age where dishonor is celebrated as authenticity and rebellion is packaged as independence. But honor is not submission to control; it is agreement with divine order. To honor is to recognize where God has chosen to dwell, in Himself, in His Word, and in His people.

Everywhere honor is missing, something dies, relationships wither, revelation dims, authority weakens, and worship becomes performance. But wherever honor is restored, life flows again.

This book is written for a generation that longs to see the culture of Heaven made visible on earth. It is for those who sense that something sacred has been lost, and that we cannot build Kingdom communities or steward divine presence without recovering it.

Honor is not flattery; it is not silence; it is not fear. Honor is appropriated value; it is to receive rightly what God has placed before you. It is the act of saying, "I see you; I value what Heaven has placed in you, and I make room for it."

When we speak honor, we echo Heaven's sound. And when sons learn that language again, earth will begin to sound like the Father's house.

INTRODUCTION
FATHER'S CRY FOR A GENERATION WITHOUT HONOR

I did not begin writing this book because I needed another title on a shelf or another project to complete. I began writing it because honor was dying in a generation that desperately needs fathers, alignment, and the culture of the Kingdom. I began writing it because I have lived on both sides of honor, its absence and its power, and because the Father has made me a witness to what happens when honor is restored in the lives of sons and daughters.

Honor became real to me long before I ever studied it. It became real in the places where I lacked it, where I longed for it, and where I learned its weight the hard way.

I grew up without the steady presence of a father, and when you grow up without honor being modeled in the home, you learn to survive without it. You learn to protect yourself. You learn to measure people quickly. You learn to stay guarded. You learn independence as a necessity, not a virtue. You learn to value strength over vulnerability, performance over identity.

And then you come into the Kingdom...and discover that none of those survival skills translate. Because sons cannot be raised in an atmosphere of self-protection. And the Kingdom cannot be built by men who only know how to honor conditionally.

When God brought a spiritual father into my life, I saw something I had never seen before, a man who valued me before I produced, who affirmed identity before assignment, who loved without demanding perfection, and who carried a language I had never heard spoken over me: honor.

It was Bishop Gary Clowers whose voice first struck the chord of fatherhood in my spirit. I didn't understand it then. I couldn't articulate it. But something in me came alive the moment honor touched what had been starved. God was not simply giving me a mentor, He was fathering a son.

From that moment forward, honor was no longer a sermon topic.
It became a lifeline.
It became a revelation.
It became a foundation.

I began to realize that honor is the environment where sons grow, and dishonor is the environment where orphans strive. Honor is the weight of Heaven. Honor is the language of the Father's house. Honor is the soil where identity takes root. Honor is the boundary that protects relationships and the currency that sustains spiritual family.

But honor is also the missing ingredient in most churches, ministries, families, and relationships today.

We have mistaken talent for maturity.
We have substituted gifting for formation.
We have built ministries that attract crowds but fail to raise sons.
We have celebrated influence while neglecting identity.
We have platformed charisma while ignoring character.
We have empowered the gifted while overlooking the dishonored.

And as a result, we have gathered people who know how to serve…but do not know how to honor. We have raised leaders who know how to do ministry…but do not know how to be sons.

This book is my attempt, by the grace of God, to help restore the culture of honor in the earth. Not the honor of empty compliments, false submission, or religious politeness. Not the honor that manipulates. Not the honor that flatters. But the honor of the Kingdom, the honor that recognizes the God-image in every person, the divine order God establishes, the spiritual lineage He assigns, and the identity He breathes into His sons and daughters.

It is the honor that Jesus lived, taught, and demonstrated.
It is the honor that builds families.
It is the honor that strengthens churches.
It is the honor that heals hearts.
It is the honor that reveals the Father.

Honor is not something we do; honor is something we become.
It is the language of sons.

This book was written with an ache in the heart of a father, a weight in the spirit of a son, and a mandate from the Holy Spirit to help heal a generation that has been fractured by dishonor. Every page carries the cry of the Father, the wisdom of Scripture, and the lessons I have learned through both wounds and wins, failures and victories, mistakes and mercy.

If you allow it, this book will:
- confront dishonor at its roots
- reorder your heart
- restore your identity
- realign your relationships
- and reshape the way you see people

It will help you step into the culture of Heaven and speak the language of sons.

Welcome to the journey.
Welcome to the restoration of honor.
Welcome home.

CHAPTER 1

THE SOUND OF HEAVEN'S CULTURE

Section 1 – The Sound of Heaven

Before there was spoken light, there was language. Before creation ever appeared, Heaven already had a sound. It was not noise, but harmony, not competition, but communion. In that realm, every being and every breath moved in rhythm with one eternal tone, honor.

When I think of Heaven, I do not first imagine golden streets or shining crowns. I hear something. I hear the endless echo of value flowing in every direction: the Father honoring the Son, the Son glorifying the Father, and the Spirit bearing witness of both. Around the throne the living creatures cry, "Holy, Holy, Holy," and the elders cast their crowns in response (Revelation 4). It is not ritual; it is reflex. In that place, honor is not taught, it is instinctive. Everything that lives, breathes, or burns in that atmosphere understands its source and gives it back.

That is why Heaven never grows old. There is no decay where there is perfect value. Glory is sustained because honor never stops circulating. The glory we long to see on earth is not a random outpouring, it is the sound of that same circulation restored.

The Circulation of Glory

In John 17:1–5, Jesus pulled back the veil and let us hear Heaven's dialogue. He prayed,

"Father, glorify Your Son, that the Son may glorify You… and now, O Father, glorify Me together with Yourself, with the glory which I had with You before the world was."

That is the sound of Heaven's culture: mutual glorification, value flowing back and forth between Father and Son. The Son does not demand glory; He reflects it. The Father does not withhold it; He shares it. That exchange is the pulse of eternity, the circulation of divine life.

Where honor circulates, life flows. Where honor ceases, death begins. Every created order mirrors this law: rivers die when they no longer give what they receive; hearts fail when they cease to circulate blood; relationships wither when value stops moving between them.

The Atmosphere That Sustains the Throne

Isaiah 6 describes the seraphim above the throne crying one to another, "Holy, holy, holy." Notice, they do not speak directly to God but to one another about Him. Even angels understand that honor must move horizontally as well as vertically. They magnify God by reminding each other of His worth. Heaven is sustained by that exchange; dishonor would be suffocation.

When I stood in Corinth at the ancient Bema and thought about Paul's words, "We must all appear before the judgment seat of Christ," I realized Heaven's court is not defined by punishment but by rightness. Everything there honors what is true. That atmosphere of rightness is glory's habitat.

Honor: Heaven's Gravity

Glory and honor are inseparable. Glory is the manifestation of value; honor is the recognition of it. Glory shows what something is worth; honor agrees with that worth. In Heaven, nothing rises above the throne because honor keeps everything rightly ordered. Honor is Heaven's gravity; it keeps glory from drifting into self-exaltation.

Lucifer's fall began when he tried to rise above the gravity of honor. He wanted light without reverence, position without posture. When he said, "I will ascend," he broke the circulation. Dishonor was the first sound of rebellion, and silence followed. Wherever dishonor enters, Heaven's sound stops.

Section 2 – The Silence of Dishonor and the Fracture in Creation

When Lucifer fell, Heaven lost no power, but something in creation lost its sound. The rebellion of one being interrupted the rhythm of honor that had always filled the cosmos. What was once a song became static.

I have often wondered what Heaven must have felt in that moment, the sudden absence of resonance, the void where worship used to rise. Dishonor is more than disobedience; it is dissonance. It introduces a note that does not belong, a vibration that contradicts the heart of God.

From that moment forward, the earth inherited the echo of that dissonance. Adam and Eve were created in perfect harmony, naked and unashamed, fully valued, fully honoring one another and their Maker. Yet when the serpent whispered, "Has God indeed said…?" he was not merely tempting them to sin; he was re-introducing dishonor. He questioned God's integrity, implying that the Creator was withholding something good. Doubt toward goodness is the first step toward dishonor, because you cannot truly honor what you no longer trust.

When Adam and Eve believed that lie, they broke the circulation of honor. Instead of reflecting God's image back to Him, they turned inward, hiding from the Presence that once clothed them. The moment honor was lost, glory departed. Their eyes were opened to see themselves apart from Him, and the sound of their steps in the garden changed. What had been harmony became hesitation.

Dishonor always produces distance. You cannot keep value flowing when you're covering yourself in shame. The world's first religion was not idol worship, it was self-covering. They tried to fix the loss of glory by sewing their own garments, but no human effort can replace the atmosphere of honor.

Dishonor in Nazareth: The Echo Continues

Centuries later, the same sound of dishonor surfaced again, this time in a synagogue in Nazareth. Mark 6 records that Jesus returned to His hometown, the very soil that had watched Him grow, and there the people said, "Is this not the carpenter, the son of Mary?" They acknowledged His existence but not His essence. Familiarity made them blind.

And Scripture says, "He could do no mighty work there." He did not lose power; they lost access. The door of Heaven was standing open, but dishonor closed it from their side.

I often pause on that phrase, He could not. The omnipotent Son of God restricted not by demons, not by Rome, but by dishonor. Heaven's sound was present, but no heart tuned to it. The same principle that sustained glory in Heaven was silenced on earth.

When you dishonor what God sends, you silence what Heaven speaks. The people of Nazareth heard words but missed the Word. They were in proximity to Presence yet lived as if nothing divine stood among them.

The Quiet Judgment

Dishonor's judgment is rarely thunder or fire; it is silence. God often responds to contempt by withdrawing conversation. There are seasons when the worst thing that can happen to a person or a church is that Heaven stops talking. When the voice that once stirred becomes faint, it is not always that God is absent, sometimes it is that dishonor has deafened the ear.

That silence hovered over four hundred years between Malachi and Matthew. Heaven did not run out of things to say; earth ran out of honor to hear them. Dishonor can turn the tuned ear away from the frequency of His voice. This is not absolute, there could be other causes for seasons of not hearing, but dishonor is a predominant one.

Yet even in silence, mercy was preparing a new sound. When the Word became flesh, Heaven's language walked among us again.

Section 3 – The Restoration of Heaven's Sound Through Christ

When the Word stepped into flesh, Heaven's frequency returned to earth. The sound that had been silenced in Eden began to vibrate again in the cries of an infant in Bethlehem. Angels heard it first; shepherds heard it next. They said, "Glory to God in the highest, and on earth peace, goodwill toward men." Glory, honor upward. Peace, honor outward. Goodwill, honor downward. In one announcement Heaven revealed its entire vocabulary: value moving in every direction.

Jesus did not merely preach honor; He embodied it. Everything He said and did restored the proper value of things. He honored the Father by doing nothing independently: "The Son can do nothing of Himself, but what He sees the Father do" (John 5:19). He honored humanity by entering its weakness without contempt. He honored creation itself by calming its storms instead of condemning them. Every miracle was an act of restoration, a moment when the earth remembered its original sound.

When He touched lepers, honor spoke louder than disease. When He dined with sinners, honor silenced accusation. When He washed the disciples' feet, honor re-ordered greatness. When He hung upon the cross, He honored the Father's will above His own. He restored value where shame had reigned, and that act became the new melody of creation.

The Cross: Honor's Highest Note

The crucifixion was not the loss of honor, it was its crescendo. The cross is Heaven's proof that honor never stops giving, even when dishonored. Jesus was spit upon, stripped, mocked, and pierced, yet He refused to return dishonor for dishonor. He said, "Father, forgive them." That was not resignation; it was revelation: the sound of Heaven cannot be silenced by cruelty. Love keeps singing.

In that moment the Son honored the Father, the Father honored the Son, and the Spirit bore witness in the earth through signs and trembling ground. The curtain in the temple tore from top to bottom because honor had opened the door again. For the first time since Eden, humanity could hear Heaven without a veil.

The resurrection was Heaven answering honor with honor. The Father glorified the Son because the Son had glorified the Father. When Jesus walked out of the tomb, He carried more than victory, He carried the atmosphere of Heaven back into human form. Every encounter after the resurrection dripped with that atmosphere. He breathed on the disciples and said, "Receive the Holy Spirit." That breath was the reintroduction of Heaven's tone into human lungs.

The Spirit: Heaven's Sound Within

When the Holy Spirit descended at Pentecost, the language of honor filled a room and then a city. The disciples began speaking with tongues, but the greater miracle was not linguistic, it was relational. "They were all with one accord in one place." Honor had unified hearts before it ever inspired words. That is why the wind came, why fire sat upon each of them: Heaven had found an echo.

The Spirit is the voice of honor inside us. He teaches us how to value rightly, how to call holy what the Father calls holy, how to love what He loves, how to receive who He sends. Every prompting of the Spirit is an invitation to continue Heaven's sound on earth.

Restored Circulation

When honor flows again, glory returns. The Church was born not in strategy but in shared esteem. They "continued steadfastly in the apostles' doctrine and fellowship, in the breaking of bread, and in prayers." Each of those actions was an expression of value, toward God, toward leaders, and toward one another. The result? "And great grace was upon them all." Grace is Heaven's response to honor.

Every revival, every outpouring, every fresh move of God begins when people start valuing His presence more than their preference. The sound of Heaven is not thunder or hype; it is the quiet hum of value moving freely among hearts that revere God and regard one another.

Section 4 – Sons Who Carry the Sound

When the Spirit came, the sound of Heaven was no longer confined to a throne room or an upper room. It entered people. Every son and daughter reborn by the Spirit became an instrument of that same harmony. The atmosphere that once surrounded the throne now abides within hearts. We are living temples resonating with the frequency of honor.

The Father's design has never changed: Heaven would fill the earth by filling His sons. What was once sung by angels is now lived by believers. The phrase "on earth as it is in heaven" is not a poetic wish, it is a mandate for manifestation. When honor flows through sons, Heaven is heard again in human tone.

Honor as Expression, Not Effort

To carry the sound does not mean to perform perfection; it means to live aware of value.

When I honor God, I keep His worth before my eyes. When I honor people, I keep His image before my heart. When I honor myself, I keep His workmanship before my conscience.

This is not exhausting obedience; it is effortless resonance. The same way a tuned string vibrates when a matching note is played, a son's spirit vibrates when the Father's tone is near. That is what walking in the Spirit feels like, life moving in sync with Heaven's rhythm.

Honor in Daily Life

Heaven's sound is not confined to pulpits or worship gatherings; it hums through ordinary moments. It speaks when you greet someone with dignity, when you listen without interrupting, when you refuse gossip because you see image where others see imperfection. Every time you treat another as valuable, you amplify Heaven's music in the earth.

A culture of honor begins privately before it becomes public. It begins when you stop speaking harshly about yourself, when you treat your own soul as a temple of God. It deepens when you celebrate another's success as though it were your own, because in the Kingdom, it is. It matures when you can disagree without dishonoring, correct without condemning, lead without lording.

Honor is not weakness; it is weight.

It takes more strength to value someone than to judge them, more courage to bless than to belittle. Every time we choose value over vengeance, we keep Heaven's sound pure.

Heaven's Tone Through Earthly Voices

Creation still groans, waiting for the manifestation of sons (Romans 8:19).

What is creation waiting to hear? The same sound it heard at the beginning, honor. The trees, the tides, and the nations are listening for a people who will mirror the Father's heart again. When we honor rightly, even the natural world responds, peace replaces chaos, order replaces confusion, and glory fills the air.

I believe the final revival will not be defined by louder worship or larger crowds but by a deeper culture of honor, a people who make room for God and for one another until Heaven's language becomes humanity's lifestyle.

The Call

The Lord is calling us to become translators of that language. Heaven has spoken; will the earth echo? Every son who learns to value presence, people, and purpose becomes a conduit through which Heaven's sound travels.

You are that conduit.
You are a carrier of the culture.

Let your life become the reverberation of the throne, wherever you go, let the atmosphere shift because honor walked in.

When sons speak this way, the world begins to remember the melody it has forgotten.

And one day, when every tongue confesses and every knee bows, the sound of Heaven will cover the earth again, not as noise, but as honor restored.

Chapter 1 Review & Reflection
The Sound of Heaven's Culture

Core Revelation

Honor is the atmosphere of Heaven, the circulation of value that sustains glory. In the throne room, glory is not achieved by performance but maintained by mutual esteem. The Father glorifies the Son, the Son honors the Father, and the Spirit bears witness of both. When that circulation stopped in Lucifer's rebellion, the sound of Heaven was silenced on earth. When Christ came, the sound returned, Heaven once again found expression in human form.

Kingdom Principle

Where honor flows, Heaven follows. Glory is the manifestation of value; honor is the recognition of it. To restore honor on earth is to reintroduce Heaven's culture to creation.

Scripture Focus

- Revelation 4–5 – Worship as Heaven's natural reflex.
- Isaiah 6 – The seraphim cry "Holy" one to another: horizontal honor sustains vertical glory.
- John 17:1–5 – Mutual glorification within the Godhead.
- Mark 6:1–6 – Jesus "could do no mighty work" in Nazareth; dishonor closes Heaven's door.
- Acts 2:1–4 – Unity and value created the environment for the Spirit's sound.

Truths to Remember

1. Honor is Heaven's gravity. It keeps glory from drifting into self-exaltation.

2. Dishonor produces silence. Heaven stops speaking where it is not valued.
3. The cross is the crescendo of honor. Jesus honored the Father's will above His pain.
4. The Spirit restores Heaven's tone within us. Pentecost was Heaven finding an echo in humanity.
5. Sons are instruments of harmony. Every act of value amplifies Heaven's sound on earth.

Application

- Speak honor into your ordinary spaces. Value people as image-bearers, not as inconveniences.
- Guard your language, complaint and gossip are dissonance in Heaven's symphony.
- Let worship become reflex, not ritual. Where God is valued, His presence rests.
- When correction or authority feels uncomfortable, honor the order rather than resist it.
- In moments of silence, listen, Heaven is tuning hearts before releasing new sound.

Reflection Questions

1. Where in my life has dishonor silenced God's voice?
2. How can I re-establish circulation of value in my relationships?
3. What practical actions communicate value to God, to leaders, to peers, and to the "least"?
4. Am I willing to become a carrier of Heaven's sound even if no one else around me speaks its language?

Declaration

"Father, let my heart be tuned to Your tone. Where dishonor once deafened me, restore my hearing. Let honor flow through me like

breath in word, in action, and in attitude. Make me a living echo of Heaven's culture on earth."

CHAPTER 2
THE LANGUAGE OF SONS

Section 1 – The Voice of Belonging

When I was a boy, I learned to speak by imitation. I watched my parents' mouths form words, I listened to their tone, and my tongue slowly learned to echo theirs. That is how every child learns language, by exposure to belonging. The same is true in the Spirit. Sons learn Heaven's language by being near the Father.

Servants learn commands, but sons learn conversation. Servants memorize what to say; sons absorb how the Father sounds. They carry His inflection, His compassion, His timing, His restraint. That is why Jesus said, *"My sheep hear My voice."* He didn't mean they recognize a sound; He meant they understand a tone.

Heaven's tone is honor.

Identity Determines Vocabulary

The way you see yourself decides how you speak. If you believe you are a servant trying to earn approval, your words will be filled with striving, apology, and fear. But when you know you are a son already accepted, your words carry assurance, peace, and value. Honor becomes effortless when identity is settled.

Jesus never apologized for His relationship with the Father. He said, *"I and the Father are one."* He spoke from sonship, not for it. When He addressed the Father, there was no distance in His tone, only delight. That is why demons obeyed Him and storms responded: creation recognizes the sound of belonging.

Language of the Heart

Every language is more than words; it carries the heart of the speaker. Heaven's language cannot be learned academically, it must be caught relationally. When the heart is healed of orphan thinking, honor flows without effort.

The orphan speaks suspicion; the son speaks security. The orphan withholds value; the son releases it. Honor is not what the **son does** to please the Father; it is what the **son is** because of the Father.

I've watched believers struggle to speak honor because they still feel disconnected. They mimic the vocabulary of the Kingdom without the heart of sonship, so their words sound right but ring hollow. True honor is not learned by repetition; it's born from revelation, I belong to Him, therefore I reflect Him.

The Father's Affirmation

Before Jesus performed one miracle, He heard the Father say, *"This is My beloved Son, in whom I am well pleased."* That affirmation became His language base. He healed the sick, taught the multitudes, and faced the cross all from the security of that sentence. When you know you are already beloved, you no longer need to speak from insecurity or demand validation. Honor flows because you have been honored by God Himself.

Many try to produce honor as a discipline, but Heaven produces it through delight. When the Father's pleasure becomes your atmosphere, your words change. You stop competing, comparing, and correcting others to prove yourself. Instead, you start valuing what God values. That is the language of sons.

Learning by Listening

Jesus said, *"The words that I speak to you are spirit and life."* When we listen to Him, we are being re-taught the vocabulary of Heaven. Prayer is not primarily about presenting requests; it is about exposure to sound. Every moment in His presence retrains your tone. You begin to think in honor, to react in peace, to speak with weight. The more you listen, the less you strive to sound spiritual, because His voice becomes yours.

Section Transition

Honor doesn't begin in the mouth; it begins in the mirror. You cannot speak like a son while thinking like a servant. Before honor becomes a language to others, it must become your internal dialogue with God and yourself.

Section 2 – The Mirror of Sonship: Seeing What the Father Sees

When you stand before a mirror, the image you see determines how you present yourself. You fix what you see wrong, you smile when you like what reflects. But in the Spirit, the mirror works differently. You don't see your own flaws; you see the Father's likeness staring back. Honor begins the moment you agree with that reflection.

Paul said, *"We all, with unveiled face, beholding as in a mirror the glory of the Lord, are being transformed into the same image"* (2 Corinthians 3:18). The more clearly you see Him, the more accurately you see yourself. And the more you value what you see, the more you reflect it. This is why the enemy's first assignment is to distort the mirror, to convince sons that they are servants, sinners, or strangers. Dishonor begins in the mirror. If he can make you despise yourself, he can make you dishonor everything around you.

The Orphan's Mirror

The orphan looks into the mirror and sees absence. He defines himself by what he lacks, approval, position, or success. So, he speaks from insecurity and reacts from fear. Every correction feels like rejection. Every delay feels like punishment. The orphan cannot speak honor because he lives in survival mode; his words defend what he doesn't believe he already has.

That's why Heaven's first work in restoration is not instruction but revelation. God doesn't start by telling us what to do; He starts by showing us who we are. He told Gideon, *"You mighty man of valor,"* while Gideon was hiding in a winepress. He called Abraham the father of many nations while the man had no son.

"He identified David as a man after His own heart while David was still a boy, likely twelve to fifteen years old, unseen by men but already known by God."

God's language always honors **potential** before **performance**. He speaks to essence, not evidence. Potential is the God-given **potency** embedded within a life before performance ever reveals it.

The Son's Mirror

The son, however, looks into the mirror and sees abundance. He recognizes grace where others see guilt. He sees inheritance where others see insufficiency. He doesn't have to inflate himself, because his reflection already carries glory. Honor flows naturally from that awareness: I am valued; therefore I value.

Every time I look into the mirror of His Word and see His image forming in me, my heart grows quieter. I stop striving for significance and start reflecting significance. Honor becomes instinctive, like breathing. I no longer respond to people based on how they treat me; I respond based on how He sees them.

Agreement Produces Reflection

To speak Heaven's language, you must agree with Heaven's view. When you call yourself, what God calls you, you give Heaven permission to echo through you. When you contradict His view, when you call unclean what He calls holy, you interrupt the reflection.

The Father is not glorified when His children shrink in shame. He is glorified when they shine with likeness. Jesus said, *"By this My Father is glorified, that you bear much fruit."* Fruitfulness is reflection, it proves that the seed took root. Sons honor the Father by becoming living mirrors of His nature.

Healing the Mirror

If the mirror has been cracked by shame or clouded by condemnation, the Spirit is a gentle restorer. He doesn't replace you; He polishes you. The longer you stay in His presence, the clearer you see. Revelation isn't lightning; it's polishing. Every layer of guilt removed is another layer of glory revealed. And when the mirror clears, your language changes. You begin to speak to others from clarity, not distortion.

That's why worship is essential to honor, it cleans the mirror. You can't keep bitterness and behold beauty at the same time. As you exalt Him, your reflection resets, and you begin to sound like where you came from, Heaven.

Section Transition

To speak the language of sons, you must first see as sons. Once you know how the Father sees you, you can begin to see, and honor, what He sees in others. The next section unfolds how sons extend that vision outward, creating a culture where honor becomes contagious.

Section 3 – The Culture of Communication: How Sons Speak to Heaven and to One Another

Language is never neutral. Every word carries an atmosphere. When sons speak, they are not merely transferring information, they are releasing environment. That is why Jesus said, *"The words that I speak to you are spirit and life."* Each syllable carried the fragrance of the Father's heart.

When Heaven hears a son speak, it recognizes its own accent. It sounds like peace. It smells like grace. It feels like rest. The sons of God are translators of that tone in a world that only knows accusation.

Speaking to Heaven

Prayer is not about volume; it is about value. Servants petition for permission, but sons commune from position. When I pray, I am not trying to convince God; I am aligning with Him. Honor in prayer means I approach His presence with awareness, not anxiety. I do not rush in with noise; I enter with recognition: You are holy, and yet You call me son.

Honor filled prayer sounds less like begging and more like breathing. It begins with thanksgiving, moves through trust, and ends in rest. When you pray from that place, Heaven hears harmony, not desperation. That's why Jesus taught, *"Our Father in heaven, hallowed be Your name."* Before any request, He established relationship and reverence, the twin notes of Heaven's language.

Speaking to One Another

The first evidence that a heart has been fathered by God is the way it speaks to people. Paul wrote, *"Let your speech always be with grace, seasoned with salt."* Grace gives life, salt preserves value. Every conversation becomes an opportunity to practice Heaven's culture.

Honor in conversation means I treat people's hearts as holy ground. I measure my words not by how clever they sound but by how much life they leave behind. If my words wound needlessly, I have forgotten whose image I'm addressing.

This is why gossip is more dangerous than most realize, it is linguistic dishonor. It trains our mouths to devalue what Heaven treasures. When I speak lightly of someone God died for, I fracture the language of sons. The Kingdom cannot flow through a mouth that curses its own family.

Tone Matters

Sons not only speak truth; they carry tone. Heaven's tone is gentle yet firm, strong yet safe. Jesus could rebuke a storm and cradle a child with the same voice because His tone never left the frequency of honor. You can say the right thing in the wrong tone and lose Heaven's sound. Honor guards' tone, it keeps truth from turning into arrogance and correction from turning into control.

Before I speak, I often ask, does this sentence carry the weight of value or the sting of ego? That question realigns my heart with Heaven's dialect.

Mutual Edification

Paul wrote, *"Let no corrupt communication proceed out of your mouth, but only that which is good for edifying, that it may impart grace to the hearers."* Edify means to build. When sons talk, walls go up, not between people, but around them, structures of safety, belonging, and dignity. That is the architecture of honor.

The early Church spoke that way. They encouraged one another daily. They confessed, they prayed, they sang psalms together. Their words-built community where systems could not. The Holy Spirit still longs to construct such spaces through the tongues of sons.

Listening as Language

Honor also listens. Silence is not absence of speech; it is space for another's value. When I listen with attention, I am saying, You matter enough for me to pause. The Father listens this way. He hears before He answers. To mirror Him, we must learn to value presence over performance in every conversation.

Section Transition

When sons speak this way, to Heaven in reverence, to one another in grace, they form a living echo of divine communion. Their community begins to sound like the Trinity itself: mutual deference, shared delight, unbroken flow.

In the next section we'll explore how that sound becomes governance, how sons steward authority through honor rather than control.

Section 4 – The Government of Honor: Authority Expressed Through Likeness

Every kingdom has a government, but not every government carries glory. Earthly systems rule by position and power; Heaven governs by likeness. In the Kingdom of God, authority does not descend from office, it flows from image. Whoever most resembles the Father carries the greatest weight. That resemblance is measured not by miracles or eloquence but by honor.

Jesus never forced allegiance; He revealed likeness. His authority was magnetic because it was familiar. When He spoke, Heaven recognized itself in His tone. The demonic realm yielded because it heard its Creator's sound in human flesh. His government was honor embodied.

Authority Without Control

When you understand that honor is Heaven's government, you stop trying to control people. Control is counterfeit authority. It uses fear to create compliance. Honor uses love to cultivate agreement. Control silences voices; honor tunes them. Control protects ego; honor protects order.

The centurion understood this. He said, *"I also am a man under authority."* His revelation was not about rank, it was about flow. He knew that real authority is the right to represent, not the power to dominate. That's why Jesus marveled: He heard Heaven's government in the centurion's language. Faith and honor spoke the same sentence.

Likeness Releases Authority

Genesis reveals that dominion was given to man because he was made in the image of God. Image precedes influence. The more we look like Him, the more creation listens. That is why sons must never chase authority; they must chase likeness. Honor is the practice that preserves that likeness, it keeps the heart aligned with the Father's posture.

When you carry honor, you don't have to announce authority. It becomes visible. The way you handle people, the way you speak truth, the way you steward presence, all testify that Heaven trusts you. Authority is not taken; it's recognized. Honor makes it recognizable.

Governed by the Spirit

The Holy Spirit is Heaven's governor within us. His task is not to coerce but to conform. He governs by reminding, convicting, and empowering, never by shaming. His government feels like invitation. When we yield to that inward government, we manifest outward order.

That's why Paul wrote, *"The Kingdom of God is righteousness, peace, and joy in the Holy Spirit."* Righteousness, things in right order. Peace, no competition of wills. Joy, the delight of harmony. This is government by honor: every heart voluntarily aligned with divine rhythm.

The Weight of Representation

Honor makes you safe to represent the King. To represent means to re-present, to present again. God re-presents Himself through sons who mirror His nature. When people meet you, they should sense the same safety, truth, and value that mark His throne. That is Kingdom government in human form.

Leadership in the Body of Christ is not about how many follow you but how much Heaven follows your words. Heaven follows honor. The Spirit endorses those whose hearts carry the Father's weight. True government is not established by charisma but by character that refuses to dishonor God or people for personal gain.

From Rule to Reign

When sons walk in honor, they don't just manage environments, they reign in them. Reigning is rule through rest. It is the effortless influence of one who knows he is trusted by Heaven. Romans 5:17 says, *"Those who receive abundance of grace and of the gift of righteousness will reign in life."* Notice, it begins with receiving, not striving. Grace is Heaven's authorization, and honor is its administration.

Wherever dishonor is tolerated, chaos multiplies; wherever honor is practiced, government emerges. Families stabilize, churches mature, regions awaken. The sound of Heaven's government is not a gavel, it is harmony.

Section Transition

The language of sons is the language of government, honor in word, posture, and tone that re-presents the Father's rule. In the next chapter we will look upward to the fountainhead of all honor, God Himself, and see how honoring Him restores every other alignment.

Chapter 2 Review & Reflection

The Language of Sons

Core Revelation

Honor is the native language of sonship. Sons don't imitate Heaven's speech, they echo it. The more we behold the Father, the more our vocabulary changes. Servants repeat commands; sons reproduce conversation. The Father's affirmation, *"This is My beloved Son"*, is the sound every believer must learn to live from. Once you know you are valued, you begin to value everything He values.

Kingdom Principle

Identity determines expression. What you believe about who you are shapes how you speak and how you treat others. The language of sons flows from likeness, not labor.

Scripture Focus

- 2 Corinthians 3:18 – We behold and reflect the Lord's glory.
- Matthew 3:17 – The Father's voice of affirmation establishes identity.
- Ephesians 4:29 – Words that edify impart grace.
- Matthew 8:9–10 – The centurion reveals Heaven's government through honor.
- Romans 5:17 – Those who receive grace reign in life.

Truths to Remember

1. Sons speak from belonging, not for it.
2. The orphan's mirror distorts; the son's mirror reflects.
3. Honor in speech builds environments where Heaven feels at home.

4. Tone carries authority, truth without honor becomes tyranny.
5. Heaven's government is likeness: control fails, character reigns.

Application

- Spend time daily listening before speaking; let your words be tuned by His presence.
- Replace self-criticism with gratitude, speak to yourself the way the Father speaks to you.
- Practice honor in ordinary conversations: pause, listen, affirm value.
- When leading or correcting, ask whether your tone protects dignity as well as truth.
- Seek likeness over leverage; authority flows through resemblance, not rank.

Reflection Questions

1. How does my inner dialogue reflect my belief about being a son or servant?
2. Where have I allowed orphan thinking to shape my tone toward others?
3. What practical changes in my communication can make my home or ministry sound more like Heaven?
4. Am I governing by control or by honor? How would those I lead describe the difference?

Declaration

"Father, thank You for calling me Your child. Tune my voice to match Yours, gentle, truthful, full of grace. Heal every distortion in the mirror of my heart, and let my words build what You love. Through my life, may the language of Heaven be heard again on earth."

CHAPTER 3
HONORING GOD: THE FOUNTAINHEAD OF VALUE

Section 1 – Where All Honor Begins

Every river begins somewhere. However wide it becomes, however far it runs, it has a single spring where the first drop rises. Honor is the same. Every stream that touches people, leaders, or nations finds its source in one fountain, the way we value God.

If honor toward Him dries up, every other relationship eventually becomes a desert. You may still have order, rules, even respect, but the living flow of worship disappears. When a generation forgets how to honor God, they will inevitably misuse everything that carries His image.

The first words of Scripture already carry this sound: *"In the beginning, God."* That statement alone is a posture. It places Him first, not merely chronologically but pre-eminently. Honor starts there: putting Him first in thought, affection, and intention.

The Posture of Reverence

When Isaiah saw the Lord high and lifted up, he didn't begin with questions, he began with awe. Honor opens with awareness. Reverence is not fear of punishment; it is the stillness that comes when presence fills perception.

I have learned that when you truly sense His nearness, explanations shrink, and worship expands. Your heart bows even if your knees don't. Reverence is not ceremony; it's alignment. Everything in you recognizes, You are the Source, and I am sustained.

The Hebrew word for *"glory,"* kabod, means weight. The more weight you give Him, the more your world finds balance. Dishonor, by contrast, is lightness, treating what is holy as common, what is eternal as optional. When the ark of God was mishandled in Israel, it wasn't ignorance that killed Uzzah, it was casualness. Heaven's government runs on reverence.

Worship as Value Returned

Worship is not entertainment; it is valuation. To worship is to return value to its Source. Every raised hand, every whispered *"holy,"* is a declaration: You are worth everything.

Cain and Abel illustrate the difference. Abel offered the first and the best; Cain offered leftovers. The Father was not counting sheep and vegetables, He was reading value. Abel honored God; Cain honored convenience. Only one offering still speaks.

Whenever I give, whether time, attention, or treasure, I am placing worth on someone. Worship simply directs that worth correctly. When I worship, I am saying, "God, You deserve the weight of my focus." And the astonishing thing is that the more value I return to Him, the more value He reveals in me. That is the circulation of glory restored.

The Heart of the First Commandment

Jesus summarized all law and prophecy in a single statement: *"You shall love the Lord your God with all your heart, soul, mind, and strength."* That is not obligation; it is orientation. The heart governs affection, the soul governs identity, the mind governs perspective, and strength governs action. To love Him with all means that no part of life operates independently of value for Him.

When we fragment love, Sunday affection without weekday awareness, we lose continuity. Honor unifies. It gathers every faculty of life and directs them toward the Source. That is why the command to love God precedes the command to love neighbor: only a heart filled with divine value can distribute it properly to others.

The Weight of His Name

Honor for God begins with honor for His name. In Scripture, His name is more than a label; it is His nature revealed. To take His name *"in vain"* is not only profanity, but also to carry it without weight. Every time I represent Him lightly, every time I attach His name to my ambition, I am misusing the name that carries the universe.

That realization doesn't condemn me; it humbles me. It reminds me that the name I bear as Christian, *"little Christ"*, is holy ground. My speech, conduct, and attitude all speak that name. To honor it is to ensure that what I express matches who He is.

"To honor it is to ensure that what I express matches who He is."

The Weight of His Name in Prayer

We often attach God's name to our prayers as though adding *"in Jesus' name"* obligates Heaven to respond. But Jesus never instructed us to pray **using** His name, He said to pray **in** His name (John 14:13–14; 16:23–24). To pray using His name is to add it as a closing signature. To pray in His name is to enter the prayer as if we were Christ Himself, carrying His nature, His posture, and His alignment.

This is beautifully illustrated in the story of Jacob. He desired the blessing that belonged to the firstborn (Esau), just as we often desire what is reserved for the Son. Knowing he could not approach in his own name, Jacob clothed himself in Esau's garments. Isaac said, *"The voice is Jacob's voice, but the hands are the hands of Esau"* (Genesis 27:22). He was speaking like himself but feeling like his elder brother.

So it is when we pray in Christ's name, we may speak with our human voice, but we approach the Father clothed in the identity of the Firstborn Son. To honor His name is to **pray from His nature**, not merely mention His title. It is to stand before the Father as if we are Jesus, fully aligned with His will and character.

To misuse His name is to carry it lightly. To pray in His name is to carry His nature faithfully.

This changes how I pray, not as someone trying to convince Heaven, but as someone seated with Christ (Ephesians 2:6), agreeing with Heaven.

Section Transition

Every form of honor originates here: the recognition of God's unmatched worth. Until He is rightly valued, everything else we value becomes distorted. In the next section we'll look at how this vertical honor, our reverence and worship, reorders every other part of life, restoring divine alignment and releasing Heaven's flow through us.

Section 2 – The Alignment of Honor: How Valuing God Reorders Life

Honor is Heaven's compass. When it points true north, toward God, everything else in life aligns itself. But when that compass is ignored, direction becomes confusion and priorities lose gravity.

I have learned that dishonor toward God does not begin with rebellion; it begins with replacement. It's when something else quietly receives the attention, trust, or dependence that only He deserves. It can be success, ministry, even family, good things made ultimate things. Whatever you honor most becomes your authority. That is why idolatry always precedes instability.

Honor Restores Order

When I place God first, chaos loses jurisdiction. It's not that problems vanish; it's that they bow to hierarchy. The moment I return value to Him, I re-establish the flow of grace that was always meant to govern me. Peace is simply the by-product of right order.

David understood this. When the ark, the symbol of presence, was returned to its rightful place in Jerusalem, the nation stabilized. His throne prospered because God's throne was prioritized. The pattern has never changed: where God is valued, government is sound.

Honor is Heaven's architecture; it builds structure around blessing. Without it, even miracles become unsustainable. Israel saw wonders in the wilderness but died there because they honored what God did without honoring who He was. They loved provision but questioned Presence. That imbalance still breaks flow today.

Time, Treasure, and Thought

Three areas continually reveal alignment:
1. **Time** – Whatever owns my schedule owns my worship. When I give God my first attention, the rest of my day becomes ordered around peace instead of panic. Honor redeems time because it brings rhythm back to purpose.
2. **Treasure** – Giving is not fundraising; it's firstfruits. Every seed declares, You are my Source. When I tithe, sow, or bless others, I am not losing resources; I'm keeping resources within the current of honor. Money multiplies where value is right.
3. **Thought** – Paul wrote, *"Whatever things are true, noble, just, pure... think on these things."* Our thought life is an altar. What we meditate on reveals what we magnify. Honor begins in imagination, seeing God as larger than the problem, heavier than the distraction.

When these three align, the rest of life harmonizes around them like instruments tuned to the same key.

The Gravity of the Throne

John saw a throne set in Heaven and One seated upon it (Revelation 4). The throne is not a piece of furniture, it's the axis of reality. Everything orbits the weight of that seat. When I honor God, I consciously return to that orbit. My will, emotions, and ambitions stop colliding; they start revolving around Him. That is what Scripture calls righteousness, right alignment under rightful authority.

Dishonor throws life out of orbit. When I attempt to center the universe around myself, relationships become strained, purpose becomes scattered, and peace becomes impossible. But one moment of sincere worship re-centers everything. A bowed heart recalibrates an entire life.

The Flow of Grace

Honor not only reorders life; it reopens channels of grace. Peter wrote, *"God resists the proud but gives grace to the humble."* Pride is self-exaltation, an attempt to make self the source. Humility is God-honor, an admission that He is. Grace flows wherever humility builds a path. If you feel grace missing in a season, examine honor. Where He is rightly valued, favor follows naturally.

Living in Continuous Alignment

Alignment is not a single act but a lifestyle of adjustment. Planes stay airborne by constant correction; the same is true for sons. Every day the Spirit whispers, *"Re-center here. Shift your gaze."* Those gentle corrections are grace at work, Heaven ensuring that the compass keeps pointing home.

When I awaken each morning and whisper, *"Good morning, Father,"* I am not performing ritual; I am acknowledging the Fountain again. That single act of value draws order into my day. Honor keeps Heaven's gravity intact.

Section Transition

When the Fountainhead is honored, every tributary carries life. That is why the next movement of this chapter will explore how honor becomes obedience, not as duty but as delight, how valuing God's will becomes the joy of sons who trust His heart.

Section 3 – Obedience as Delight: When Honor and Will Become One

Obedience was never meant to feel like slavery; it was meant to feel like synchronization. When honor fills the heart, the will and the Word move in rhythm. You no longer obey to earn favor; you obey because you agree with love.

Every parent knows the difference between a child who obeys out of fear and one who obeys out of trust. Fear produces momentary compliance; love produces continuous cooperation. Heaven has always desired the second kind. That is why Jesus said, *"If you love Me, keep My commandments."* Love is the engine, obedience the echo.

From Command to Communion

In Eden, obedience was not a test; it was communion. The boundary God gave, *"Don't eat of that tree"*, was an invitation to trust His wisdom above their own. Honor made that boundary holy. The moment they questioned His goodness, obedience turned to obligation, and the flow broke.

When Jesus came, He redefined obedience as fellowship. He said, *"I always do those things that please the Father."* That statement doesn't describe restriction; it describes rhythm. The Son delighted in the Father's will because He trusted the Father's heart. The greatest evidence of honor is not blind submission but willing alignment.

The Joy of Agreement

Psalm 40 records a prophetic whisper of the Messiah:

"I delight to do Your will, O my God, and Your law is within my heart."

Delight is the **sound of honor perfected**. It is the moment when commands become conversation, when you stop asking, *"How much do I have to do?"* and start asking, *"How much can I give?"*

I've discovered that the more I honor God, the more His desires feel like my own. His preferences become my pleasure. That is not brainwashing; it is bonding. The Spirit writes His nature on our hearts until obedience feels natural and rebellion feels foreign. Heaven calls that maturity.

Obedience Reveals Value

To honor is to assign worth, and nothing reveals worth like what you obey. Every choice is an altar. When I obey His prompting at personal cost, I declare that He is worth more than comfort. When I forgive instead of retaliating, I am saying His peace is worth more than my pride.

Jesus' obedience unto death is the clearest mirror of divine value: the Son valued the Father's purpose above His own preservation. And because of that, *"God highly exalted Him."* Honor always returns honor. When I submit my will to His, I am not losing myself; I am finding my true self. The surrendered life is not smaller, it is centered.

Obedience and Timing

True obedience also honors when God speaks, not just what He says. Saul lost his kingdom not because he ignored instruction but because he hurried it. Partial timing is partial trust. Honor waits even when understanding lags. Waiting is worship in slow motion.

I have learned that God's instructions are never random; they are relational. When He says *"wait,"* He is guarding me. When He says *"move,"* He is trusting me. Either way, honor keeps the conversation open.

Obedience as Worship

Worship that ignores obedience is flattery. The song must eventually become surrender. Abraham proved this when he raised the knife over Isaac; the angel called his act worship. He wasn't singing, he was yielding. Honor hears God's voice and responds, even when the request cuts close to the heart, because it believes resurrection is hiding on the other side.

Every yes refines your capacity for glory. Each time you obey, you widen the channel through which His presence flows. The obedient heart becomes Heaven's favorite habitat.

Section Transition

When honor and will become one, the believer no longer fights God's directions; he flows with them. That flow is what gives life its melody, obedience as harmony, not burden.

The next section will show how this vertical honor, loving and obeying God, translates into tangible acts of worship that shape environments, not just moments.

Section 4 – Worship as Atmosphere: Building Habitations for His Honor

Every heart builds a house for what it values most. Some erect monuments to memory, some sanctuaries to fear, others, palaces to ambition. Worship is simply the construction of atmosphere around affection. When we honor God, we begin to host Him, not just acknowledge Him.

David wrote, *"You are holy, You who inhabit the praises of Israel."* Inhabitation requires environment. Praise becomes timber; gratitude becomes foundation; obedience becomes roof. Together they create a dwelling where the Presence finds rest.

From Visitations to Habitations

Many believers experience God in brief visitations, moments when His nearness breaks in during a song or service, but honor transforms visits into residence. A visiting presence excites; a dwelling presence governs. The difference is sustained value. When the Ark rested in Obed-Edom's house, everything in that house prospered because honor made room. He treated what others handled casually with reverence. Honor upgrades presence from guest to governor.

Every revival in history began as a visitation and either became habitation or history, depending on how people stewarded honor. **The Kingdom never withdraws; people simply stop valuing.**

Worship Beyond Music

Music expresses worship but **does not define it**. Worship is any act that declares, You are worth it. A quiet commute, a patient response, a generous gift, each can be incense if it rises from value. The melody Heaven hears is obedience played in daily keys. To live aware of His worth is to walk inside perpetual praise.

I have stood in rooms thick with sound but thin with substance, people singing about God without yielding to Him. Noise cannot replace nearness. True worship always carries weight; you can feel it when it enters. The air stills. Attention shifts. That is what happens when honor becomes atmosphere.

The Architecture of Honor

Every house of worship should mirror Heaven's order:
1. **Throne** – Center: Everything revolves around His presence, not personality.
2. **Table** – Communion: Relationship replaces ritual; sons gather as family, not crowd.
3. **Altar** – Surrender: Sacrifice keeps self-off the throne.
4. **Gate** – Gratitude: Thanksgiving keeps access open.

When these elements align, the Spirit finds a familiar environment, the blueprint of Heaven reproduced on earth. Honor is the architect that keeps the proportions right.

Honor and Hosting His Presence

Hosting presence means staying sensitive. The Holy Spirit is not fragile, but He is particular. He will not compete with pride, distraction, or performance. I have felt Him lift in rooms still filled with noise, because honor left first. The Spirit doesn't depart in anger; He withdraws in grief. But when humility and reverence return, He returns instantly.

To host Him is to notice Him. Every time you pause mid-day and whisper, *"I know You're here,"* you are laying another brick in a habitation. Eventually that awareness grows until whole communities breathe in rhythm with His presence.

The Scent of Honor

Heaven recognizes places by aroma, not address. Honor releases fragrance, Mary breaking her alabaster jar filled the room. That scent became a prophetic environment announcing the cross. Every time you pour affection without calculation, you perfume the atmosphere with honor. God remembers that fragrance long after others forget your act.

When Atmosphere Becomes Authority

A life that honors God consistently carries environmental authority. Jesus changed weather patterns because He lived under unbroken worship. Paul and Silas sang in prison and chains fell off, not because of volume, but because Heaven heard a familiar climate and entered it. Wherever honor rises, liberty follows. Worshiped-in spaces become governed spaces.

Section Transition

Honoring God through worship is the foundation of all other honor. When His presence is properly housed, His likeness naturally flows into every other relationship.

In the next chapter we'll step diagonally, from Heaven to representation, and explore how honoring God's sent ones becomes the bridge between Presence and people.

Chapter 3 Review & Reflection

Honoring God: The Fountainhead of Value

Core Revelation

All honor flows downward from one spring, how we value God Himself. When He is rightly enthroned in our affection, every other relationship finds gravity and grace. To honor God is to recognize Him as Source: the first thought, the central focus, the final authority. Where He is valued, chaos loses voice and peace takes seat.

Kingdom Principle

Order follows honor. The degree to which God is valued determines the degree to which life stays aligned. Honor establishes habitation; dishonor invites drought.

Scripture Focus

- Genesis 1:1 — "In the beginning, God …" Honor's posture
- 1 Samuel 2:30 — "Those who honor Me I will honor."
- Isaiah 6:1–3 — Reverence before revelation.
- Psalm 40:8 — "I delight to do Your will."
- John 4:23–24 — True worshipers in spirit and truth.
- Romans 5:17 — Reigning through received grace.
- Revelation 4 — The throne as the universe's center of gravity.

Truths to Remember

1. Reverence is not fear, it is awareness of worth.
2. Worship is value returned to its Source.
3. Whatever you honor most becomes your authority.
4. Obedience without delight is survival; delightful obedience is sonship.

5. Honor turns visitation into habitation.
6. Presence leaves where casualness enters.
7. The fragrance of broken worship still fills Heaven's memory.

Application

- Begin each day by acknowledging His presence before planning tasks.
- Guard against the subtle replacements of honor, ambition, routine, even ministry.
- Offer firsts: first thought, first time, first treasure.
- Practice waiting; timing reveals trust.
- Create worship atmospheres in ordinary spaces, car, kitchen, office, until awareness becomes habit.
- Treat His name as weighty: speak, post, and represent it with care.

Reflection Questions

1. What competes most often for my primary attention or trust?
2. How does my use of time and thought reveal what I truly honor?
3. Have I turned worship into performance rather than habitation?
4. In what areas is God asking me to transform obedience from duty into delight?
5. How can I make my home or ministry a continual atmosphere of honor?

Declaration

"Father, You are first and central. Every breath and boundary belongs to You. I return value to its Source; I enthrone You in my affection. Let my obedience become joy, my worship become habitation, and my life a living altar where Your presence feels at home."

CHAPTER 4

HONORING AUTHORITY: RECEIVING THE SENT ONES

Section 1 – The Pattern of Representation

Honor does not end in Heaven; it extends through vessels.

Every move of God arrives through men and women who carry His commission. From Moses to Paul, divine purpose has always worn human skin. To dishonor the vessel is to disrupt the flow.

Jesus said, *"He who receives you receives Me, and he who receives Me receives Him who sent Me."* (Matthew 10:40). That single sentence establishes Heaven's order of transmission. The Father sends the Son; the Son sends the Spirit; the Spirit sends people. The line of honor is unbroken, unless reception fails.

The Divine Chain of Trust

When God entrusts His purpose to a person, He invites us into relational discernment. We are not worshiping man; we are recognizing divine investment. Authority in the Kingdom is stewardship, not superiority. The apostle, prophet, pastor, or teacher is a conduit, not a competitor with Christ.

I have learned that God rarely answers prayers directly; He answers them through people. The blessing you've been waiting on may already be standing at your door in human form. Whether you receive it depends on whether you can see God's hand beneath human frailty.

The Test of Nazareth

Jesus faced the greatest resistance not from demons but from familiarity. *"Is this not the carpenter's son?"* they asked, and Scripture records that He could do no mighty work there except lay His hands on a few sick folks. (Mark 6:5). **Power was present, but honor was absent.**

Nazareth teaches us that the **absence of miracles** is not the **absence of God**, it is the absence of reception. Familiarity blinds perception: dishonor disables demonstration. The same anointing that raised the dead in Capernaum was neutralized by casualness in Nazareth.

I often wonder what Heaven wanted to do in that city but couldn't because men had reduced divinity to a résumé. Every generation faces its own Nazareth: the temptation to trivialize what it's too accustomed to.

Recognizing the Gift

Paul wrote, *"We have this treasure in earthen vessels."* That phrase keeps me both humble and perceptive. The vessel may be clay, but the content is glory. Honor is the ability to distinguish between the two, to handle humanity without despising divinity.

When you receive a messenger, you receive his measure. Jesus said, *"He who receives a prophet in the name of a prophet shall receive a prophet's reward."* Honor is Heaven's exchange rate. Whatever level you recognize is the level you can receive from. To treat every gift as common is to live beneath your inheritance.

Honor in Leadership and Followership

True authority is never imposed; it is invited by honor. Leaders don't demand it, they demonstrate it. They lead from likeness, not leverage. When leaders honor those, they serve, and sons honor those who lead, a reciprocal current of grace forms. That current is what Scripture calls unity of the Spirit in the bond of peace.

I have seen teams operate in talent but crumble in tension because honor was missing. Where competition replaces celebration, government fractures. But where mutual esteem abides, the smallest group can move mountains.

Receiving Without Idolatry

To honor authority is not to deify humanity. It is possible to respect an office without surrendering discernment. Spiritual manipulation begins where honor mutates into hero worship. The antidote is simple: keep your gaze on the Sender while receiving those He sent.

When the people of Lystra tried to worship Paul and Barnabas as gods, they tore their clothes and redirected attention to Christ. Healthy leaders deflect glory upward. Healthy sons reflect glory outward. That cycle keeps the Kingdom pure.

Transition

Every divine relationship begins with recognition. The **way** you receive determines **what** you receive. In the next section, we'll explore the posture of receiving authority, how sons position their hearts to draw grace from those God places in their lives.

Section 2 – The Posture of Reception: Drawing Grace Through Honor

You can sit in the same room with greatness and still receive nothing if your heart is closed. The woman with the issue of blood proved that proximity is not enough; posture determines flow. Crowds pressed Jesus, but only one touch drew virtue. Honor reached where curiosity could not.

Every relationship God ordains carries a measure of grace. That grace must be drawn out, and drawing requires posture, humility, expectancy, and recognition. Without those, the anointing present remains potential instead of power.

1. Humility — The Lower the Vessel, the Higher the Flow

Grace only travels downhill. Pride builds dams; humility digs channels. When you choose to humble yourself under God's mighty hand, you position your life beneath His flow. That *"hand"* often comes in the shape of human leadership. To resist the hand because you dislike its form is to resist the grace it carries.

I've learned that humility is not thinking less of yourself, it's thinking rightly of God in others. It's the willingness to kneel to the God who hides in clay.

2. Expectancy — Faith Turns Recognition into Reception

Honor without faith is admiration; honor with faith is activation. The Shunammite woman exemplified this. She perceived Elisha as a man of God and prepared a room for him. Her honor created atmosphere; her expectancy invited miracle. Years later, that same room became the setting for her son's resurrection.

Expectation gives honor a voice: *"Something divine is in this connection, and I will not treat it lightly."* That awareness pulls grace from potential into manifestation.

3. Recognition — Seeing God in the Ordinary

Recognition is revelation wrapped in awareness. God often disguises answers in everyday appearances, a carpenter's son, a neighbor's counsel, a pastor's correction. If you require glamor to discern God, you'll miss Him every time He comes quietly.

Honor trains the eyes to see glory in disguise. When I discern Him in others, I'm not flattering humanity; I'm acknowledging divinity at work. That recognition opens the valve of spiritual exchange.

The Silent Posture

Sometimes reception doesn't look like activity at all, it looks like listening. The Kingdom moves at the speed of attention. When you quiet your assumptions long enough to truly hear, grace has space to enter. Many miss impartation because they talk while Heaven is pouring. Silence is not passivity; it's availability.

Guarding the Heart While Receiving

Posture also means guarding the inner gate. Submission without discernment can invite abuse, discernment without submission breeds rebellion. Honor walks the narrow road between. It listens for God's voice through leadership but never worships leadership as God.

Healthy reception always keeps one ear tuned upward. If the instruction contradicts Scripture or character, honor responds with humility and truth, not rebellion. True sons protect the flow and the standard.

The Result of Proper Posture

Where posture is right, grace multiplies. Elisha served Elijah with that heart, pouring water on his hands until Heaven poured mantle on his life. The double portion was not favoritism; it was proximity plus posture. Likewise, Timothy inherited Paul's ministry not because of bloodline but because of honor-line. He drew what others only admired.

Honor positions you under spouts others stand beside. It turns mentors into portals, fathers into fountains, and relationships into rivers. The Spirit loves that alignment; He recognizes His own government in it.

Transition

Once posture is established, reception turns into partnership.

In the next section we'll explore how those who honor authority become co-laborers with it, how sons help build what fathers carry, extending Heaven's pattern through agreement and service.

Section 3 – *The Partnership of Honor: Serving the Grace You Receive*

Honor is not complete when you receive; it is fulfilled when you serve what you've received. When God joins your life to a leader, a father, or an apostolic assignment, He is not just giving you a teacher, He is inviting you into co-labor. Grace is never meant to sit still; it multiplies through partnership.

Paul called the Philippians *"partakers of grace with me."* They did more than listen to his sermons, they shared in his mission. Every offering they sent, every prayer they prayed, every obedience they walked in became an extension of apostolic flow. That's what partnership looks like: shared grace, shared burden, shared glory.

Serving the Grace, Not the Personality

In every generation, people are tempted to attach themselves to personalities rather than purposes. But true sons and daughters discern assignment over charisma. They don't serve for access or approval; they serve because they recognize God's grace at work and want to strengthen it.

When Elisha poured water on Elijah's hands, it wasn't because he lacked identity, it was because he valued impartation. He wasn't following a man; he was stewarding a mantle. That heart posture releases Heaven's continuity. Serving grace means I guard it, pray for it, and advance it. I build altars, not brands.

Carrying the Weight Together

Honor turns followers into builders. It says, *"I see the burden you carry, and I'll shoulder part of it."* When Moses' arms grew heavy, Aaron and Hur lifted them. That act of honor secured victory for Israel. One man's obedience became a nation's breakthrough. The pattern remains: when sons support what fathers sustain, the Kingdom advances without interruption.

Serving grace may look simple, showing up on time, executing vision with excellence, protecting reputation, but in Heaven it registers as governance. Every practical act is a spiritual investment.

The Currency of Agreement

Partnership is sustained by agreement. Amos asked, *"Can two walk together unless they be agreed?"* Agreement is not identical thought; it is shared direction. When hearts move in the same rhythm, God amplifies impact. Jesus promised, *"If two of you agree on earth concerning anything, it shall be done by My Father in Heaven."* Honor preserves that rhythm. It resists offense, corrects quietly, and values unity above ego.

Offense is partnership's assassin. The enemy knows he cannot out-preach truth, so he tries to out-persuade hearts through suspicion. The moment you entertain dishonor, you cut yourself off from the grace you once drew. Honor keeps the line open and the current pure.

Serving Is Sowing

When you serve, you are sowing into your own future. Elisha's faithfulness birthed succession. Ruth's loyalty unlocked redemption. Joshua's service to Moses positioned him for leadership. None of them chased promotion; they chased purpose. In the Kingdom, God never forgets hands that serve honorably. He writes their names into the storyline of His plans.

Service doesn't diminish you; it develops you. The soil of someone else's vision becomes the training ground for your own. Every seed of honor you plant there guarantees harvest when God entrusts you with your own field.

Guarding the Grace You Carry

Partnership also demands protection. The enemy aims at dishonor because he knows dishonor breaks continuity. Paul warned Timothy to guard the deposit entrusted to him. Honor is the guardrail that keeps grace from leaking through neglect or pride.

To serve grace well, you must stay both submitted and sanctified. Submission keeps you connected; sanctification keeps you clean. Without those two, partnership turns into performance. But when the heart stays pure, the flow never ends. Grace multiplies down generational lines.

Transition

Partnership is proof of maturity. Children consume grace; sons cultivate it. Those who truly honor authority move from admiration to administration, they help carry the Kingdom forward.

In the next section we'll look at what happens when honor is broken, how dishonor interrupts grace, and how God restores it when hearts return to reverence.

Section 4 – *The Breach of Honor: When Grace Is Interrupted*

Honor is the circuitry of Heaven's government. When that circuit breaks, the current stops flowing. You can have the same people, the same gift, the same setting, but without honor, grace flickers like a light disconnected from its source.

I've seen churches filled with activity yet void of anointing, families that quote Scripture but live in tension, all because the unseen wiring of honor was severed. Grace doesn't vanish; it waits for reconnection.

When Hearts Harden

Dishonor rarely begins as rebellion; it begins as offense unhealed. A word misunderstood, a correction misinterpreted, a moment unmet by expectation, and the heart closes. Once the heart closes, perception darkens. You no longer hear with the same ears or see with the same eyes. The person you once called *"a gift from God"* becomes *"just a man."*

Jesus said, *"Blessed is he who is not offended because of Me."* Offense is the devil's backdoor into the garden of grace. If he can plant offense, he can grow dishonor, and dishonor always leads to disconnection.

The Pattern of Saul

King Saul began in humility. Scripture says he hid among the baggage, unassuming, chosen by God. But honor turned inward became pride. When he began seeking approval more than obedience, grace lifted. His obsession with self-image destroyed his ability to honor Samuel, David, or even God.

Dishonor turns the heart from steward to competitor. Saul's greatest tragedy wasn't losing his throne; it was losing his posture. Once you start defending your title, you've already lost your authority. Honor protects both.

How Dishonor Spreads

Dishonor is contagious. It speaks in whispers, sows in corners, and disguises itself as "concern." It can hide behind phrases like *"I just think we should…"* or *"Did you notice…?"* But beneath those words lies a subtle transfer of weight, taking value from what God has anointed and placing it on personal opinion.

Lucifer invented that language. His fall began with an internal re-evaluation: *"I will ascend…I will be like the Most High."* Dishonor starts by changing the conversation around value. The moment you question God's order through comparison, the sound of Heaven's harmony fractures.

The Silence of Dishonor

When honor breaks, Heaven goes quiet. Prophecy turns mechanical, worship feels hollow, and communication loses weight. Eli's sons mishandled sacred things, and the lamp in the temple went dim. God still desired to speak, but dishonor had deafened the room.

The Holy Spirit is sensitive to atmosphere. He doesn't operate through intimidation or competition. When dishonor fills the air, He waits until the air clears. That's why revival never lasts where pride remains.

The Way Back: Repentance and Restoration

The good news is that breaches can be repaired. Grace never expires; it waits for humility. The moment a heart repents, truly turns from self-defense back to reverence, the current returns. Peter dishonored Christ in the courtyard, but one look from Jesus restored the circuit. His tears rewired his heart for Pentecost.

Repentance is not humiliation; it is restoration. It rebuilds connection. The Father never withholds grace; He simply will not force it through pride. Honor opens what humility unlocks.

When I feel the flow lessen in any relationship or assignment, my first prayer is not, *"Lord, change them,"* but *"Lord, check me."* Sometimes the blockage is an unseen attitude, a subtle cynicism or fatigue that dulled awareness of value. When I realign, the current returns.

Protecting the Flow

To keep honor unbroken, guard your heart against three enemies:
1. **Comparison** – It breeds competition.
2. **Familiarity** – It breeds contempt.

3. **Complaint** – It breeds confusion.

Each one reroutes affection away from value. But gratitude keeps circuits alive. A thankful heart cannot host dishonor; it's too full of remembrance.

Transition

Dishonor interrupts grace; repentance restores it. When honor is repaired, the flow resumes stronger than before. In the next section, we'll complete this chapter by examining the reward of honor, how God responds when hearts and houses uphold His order with reverence and joy.

Section 5 – *The Reward of Honor: Heaven's Response to Reverence*

God never allows honor to go unrewarded. Every act of reverence releases a corresponding response from Heaven. When you give weight to what He values, He gives weight to what you carry. That's the promise of 1 Samuel 2:30 - - *"Those who honor Me I will honor."* Honor always returns to its source multiplied.

The Circle of Glory

Honor forms a divine circulation, glory rising and descending in rhythm. When the creature honors the Creator, Heaven releases reflection: God shares Himself through those who revere Him. Moses' face shone because he gave God undivided attention. That light wasn't reward points; it was participation. The more you value Him, the more He entrusts you with visibility of Himself. Honor makes you luminous

In that same pattern, when you honor the people He sends, their grace mirrors back on you. The Shunammite honored Elisha and gained resurrection in her household. Cornelius honored God with generosity and devotion, and the Gentile world was opened through his house. Honor never dies where it is planted; it resurrects where it is needed most.

Access Through Honor

Honor is the Kingdom's master key. It opens doors that gifting cannot pick. Many pray for open heavens while speaking with closed hearts. But Heaven's atmosphere recognizes its own tone, reverence. When Jesus thanked the Father before multiplying bread, He unlocked divine economy through gratitude. When He lifted His eyes before raising Lazarus, He accessed resurrection by honor. Thanksgiving is verbalized honor, and it still opens impossible doors.

Honor Attracts Increase

Whatever you honor grows; whatever you dishonor withers. It's a law as old as Genesis. When Adam named the animals, he was honoring order, assigning purpose by recognition, and creation responded with fruitfulness. When Cain dishonored God's altar, his field resisted him. Honor is the invisible fertilizer of destiny.

That's why the centurion's household received healing at a distance: he understood how authority worked and spoke the language of honor. Faith and honor intertwine, faith believes what God can do, honor values who He is. Together they multiply results.

The Reward of Presence

The highest reward of honor is not possessions, it's presence. When Solomon finished dedicating the temple, fire fell, and glory filled the house. Heaven responded not to the architecture but to the attitude: *"The priests could not stand to minister because of the cloud."* That cloud wasn't earned; it was invited. God always sits where He is esteemed.

I've discovered that when a house, a ministry, or a heart exalts Him above preference, the glory becomes heavy again. Miracles follow, but they are by-products of habitation. The true reward is not what you receive from Him, it's that you can feel Him resting among you.

Honor and Generational Continuity

Heaven honors not just individuals but lineages that steward reverence. God said of Abraham, *"I know him, that he will command his children after him."* Honor builds legacy. When fathers model reverence, sons inherit rhythm. When sons sustain honor, generations remain aligned. The lamp in such houses never goes out.

That's why Elisha could strike the Jordan and cry, *"Where is the Lord God of Elijah?"*, and Heaven answered. Honor connects eras; it keeps grace traveling from one mantle to the next. God is not looking for celebrity; He is looking for continuity.

Heaven's Endorsement

When Heaven honors a person, it looks like favor that man cannot manufacture doors opening without explanation, resources finding assignment, influence resting on humility instead of ambition. God endorses what reflects Him. Honor reproduces His likeness in the earth, so He backs it publicly. That endorsement is not for ego; it's for expansion, the Kingdom made visible through reverent lives.

Conclusion: The Unbroken Line

Honor toward authority is not subjugation, it's synchronization. It links earth's voices with Heaven's sound. When you receive God's sent ones rightly, you partner with His purpose, preserve His flow, and participate in His reward. The line of honor remains unbroken, from the throne to the field, from the Father to the family, from Heaven to your heart.

Transition

The next chapter turns from vertical and representative honor to horizontal honor, how we esteem all people, as Peter commanded:

"Honor all men. Love the brotherhood. Fear God. Honor the king." (1 Peter 2:17)

We'll explore how the culture of the Kingdom transforms relationships, workplaces, and society} when honor becomes our default language.

Chapter 4 Review & Reflection

Honoring Authority: Receiving the Sent Ones

Core Revelation

Honor for authority is not about rank; it's about recognition. God moves through representation; He hides His glory in people. To receive those, He sends is to receive the One who sent them. When honor flows through that order, grace flows with it. When dishonor breaks it, Heaven's circuit pauses until hearts return to reverence.

Kingdom Principle

Honor is Heaven's delivery system. God rarely sends blessings wrapped in clouds; He wraps them in people. The measure you recognize determines the measure you receive.

Scripture Focus

- Matthew 10:40–42 – *"He who receives you receives Me."*
- Mark 6:4–6 – The Nazareth principle: honor limits or releases power.
- 1 Samuel 2:30 – *"Those who honor Me I will honor."*
- 2 Kings 2:9–15 – Elisha's double portion through service.
- Philippians 1:7 – *"You are partakers of grace with me."*
- Amos 3:3 – *"Can two walk together unless they are agreed?"*

Truths to Remember

1. Authority is stewardship, not superiority.
2. Grace travels through relationship; posture determines flow.
3. Humility attracts grace; pride repels it.
4. Honor without faith is admiration, honor with faith is activation.
5. Partnership fulfills reception; you serve what you value.

6. Offense is dishonor in disguise.
7. Dishonor silences Heaven, but repentance restores flow.
8. Every act of honor yields divine reciprocity; Heaven responds to value.

Application

- Practice recognizing God's hand in ordinary people.
- Guard your heart from offense; speak directly, forgive quickly.
- Serve faithfully in another's vision; it prepares you for your own.
- Honor correction as protection, it keeps the flow clean.
- Resist comparison; celebrate grace in others as evidence of God's generosity.
- When conflict arises, choose alignment over argument.
- Speak well of leadership in private; Heaven hears the whispers of both faith and complaint.

Reflection Questions

1. Do I recognize God's grace in those He has placed over me or beside me?
2. Have I allowed familiarity or offense to diminish my receptivity?
3. How can I actively serve and strengthen the grace I've received?
4. What does partnership look like in my context, home, ministry, work?
5. Am I guarding the flow of honor or contributing to its breach?

Declaration

"Father, thank You for the gifts You've placed in people.

Teach me to see You in them and to receive grace without pride or fear. I choose humility, agreement, and faith. Let my posture keep the flow open, that through honor, Heaven may move freely on earth."

CHAPTER 5

HONOR AMONG MEN: THE CULTURE OF THE KINGDOM

Section 1 – *The Weight of Every Image*

When Peter wrote, *"Honor all men,"* he wasn't giving etiquette lessons, he was describing Kingdom culture. In Heaven, honor isn't reserved for thrones or titles; it's the air everyone breathes. Every person carries God's imprint, so every encounter becomes sacred space.

I have learned that the Kingdom doesn't measure people by usefulness but by likeness. To honor all men is to recognize divine fingerprints even where sin has smudged them. It's to look past behavior into design, past dust into destiny.

Seeing the Image Beneath the Ashes

When I look at another person, I'm not seeing **competition**; I'm seeing **creation**. Genesis says, *"Let Us make man in Our image."* That verse doesn't have an expiration date. Though the fall distorted the image, it did not delete it. Christ came to restore it, and sons are called to recognize it.

Jesus honored people the world had written off, lepers, women, Samaritans, tax collectors. He saw worth where culture saw waste. He spoke to fishermen like future apostles, to the demonized like dormant evangelists, to the adulterous like a woman with untapped worship. He never ignored sin, but He never let sin define worth. That is the essence of Kingdom honor.

The Measure of Maturity

Spiritual maturity is revealed not by how we treat those above us but how we treat those beneath us. Anybody can honor power; it takes Kingdom eyes to honor the powerless. When Jesus washed His disciples' feet, He wasn't lowering Himself; He was revealing Heaven's definition of greatness. He said, *"I am among you as one who serves."*

Honor doesn't flow down a hierarchy; it circulates through family. The King of Glory wrapped a towel around His waist to teach sons how the government of Heaven works, not by control but by compassion. Serving is not weakness; it's divine strength expressed through humility.

Honor as Spiritual Vision

To honor rightly, we must see rightly. When the eyes of honor are open, value appears everywhere. When they close, cynicism becomes vision's substitute. The Pharisees looked at Jesus and saw a threat; the blind man looked and saw Lordship. Sight was not the issue, seeing value was.

The Kingdom restores the ability to see accurately, to discern the treasure hidden in earthen vessels. That's why Paul said, *"We regard no man after the flesh."* Once you've seen Christ in yourself, you start seeing Christ in others. That recognition is the beginning of transformation in communities and nations.

The Language of Value

Honor is expressed in speech before it's seen in action. The words we use either build identity or bury it. When we speak to people according to their past, we imprison them there. But when we speak according to design, we pull destiny to the surface.

Jesus called Simon *"Peter"* long before he was stable.

He used Heaven's language, not history's. When you name someone according to Heaven's vision, you participate in their restoration. That's why gossip, criticism, and sarcasm are poison to Kingdom culture, they corrode value and normalize dishonor.

Heaven's Culture on Earth

Imagine a people who greet strangers as if they were sent ones, who esteem coworkers as image bearers, and who honor the poor as carriers of potential. That's not idealism, that's the atmosphere of Heaven finding residence on earth. The Kingdom advances through culture, not coercion. Every act of honor builds an embassy of Heaven wherever it's expressed.

In a world starving for dignity, honor becomes evangelism. You don't need a pulpit to preach; you need perception. People recognize divine love long before they understand doctrine. When they feel seen, they begin to see Him.

Transition

The culture of honor among men begins with vision, seeing God's image in every person. In the next section, we'll explore how honor functions in relationships, from families to friendships, from coworkers to communities, and how Kingdom culture reforms natural environments through spiritual perception.

Section 2 – Honor in Relationships: The Culture of Value Made Visible

Honor must wear skin to become believable. It cannot stay an idea; it must enter conversation, decision, and relationship. If honor never leaves your mouth or calendar, it's admiration, not transformation. The Kingdom becomes visible when value becomes visible.

I have learned that every relationship is a classroom for honor.

The home trains affection, the church trains submission, the workplace trains humility, and the world tests consistency. Wherever people are, God hides lessons in them about Himself. He designed relationships not merely for companionship but for formation, a mirror where we learn to see His image in others.

Honor in the Home

The first commandment with a promise was relational: *"Honor your father and your mother, that your days may be long."* That verse reveals two things: **honor brings longevity**, and **dishonor shortens legacy**. When the family learns honor, generations flourish; when it's lost, time itself seems to work against them.

In the home, honor sounds like gratitude and looks like patience. Spouses practice it by listening without leverage; children learn it by obedience that grows into empathy. No house is perfect, but when honor governs tone, healing enters rooms that counseling alone cannot fix.

To dishonor those closest to you is to curse the soil God gave you to grow in. Every family is sacred ground because it holds the fingerprints of divine design, even the broken ones. Honor rebuilds what dysfunction destroyed.

Honor Among Friends

Real friendship thrives where honor protects vulnerability. David and Jonathan teach us that loyalty is a form of worship. Jonathan knew that David's rise meant his own throne would fade, yet he defended him anyway. That's Kingdom friendship, celebrating another's anointing even when it outshines your own.

Dishonor in friendship begins when comparison replaces covenant. You stop seeing grace and start seeing threat.

Honor preserves connection by refusing to weaponize knowledge. A true friend carries your flaws like secrets between altars, not ammunition in arguments.

Honor in the Workplace

The workplace is one of the greatest testing grounds for Kingdom culture. Paul told servants to work *"as unto the Lord."* He was teaching that your supervisor is not your source, God is. When you honor through excellence, punctuality, and integrity, you're not performing for promotion; you're revealing Heaven's standards in earthly systems.

Honor at work also means how you treat peers and subordinates. Those who carry authority must model Heaven's heart, not Babylon's hierarchy. Authority without honor becomes tyranny; leadership with honor becomes trust. When coworkers feel valued instead of used, they begin to see the invisible King you represent.

Honor in Community

Communities deteriorate when honor disappears. When people stop valuing one another's dignity, society devolves into competition for control. But the Kingdom restores order through love that esteems. Jesus summarized all law and prophets with love God and love neighbor. Love gives honor its motive; honor gives love its structure.

In the Kingdom, we don't honor because people are flawless, we honor because God is faithful. Every act of courtesy, every gesture of patience, every moment of listening is evangelism in disguise. Cities can be discipled through dignity long before they're discipled through doctrine.

Honor During Conflict

Conflict reveals whether honor is conviction or convenience. It's easy to value people who agree with you; it's divine to value those who oppose you. Jesus washed Judas' feet knowing betrayal was minutes away. He honored the image even when the intention was impure. That moment unmasks Heaven's culture: honor is not endorsement of behavior, it's preservation of essence.

When offense tries to infect your heart, respond with remembrance: *"This person still bears His image."* That doesn't mean you tolerate abuse or ignore truth, but you refuse to strip dignity from disagreement. You confront without contempt and correct without cruelty. Honor allows truth to heal instead of humiliate.

Honor as Witness

The world recognizes authenticity by how believers treat one another. Jesus said, *"By this all men will know you are My disciples, if you have love for one another."* Love is the motive; honor is the method. Every word of grace, every refusal to gossip, every act of preference for another's good preaches louder than sermons. Honor is evangelism translated into tone.

Transition

Honor among men turns ordinary relationships into living altars. Where people esteem each other, Heaven finds space to dwell. In the next section, we'll explore how honor heals division, how the Kingdom redefines equality, breaks prejudice, and restores unity by returning worth to every human soul.

Section 3 – *Honor Heals Division: Equality in the Light of the Kingdom*

Division is what happens when value disappears. When people forget who they are and whose image they bear, they begin to measure worth by difference, color, culture, status, gender, gift, or opinion. But in Heaven's light, those distinctions lose power; the only true measure is likeness.

Honor is Heaven's answer to every human fracture. It restores sight where prejudice blinded, hearing where pride deafened, and love where law failed. You cannot **legislate unity**; you must **restore value**. Honor doesn't erase difference, it redeems it, revealing that diversity was always part of divine design.

Heaven's View of Equality

The Kingdom's equality is not sameness; it's shared value. God never intended uniformity; He delights in variety. But in Christ, all variety flows from one Source and finds meaning in one purpose. Paul wrote, *"There is neither Jew nor Greek, slave nor free, male nor female, for you are all one in Christ Jesus."*

This oneness doesn't mean indistinction, it means equal honor. The Father doesn't love the apostle more than the usher, the preacher more than the janitor, or the strong more than the weak. He values essence, not assignment. The cross leveled the field by revealing the same price was paid for every soul.

Honor Destroys Hierarchies Built by Flesh

Religion creates ladders; the Kingdom builds tables. At ladders, people climb and compete. At tables, they commune and contribute. When honor governs, everyone has a seat, and every voice finds significance. Dishonor builds pyramids where a few stand tall on the backs of many. Honor flattens the structure until Christ alone is the head and we are members one of another.

It turns power into partnership and position into participation.
The Church becomes a family again, not a franchise.

The Spirit of Division

Division always travels with pride and fear.
Pride says, *"I'm better than you."*
Fear says, *"You're a threat to me."*
Both are dishonor wearing different masks.

Satan's oldest trick was to divide likeness: he made Eve question whether God's image was truly shared with her. The result was suspicion and shame. Every time we divide, we echo Eden's error, questioning whether another is as worthy of grace as we are. But honor sees the same blood on every believer and the same breath in every human being.

Healing Through Humility

Unity never begins with **agreement**; it begins with **humility**. You cannot heal a fracture by demanding understanding, you heal it by showing value. That's why Jesus knelt to wash the feet of the one who would deny Him and the one who would betray Him. He was healing the division before it appeared. The water in that basin was Heaven's antidote to arrogance.

When you choose humility, you disarm hell. When you honor across lines of difference, you make room for the Spirit of reconciliation. That is why Paul called the ministry of believers the ministry of reconciliation. We're not just saving souls; we're stitching humanity back together with threads of divine value.

Honor and Justice

True justice flows from honor, not anger. Anger may expose what's wrong, but honor knows how to restore what's right. Justice without honor becomes vengeance; justice with honor becomes healing. The Kingdom doesn't merely demand fairness; it reveals Father-ness, a family where everyone belongs.

When we treat people as divine image bearers rather than social categories, prejudice loses oxygen. The Spirit levels the ground beneath the cross and builds communities that reflect Heaven's equity, where difference becomes color in God's mosaic, not cracks in the wall.

The Sound of Unity

Psalm 133 calls unity *"precious oil."* Oil doesn't come from one olive; it comes from many crushed together. Unity is costly because it demands surrender, but the reward is anointing. When brothers dwell together in honor, Heaven releases fresh flow. That's why revival sounds like reconciliation, the language of restored value.

When I walk into a room where people prefer one another in love, I can feel the oil. It's thicker than atmosphere; it's Heaven's pleasure made tangible. That is the sound of the Kingdom on earth: many voices, one heart.

Transition

Honor heals what pride divides.

When we restore value to every person, we restore Heaven's image to earth. The next section will explore how this healing becomes influence, how honoring all men gives the Church credibility and power to shape culture through the aroma of Christlike dignity.

Section 4 – Honor as Influence: How Dignity Becomes Dominion

The world chases influence through visibility; Heaven gives it through credibility. God never called His sons to out-shout darkness, He called them to outshine it. Light doesn't argue with shadow; it simply reveals something more real. That's what honor does: it manifests a higher realm without needing permission.

Where honor is practiced, authority becomes effortless. When people feel valued, they open their hearts, and hearts are the true gates of cities. No amount of strategy can substitute for the fragrance of dignity. Honor is not a soft virtue; it's Heaven's strategy for dominion.

Influence Through Character

Character is the magnet of the Kingdom. Titles may impress men, but only integrity convinces Heaven. When you walk in consistent honor, speaking truth gently, treating others with value, refusing manipulation, people sense authority that cannot be faked. They may not agree with your beliefs, but they will respect your spirit.

Jesus never campaigned for credibility; He carried it. Even Pilate said, *"I find no fault in Him."* The power of His influence was purity. He represented the Father so perfectly that sinners wanted proximity more than justification. That's the gravitational pull of honor, it draws people toward the divine without coercion.

Honor Creates Platforms Heaven Can Trust

Heaven promotes only where honor has been proven. Many want stages, but God looks for stewards. The stage built on self-collapses under pressure, but the one built on reverence endures every storm. When God finds a person who values others more than spotlight, He gives them a platform that no man can close.

Joseph's honor turned a prison into a palace. He served faithfully when forgotten, spoke kindly when remembered, and used his gift without bitterness. That posture gave him authority to interpret Pharaoh's dream and save nations. His dominion was not political, it was relational. People trusted the one who refused to dishonor even those who betrayed him.

The Currency of Honor

In every arena, family, business, ministry, honor is the invisible currency of influence. You cannot withdraw what you haven't deposited. If you want to speak into lives, invest honor first. When you listen before leading, when you value before teaching, you earn the right to be heard.

Paul understood this:
He told believers to *"give honor to whom honor is due."*
He didn't say, *"Give agreement,"* but *"Give honor."*
Honor establishes credit in the spirit; once trust is earned, truth can travel freely.

Honor Disarms Resistance

Dishonor hardens hearts; honor softens them. When Stephen stood before the Sanhedrin, his face shone like an angel's. Even in accusation, he radiated reverence. His words pierced deeper because they carried no contempt. That's how Heaven speaks to rebellion, with dignity, not disdain.

In the Kingdom, confrontation doesn't have to be combat. When truth is spoken from honor, conviction lands without humiliation. That's why Jesus could dine with sinners and call Pharisees *"brood of vipers"* in the same breath, both statements were love in different languages. Honor calibrates tone so truth can heal instead of harm.

From Dignity to Dominion

Dominion begins where dignity is restored. When you treat people as image bearers, you awaken their awareness of purpose. Honor lifts others into function, and the more people walk in purpose, the more the Kingdom expands. That's dominion, not control, but cultivation.

Adam's dominion in Eden wasn't political, it was relational. He named creation, not by domination, but by recognition. To name is to honor essence. When you identify the God-given design in a person or place, you unlock it. That's Kingdom influence: discovering, declaring, and developing the glory hidden in everything God made.

Influence Through Peace

A man or woman who carries peace will always have influence. When chaos enters a room, people instinctively look for stability. Honor keeps you unoffended, unhurried, and unshaken. Peace becomes your platform; calm becomes your credibility. That's why Jesus could sleep in a storm, He ruled by rest. When you live unprovoked, you become the loudest voice in the room without raising your tone.

Transition

Honor turns servants into stewards, and stewards into standard-bearers. It transforms personal dignity into cultural dominion, governance through grace.

In the next section, we'll complete this chapter by exploring the reward and ripple of a culture of honor, how honoring all men transforms not only individuals but entire regions into reflections of Heaven's heart.

Section 5 – The Ripple of Honor: Transforming Culture Through Value

Every act of honor is a stone dropped into eternity. You may think the moment is small, a kind word, a patient pause, a respectful gesture, but Heaven never loses count of value returned to its Source. Honor never stops at the edge of your life; it ripples outward, carrying Kingdom resonance into families, workplaces, and nations.

Culture shifts not when systems are replaced, but when hearts are re-valued. When people start seeing one another through the lens of divine worth, justice finds balance, creativity awakens, and peace becomes the atmosphere instead of the goal. That is what it means to disciple nations: to teach them how Heaven esteems humanity.

Honor Turns Environments Into Ecosystems

Wherever honor abides, life multiplies. Churches that honor every gift become bodies, not businesses. Homes that honor every member become gardens, not battlegrounds. Communities that honor diversity become symphonies, not silos.

Honor is not sentimental, it's systemic. It establishes relational order that produces spiritual ecology: roots of trust, rivers of grace, fruits of righteousness. The opposite is true as well: when dishonor dominates, the soil hardens and the water dries.

From Culture War to Kingdom Culture

Many believers are fighting culture wars God never called them to fight. We win nothing by shouting louder than the darkness. The Kingdom advances by demonstrating a better world, not by condemning the current one. Honor is that demonstration.

When the Church stops arguing for relevance and starts living with reverence, society will listen again. People are not drawn to our correctness; they are drawn to our kindness. Truth clothed in honor becomes irresistible. The loudest reformers will be those who love most deeply.

The Healing Witness of Honor

Honor becomes evangelism without agenda. You can preach sermons that people forget, but they will never forget being treated with dignity. Every time you listen with patience, forgive without being asked, or serve without credit, you are revealing Heaven's nature. That is the Gospel translated into behavior.

In a cynical age, authenticity is healing. Honor restores credibility to the message of Christ because it mirrors His method, mercy. When the world tastes that mercy through us, they discover the King behind it.

Generational Ripples

Honor always outlives the moment. Children raised in honor learn instinctively how to govern. They grow up understanding that greatness is measured in service and that authority is earned by empathy. Such sons and daughters build legacies that don't have to be rebuilt every generation.

David's kindness to Jonathan's son Mephibosheth preserved covenant beyond death. That single act became a prophecy: honor never dies with the honored; it multiplies through the honoring.

Honor and the Glory to Come

Scripture says the earth will be filled with the knowledge of the glory of the Lord. That knowledge is not only revelation, but also recognition. When the nations finally know how valuable every life is, they will see His glory in each other's eyes. Honor is the education of eternity: learning how to see as God sees. Every bow of humility, every bridge of forgiveness, every word of blessing prepares the earth for that fullness.

Honor is not just culture, it is prophecy. It declares the future God has always intended: a world governed by love, filled with light, and fluent in the language of sons.

Conclusion

When Peter said, *"Honor all men,"* he was describing Heaven's social order. It's the way eternity already functions. To honor all is to let Heaven's culture run through your veins until it touches everything around you. Wherever honor flows, the King is visible. That is how sons colonize the earth with the atmosphere of home.

Transition

The next chapter moves from honoring all men to the tenderest and most difficult field of all, honoring those who have wronged us. We will explore forgiveness, restoration, and the mystery of loving our enemies, showing that honor doesn't end with agreement; it conquers through grace.

Chapter 5 Review & Reflection

Honor Among Men: The Culture of the Kingdom

Core Revelation

To *"honor all men"* is to live fluent in Heaven's language of value. Every human bears God's image, even when that image is buried beneath ashes. When we esteem others rightly, we mirror the Father's heart and manifest the Kingdom's culture. Honor transforms relationships, heals divisions, and releases influence, turning ordinary life into a visible expression of divine dignity.

Kingdom Principle

Honor is Heaven's culture manifested on earth. It dignifies every image-bearer, disarms division, and demonstrates the reality of the Kingdom through love expressed as value.

Scripture Focus

- 1 Peter 2:17 – *"Honor all men. Love the brotherhood. Fear God. Honor the king."*
- Genesis 1:26–27 – Humanity made in God's image.
- John 13:14–15 – Jesus washing His disciples' feet.
- Galatians 3:28 – Equality in Christ.
- Philippians 2:3–4 – Esteem others better than yourselves.
- Psalm 133:1–3 – The oil of unity and blessing.
- Matthew 5:44 – Love your enemies.

Truths to Remember

1. Every person is sacred space. God's image makes human interaction holy ground.
2. Honor doesn't ignore difference; it redeems it.

3. Spiritual maturity is proven in how we treat those who cannot advance us.
4. Division begins when value disappears. Honor restores both.
5. Humility heals what pride divides.
6. True justice flows from honor, not anger.
7. Dignity precedes dominion, restored value releases righteous influence.
8. Honor is evangelism with skin, it makes Heaven believable.

Application

- Speak to others according to Heaven's perspective, not history's record.
- Practice daily courtesy as worship, each act declares value.
- Replace gossip with gratitude; it changes the atmosphere.
- Value the unseen contributions of those around you.
- Honor across differences, culture, class, color, or creed.
- In conflict, remember image before issue.
- Carry peace into chaotic spaces, influence flows through calm dignity.

Reflection Questions

1. Do I see others primarily through their flaws or through their Father's image?
2. Where have I withheld honor because of offense, bias, or pride?
3. What would it look like to treat my family, coworkers, and even opponents as carriers of divine worth?
4. How can my lifestyle of honor become a testimony that shifts my environment?
5. What "ripple" of honor is God inviting me to initiate?

Declaration

"Father, open my eyes to see Your image in every person. Teach me to speak with value, act with compassion, and walk with humility.

Christopher K. Turney

Let my life release dignity where shame once ruled and let the culture of Heaven flow through me until every heart feels Your worth."

CHAPTER 6

HONOR IN ADVERSITY: LOVING THOSE WHO WOUND YOU

Section 1 – The Test No One Volunteers For

Honor is easy until it costs something. The real proof of sonship is not how we treat those who bless us, but how we respond to those who betray us. Jesus said, *"If you love those who love you, what reward do you have? Do not even sinners do the same?"* (Matthew 5:46). The Kingdom doesn't test you in comfort; it tests you in conflict.

I have discovered that the greatest classroom for honor is betrayal. Pain reveals whether honor is principle or preference. You cannot learn unconditional love without conditions that test it. And you cannot become Christlike without learning how to bless Judas.

The Scandal of the Cross

The cross is the ultimate display of honor in adversity. Jesus honored His Father and the very ones who crucified Him in the same breath: *"Father, forgive them, for they know not what they do."* He valued their redemption more than His vindication. That's the difference between the spirit of the world and the spirit of the Kingdom, the world seeks justice through revenge; Heaven restores justice through mercy.

The cross teaches that honor is not permission for abuse, it's participation in redemption. Jesus did not ignore injustice; He absorbed it to end its power. Every son will eventually face a cross moment, when you must decide whether to curse what hurt you or crucify your right to retaliation. Only one of those choices resurrects life.

Why the Enemy Uses Offense

Offense is the enemy's most efficient strategy to break divine alignment. It severs the flow between hearts, freezes faith, and paralyzes prayer. That's why Jesus warned, *"It is impossible that no offenses should come."* Offense is inevitable; carrying it is optional.

When we hold offense, we begin rehearsing dishonor internally, reliving words, redefining people, and replaying pain. What you rehearse, you reinforce. Honor, however, refuses to replay the wound; it rewrites the memory with grace. Forgiveness doesn't deny what happened; it denies the past the power to dictate your future.

The Gift Hidden in Betrayal

Every betrayal hides a promotion. Joseph's brothers sold him, but their sale funded his sending. Judas' kiss didn't end Jesus' mission, it accelerated it. When you respond with honor, what was meant to bury you becomes the seed of resurrection.

The soldiers who came to arrest Jesus did not recognize Him. They were trained in force, not familiar with His face. They knew His reputation, but not His identity. It was Judas, not a disciple of truth, but a betrayer of proximity, who said, *"The One I kiss is the Man."* Think of that. Judas revealed Jesus.

Betrayal is a revealer.

When people don't know who you truly are, how you respond in the moment of betrayal will either expose your flesh or unveil your nature. Will what comes out of you match what you say you carry? In the garden, Jesus was shaken, surrounded by fear, abandoned by friends, misunderstood by leaders, and kissed by betrayal. Yet only love flowed out… because love was all that was in Him.

If I shake a glass of water and water spills out, it isn't because I shook the glass, it's because water was already inside. Pressure doesn't create what comes out of us; it exposes what's been within us all along. No one makes me angry, they simply shake the glass. If anger comes out, it is because anger was inside.

Betrayal doesn't implant bitterness; it reveals it. When Jesus was shaken, only love emerged, because He was filled with nothing else.

Honor doesn't deny the shaking, honor determines what pours out when it comes. Betrayal presses, but honor reveals. Offense reacts, but sonship responds. Betrayal shook Jesus, and the world saw the Son.

This is why I once heard the Spirit whisper, *"Don't despise the hand that pressed you into purpose."* The betrayal that broke your heart might have broken the ground for your next season. When you stay free from offense, you inherit insight, understanding how God turns pain into pattern. Honor sees providence even in pressure. What others intended to expose in you, God intends to reveal through you.

Forgiveness Is Not Weakness

Forgiveness is not denial of pain; it's the decision to stop living in it. It's the willful act of letting God be Judge so you can remain a son. To withhold forgiveness is to drink poison hoping your enemy will thirst. To forgive is to release what isn't yours to carry.

Jesus didn't say forgive once; He said seventy times seven. He wasn't giving arithmetic; He was giving atmosphere. He meant live in forgiveness as your default posture. Honor keeps your heart light enough to love again.

When Words Cut Deep

Wounds from friends feel different. David said, *"It was not an enemy who reproached me...but it was you, my equal, my companion, my familiar friend."* That confession exposes something sacred: betrayal only hurts because love existed first. If dishonor didn't matter to you, it means value never did. But when you still choose to love through that pain, you join the fellowship of Christ's suffering, the fellowship that births resurrection power.

I have learned to stop asking *"Why did they do this?"* and start asking *"What is Heaven forming in me through this?"* Every wound that doesn't turn you bitter will turn you brilliant. Pain purified by honor becomes discernment.

Transition

The test of loving those who wound you is not to protect their behavior, it's to protect your own becoming. The next section will show how honor becomes healing, how choosing mercy not only frees others but restores your spiritual authority, peace, and perspective.

Section 2 – The Healing Power of Honor: Freedom Through Forgiveness

Forgiveness is the surgery of the Spirit. It cuts deep, not to harm, but to heal. When you forgive, you remove the foreign object from your heart, the memory that doesn't belong in your bloodstream anymore. Forgiveness doesn't change what happened; it changes what happens in you.

I used to think forgiveness was for the other person, a gift I gave to my offender. But I've learned that forgiveness is self-deliverance. It unties you from the past so Heaven can move you into tomorrow. Honor releases that healing by aligning you again with Heaven's flow.

Forgiveness Restores Spiritual Circulation

Offense clogs the arteries of the spirit. You can pray, sing, and serve, but resentment restricts flow. Jesus said, *"When you stand praying, forgive, that your Father may forgive you."* He wasn't threatening your salvation, He was protecting your circulation. The Kingdom runs on mercy; if you block it going out, you block it coming in.

When I forgive, I reopen the channel. Grace begins to move freely again, and peace returns like fresh oxygen to the soul. That's why forgiveness feels lighter, it literally removes weight. Honor is Heaven's heart surgery performed through yielded will.

Healing the Memory, Not Erasing It

Honor doesn't pretend the pain never existed. It remembers with redemption instead of resentment. The scar becomes a testimony, not a trigger. Even the resurrected Christ still had wounds, but they no longer bled. They told a story of survival and salvation.

Healing happens when you can revisit the moment without reliving the pain. That's the fruit of honor: you see the past through God's purpose, not your own disappointment. Every healed wound becomes a portal of compassion; you start recognizing hurting people by memory of your own redemption.

Forgiveness as Spiritual Warfare

People often imagine warfare as shouting at demons, but sometimes the loudest victory is silence, when you refuse to retaliate. Forgiveness disarms hell. Satan cannot dwell in a forgiving heart because there's nothing left for him to accuse. When you bless those who cursed you, you rob darkness of jurisdiction. Forgiveness is rebellion against bitterness. It's how Heaven conquers without casualties.

That's why Jesus told us to bless those who persecute us.
Blessing doesn't mean agreeing; it means refusing to mirror evil. Every time you bless where you were broken, you redeem ground the enemy thought he owned.

Reconciliation vs. Restoration

Forgiveness and reconciliation are related but distinct. Forgiveness requires one heart; reconciliation requires two. You can forgive without trusting again, and you can release someone without reentering their circle. Honor does not obligate you to stay in toxic proximity, it simply demands that you stay in pure posture.

Restoration is possible only where repentance is present, but forgiveness is possible even when it isn't. You don't wait for an apology to be free; you decide to live unchained. Heaven restores you whether or not they recognize their wrong. Honor refuses to let another person's hardness become your own.

Healing the Wound in Worship

Worship is the safest place to bleed. When words fail, tears translate. There were moments I couldn't articulate the hurt, so I laid it before Him as offering. I discovered that worship is not escape, it's exchange. Every song of surrender is a transfer of weight. You cannot simultaneously worship and worry; one will silence the other. In worship, pain loses its argument because presence redefines it. By the time you finish exalting Him, bitterness has no vocabulary left. Honor in adversity ends with raised hands, not clenched fists.

"...worship allows us to touch Him. And when we touch Him, we touch scars. Our pain has no bragging rights when we touch His scars in worship."

- Nathaniel Drake, Worship Leader/Son in the Faith

Transition

Forgiveness frees your soul, but honor goes further, it redeems your perspective. The next section will reveal how to see pain prophetically, understanding how God uses adversity as training for authority and how sons emerge from suffering carrying the fragrance of grace.

Section 3 – The Perspective of Honor: Seeing Pain Prophetically

Pain is a prophet if you learn its language. Every wound carries a word from Heaven disguised in discomfort. What feels like destruction is often divine construction in progress. The key is posture, honor allows you to see through pain rather than from it.

When your heart honors God even in affliction, the Spirit gives you new eyes. You begin to discern purpose in pressure, process in betrayal, and progress in delay. You realize that what happened to you is being used for you. That shift in vision transforms victims into vessels.

The Prophetic Eye of the Son

Honor trains your vision to interpret life through sonship rather than slavery. Remember a slave asks, *"Why is this happening to me?"* A son asks, *"What is the Father forming in me?"* That question turns confusion into classroom. When you interpret suffering through sonship, pain becomes prophecy, foretelling who you're becoming.

Joseph didn't just survive betrayal; he saw it as a setup. He told his brothers, *"You meant it for evil, but God meant it for good."* That's the vocabulary of honor, calling divine intention out of human failure. Only a healed heart can speak that way.

Pain as Preparation

Every anointing has a process, and every process has a pain threshold. The oil doesn't flow until olives are crushed. Glory doesn't rest where gratitude doesn't exist. Pain becomes preparation when you surrender outcome and trust the Potter's hand.

The pressure you're under is not punishment; it's proof of potential. You're being shaped for the weight of what's next. God never wastes pain, He repurposes it. Honor in adversity says, *"Father, if You've allowed it, You must intend to reveal something through it."*

Perspective Changes Power

The moment you stop seeing yourself as a victim, the devil loses his leverage. Victimhood anchors you to the past; vision anchors you to destiny. Paul, imprisoned and beaten, could still write, *"These light afflictions are but for a moment and are working for us an eternal weight of glory."* He called the very thing that hurt him a helper. That's prophetic sight, when pain becomes your partner in producing purpose.

Perspective doesn't minimize pain; it magnifies meaning. Honor keeps that focus pure; it refuses to curse what Heaven is using.

The Revelation Hidden in Rejection

Rejection is often Heaven's redirection. When doors close and people walk away, honor stops chasing and starts listening. God sometimes hides protection in disappointment. He removes wrong voices so you can hear His again. Every no becomes a corridor leading to a better yes.

The Spirit whispered to me once: *"I let them leave so you could learn the sound of My staying."* That single revelation turned grief into gratitude. Honor doesn't beg to be included; it trusts to be positioned.

Seeing Like Christ

At Calvary, Christ redefined perspective forever. He looked at the cross, the worst instrument of pain, and saw it as joy set before Him. He honored His Father's will and turned execution into exaltation. That's the pattern for sons: not denial of pain but dominion through it. To see pain prophetically is to stand where He stood, above circumstance, within purpose.

When you begin to see this way, adversity loses the power to deform your heart. Instead, it refines your authority. You start carrying

Heaven's calm in Hell's conditions. That's when you know the test has turned into testimony.

Transition

Once you begin to see pain prophetically, you can live peacefully, because you trust divine timing and purpose. The next section will explore how to keep honor consistent, how to guard your heart in prolonged adversity so that weariness doesn't erode wonder.

Section 4 – The Endurance of Honor: Guarding the Heart in Prolonged Adversity

Short storms reveal faith. Long storms reveal foundations. It's one thing to honor God in the first hour of pain; it's another to keep honor alive in the waiting room of delay. Time has a way of testing what moments can't. When adversity stretches, the temptation is to let honor fade into apathy, to stop expecting, stop serving, stop believing.

But endurance is worship's truest form. It's when faith becomes faithfulness, when you stay in position because of who He is, not because of how it feels. Honor that endures through delay carries a fragrance Heaven cannot resist.

The Slow Work of Glory

God does some of His best work slowly. He formed the universe in sequence, built nations through generations, and redeems souls through process. Dishonor demands speed, honor trusts sequence. Impatience is pride disguised as productivity.

In waiting, honor whispers, *"I trust Your timing more than my need for control."* That confession disarms anxiety. Every day you remain steadfast without understanding, you write a psalm Heaven will one day sing. Faith may ignite the fire, but honor keeps it burning through the night.

Guarding the Heart from Weariness

Prolonged adversity is dangerous not because of what happens around you, but because of what can grow inside you, bitterness, cynicism, numbness. That's why Solomon wrote, *"Guard your heart with all diligence, for out of it flow the issues of life."* If the heart grows hard, even miracles feel meaningless.

The key to endurance is gratitude. Thankfulness rehydrates dry hope. It doesn't deny the ache; it gives it perspective. When you thank God for what remains instead of fixating on what's missing, peace returns like morning light. Gratitude is the language of sustained honor.

The Rhythm of Rest and Resolve

Endurance is not exhaustion. You cannot maintain honor by force of will; it must be sustained by rhythm. Even Jesus withdrew to solitary places to pray. Rest is not laziness; it's reverence for your design. Honor includes stewardship of self. You cannot represent Heaven well if your soul is empty.

I have learned to schedule silence. Not as escape, but as maintenance. Stillness allows the heart to be recalibrated, reminded that results are not the reward; presence is. When rest and worship embrace, endurance becomes effortless.

When Hope Seems Delayed

The writer of Proverbs observed, *"Hope deferred makes the heart sick, but desire fulfilled is a tree of life."* Honor is the medicine for deferred hope. It keeps the heart believing when evidence is absent. It says, *"Even if it tarries, I will wait."* That waiting becomes worship; it's faith stretched to maturity.

Abraham waited twenty-five years for a promise and called God faithful before the fulfillment. That is the endurance of honor, to stay convinced of His goodness while holding empty hands. Eventually, the delay becomes delivery.

Maintaining Honor Toward People in Prolonged Trial

Sometimes the hardest part of long adversity is not God's silence but people's inconsistency. You begin the journey surrounded and finish it seemingly alone. Honor guards you from resentment in those moments. It keeps you tender toward the very people who misunderstood your process.

Jesus still called Peter *"rock"* after his denial. He honored the seed even when the fruit failed. That's endurance, to stay loving when others have left, to stay gentle when others grow cold. Heaven calls that maturity.

The Crown of Consistency

Revelation 2:10 says, *"Be faithful unto death, and I will give you the crown of life."* That crown isn't jewelry, it's authority. Consistency qualifies you for capacity. When God can trust you to remain steady in obscurity, He can trust you with influence in visibility. Honor that endures becomes glory that remains.

Every time you choose steadfastness, angels record endurance as worship. You are writing history with Heaven through patience.

Transition

Enduring honor doesn't just survive hardship, it transforms it. In the next and final section of this chapter, we'll see how enduring honor turns suffering into seed, how everything you walk through becomes something God can multiply for the healing of others.

Section 5 – *The Harvest of Honor: Turning Suffering into Seed*

Everything in the Kingdom reproduces after its kind, including pain. If bitterness conceives in you, it multiplies brokenness. But when honor conceives in you, it multiplies redemption. Suffering that is surrendered becomes seed, and seed never dies, it transforms.

The cross is the eternal proof of this: the **worst suffering ever known became the greatest harvest ever grown**. Christ's agony birthed adoption. His wounds became our doorway. When you walk through your own garden of Gethsemane with honor, what feels like crushing becomes cultivation. **You're not losing, you're sowing.**

Pain That Produces

Paul said, *"Death is at work in us, but life in you."* He understood the economy of the Kingdom: when sons absorb pain with grace, others receive life. That's why he could call his trials *"light afflictions."* They were producing something beyond sight, an eternal weight of glory.

The greater the pressure, the greater the capacity for glory. Pain is not wasted when it's worshipped through. Every tear waters the seed of future fruit. When you choose to respond with honor instead of retaliation, Heaven uses your suffering as a field of resurrection.

From Suffering to Service

The truest ministers are not those who studied the most but those who survived the most, without losing tenderness. Your authority in healing others will always grow from the wounds you've let God heal in you. Joseph could feed nations because he forgave brothers. Jesus could save the world because He honored the Father through the cross. You can't impart what you've avoided, but you can multiply what you've surrendered.

Honor turns your scars into assignments. You stop asking *"Why me?"* and start declaring *"Through me."* That's how suffering becomes service, the transformation of pain into purpose.

Multiplying Grace

Seed multiplies when it dies. Jesus said, *"Unless a grain of wheat falls into the ground and dies, it remains alone; but if it dies, it produces much fruit."* Death here means surrender, allowing the process to complete its work without pulling yourself out of the ground too early. When you stay planted in trust, resurrection becomes inevitable.

The same Spirit that raised Jesus from the dead quickens you, not just from sin, but from sorrow. Every season of submission adds spiritual weight to your words, authority to your prayers, and compassion to your leadership. Grace grows where honor has been buried.

The Fruit of Forgiveness

Forgiveness is fertile soil. It's where mercy grows into miracles. When Stephen forgave his murderers, the seeds of his prayer landed in Saul, the man who would become Paul. Your act of forgiveness may be watering someone's future transformation. That's why you can't afford to stop sowing mercy. The harvest might be beyond your lifetime, but it will still be counted to your account.

Heaven never forgets those who bless their persecutors. God multiplies every moment you choose grace over grudges. Honor doesn't just heal hearts; it expands Heaven's reach through yours.

Suffering as Apostolic Assignment

To the mature, suffering becomes stewardship. Paul said, *"I fill up in my flesh what is lacking in the afflictions of Christ, for the sake of His body."* He wasn't claiming Christ's work was incomplete, he was recognizing his role as participant. Honor invites you into that same partnership: to bear pain redemptively, carrying His fragrance into a broken world. Every time you respond to injustice with grace, you extend the Kingdom's dominion.

This is the secret of apostolic resilience, turning wounds into wells. Every place you bleed becomes a place others drink.

The Beauty of the Broken

Gold doesn't shine until it's melted. Oil doesn't flow until it's pressed. Wine doesn't pour until grapes are crushed. Likewise, glory doesn't manifest until sons are broken open in honor. In Heaven's economy, **brokenness is not loss, it's invitation**. God delights to pour Himself through those who refuse to let pain harden them.

Isaiah said, *"He gives beauty for ashes."* But He never said He removes the ashes first. He transforms them. Your ashes still preach: they sing of the God who wastes nothing.

The Law of Multiplication

Honor is Heaven's law of multiplication. Whatever you honor increases in your life; whatever you dishonor decreases. When you honor God in suffering, you increase in stature, wisdom, and favor. When you honor others despite offense, you multiply grace and peace. Every time you choose honor, you expand your harvest field. Your life becomes a landscape of redemption, what was once barren now blossoms.

Conclusion: The Echo of the Cross

When Jesus cried, *"It is finished,"* it was not resignation, it was reproduction. The seed had been sown, the soil split open, and Heaven's harvest was secured. That cry still echoes through every believer who endures hardship with honor. Every *"yes"* in adversity sounds like *"It is finished"* to hell.

Your story is not ending in suffering; it's multiplying through it. You are Heaven's seed, buried, yes, but destined to bloom. Honor ensures that even your hardest seasons will one day look like gardens.

Transition

The next chapter, Chapter 7, Honor vs Respect: The Divine Distinction, will confront the greatest counterfeit to true honor. Up to this point, we have established that honor recognizes divine intention regardless of visible maturity. In Chapter 7, we now expose how culture substituted identity-based honor with performance-based respect, and how this subtle shift has silently restructured relationships, leadership, and spiritual alignment. This is the turning point where honor transitions from general posture to discerning operation.

Chapter 6 Review & Reflection

Honor in Adversity: Loving Those Who Wound You

Core Revelation

True honor is not proven in comfort but in conflict. It's not measured by how you treat those who celebrate you, but by how you respond to those who betray you. When you honor in adversity, you don't excuse wrong, you express Heaven. You reveal a Kingdom that conquers through mercy and redeems through restraint.

Honor in adversity transforms pain into prophecy, wounds into wisdom, and suffering into seed. It is the proof of maturity and the fragrance of true sonship.

Kingdom Principle

Honor in adversity is Heaven's strategy for victory. It releases healing, disarms the enemy, and turns every injustice into an opportunity for transformation.

Scripture Focus

- Luke 23:34 – *"Father, forgive them; for they know not what they do."*
- Genesis 50:20 – *"You meant it for evil, but God meant it for good."*
- Matthew 5:44 – *"Love your enemies... bless those who curse you."*
- Romans 12:21 – *"Do not be overcome by evil, but overcome evil with good."*
- 2 Corinthians 4:17 – *"Our light affliction... works for us an eternal weight of glory."*
- Philippians 2:8–9 – *"He humbled Himself... therefore God exalted Him."*

Truths to Remember

1. The proof of honor is how you treat those who hurt you.
2. Forgiveness is not weakness, it's warfare.
3. Pain is not punishment; it's preparation for purpose.
4. Bitterness blocks circulation, honor restores it.
5. Reconciliation requires two hearts; forgiveness only one.
6. When you honor through adversity, you become unoffendable.
7. Perspective turns pain into prophecy.
8. Every act of mercy is seed sown for future harvest.
9. You cannot carry glory with a grudging heart.
10. Enduring honor qualifies you for enduring authority.

Application

- Practice immediate forgiveness. Don't wait for apology or justice, release the debt daily.
- Rehearse grace, not grievance. Speak blessings where betrayal occurred.
- Use worship as your response to wounds. Replace reaction with reverence.
- Reframe rejection. Ask what God is protecting or producing through it.
- Guard your heart from cynicism. Gratitude is your armor in prolonged adversity.
- Let pain become seed. Teach from what you've survived; heal others with what healed you.
- Maintain tenderness. The goal of honor is not survival, but transformation.

Reflection Questions

1. Who wounded me that I still inwardly rehearse rather than release?
2. What lesson might Heaven be writing inside my pain?

3. Have I mistaken delay for denial, or is God deepening trust in the waiting?
4. How can I bless, not just forgive, those who wronged me?
5. What part of my story could become seed for another's healing?

Declaration

"Father, thank You for trusting me with pain that produced purpose. I choose to honor You in every adversity, forgiving freely, loving boldly, and standing as proof that mercy wins. Let my wounds release oil, my trials birth truth, and my life reveal the fragrance of Your grace. I will love, bless, and honor, even when it hurts, because You did the same for me."

CHAPTER 7

HONOR VS. RESPECT: THE DIVINE DISTINCTION

Introduction – *Two Languages, Two Realms*

There is a vast difference between what Heaven commands and what culture negotiates. In our world, conversations about respect are relentless. People talk about earning respect, losing it, demanding it, negotiating it, withholding it, or proving themselves worthy of it. It has become a standard of relational measurement, an assessment of credibility, and a benchmark of dignity.

But when we turn to Scripture, we find an entirely different vocabulary.

The Bible rarely speaks of respect. Instead, it consistently, and unapologetically, commands honor.

This reveals something profound:

Honor is the language of the Kingdom. Respect is the language of human systems.

Honor is rooted in identity. Respect is rooted in judgment. Honor flows from Heaven's value system. Respect flows from human memory and evaluation. Honor is granted by revelation. Respect is granted through assessment.

This distinction is not minor; it is transformative. To live as sons in the Kingdom, we must understand what Heaven insists upon and what it deliberately refuses to engage. For that, we begin where God begins, in His Word.

Section 1 – Why God Commands Honor, Not Respect

Before defining honor, we must examine what God never asks us to do. Scripture is clear:

"Honor all men." (1 Peter 2:17)
"Honor the Lord." (Proverbs 3:9)
"Honor your father and mother." (Exodus 20:12)
"Let the elders who rule well be counted worthy of double honor." (1 Timothy 5:17)

Notice what is not found:
There is no verse that says, *"Respect all men," "Respect the Lord,"* or *"Respect your parents."*

Why? Because respect is a human construct, but honor is a divine one. Respect is based on perceived worthiness. Honor is based on God-given identity. Respect fluctuates based on performance. Honor remains because value remains. Respect is earned. Honor is revealed.

God commands what He Himself practices. He does not respect men; He honors them.

Transition

But to understand why this distinction matters, we must examine the essence of respect and why God refuses to align Himself with it.

Section 2 – The True Meaning of Respect and Why Heaven Avoids It

The word respect comes from re–spect, meaning "to look back, to re-inspect, or to review past behavior." Respect is fundamentally retroactive. It evaluates who a person has been, what they have done, and whether they have proven themselves worthy of favorable treatment.

It is intrinsically tied to memory. Respect depends on history: how they behaved, how they treated you, whether they failed, whether they earned trust.

This is why Scripture warns:
"It is not good to respect persons unto judgment."
Proverbs 24:23

Respect opens the door to partiality, to ranking and comparison. It teaches us to treat people based on their past, rather than their purpose. Respect causes relational distance; honor cultivates relational dignity.

Transition

To grasp this further, we must now turn our attention to the nature of God Himself.

Section 3 – Why God Is "No Respecter of Persons"

Three times Scripture repeats this truth:
"God is no respecter of persons." (Acts 10:34)
"There is no respect of persons with God." (Romans 2:11)
"Neither doth God respect any person." (Deuteronomy 10:17)

Why such emphasis? Because respect would require God to look backward, to evaluate worth based on performance. But that contradicts His nature entirely.

God does not assess value by history. He assigns value by identity. He sees:
- those made in His image,
- those created with intention,
- those loved before they were formed,
- those called before they ever performed.

Honor aligns with this divine perspective. Respect cannot. Respect is earth's way of measuring men. Honor is Heaven's way of restoring them.

Transition

Now that we know how God sees, we must consider how we see, and how honor shifts our lens from history to design.

Section 4 – Respect Judges Past Behavior; Honor Sees Original Design

Respect says, *"Show me who you have been, and I will determine how I treat you."* Honor says, *"I recognize who God created you to be, and that alone determines my posture toward you."*

Respect evaluates behavior. Honor acknowledges identity.
Respect elevates the deserving. Honor elevates the created.
Respect sees the man. Honor sees the image of God within the man.
Respect produces guardedness. Honor produces grace.
Respect examines history. Honor responds to destiny.

Transition

The effects of this divergence are far-reaching. Next, we will observe how respect fractures relationships while honor restores them.

Section 5 – Respect Divides; Honor Restores

Because respect is judgment-based, it introduces partiality, bias, comparison, and relational distance. It produces resentment when expectations are not met. It leads to favoritism and ranking.

Honor, however, does the opposite. It restores dignity, encourages unity, cultivates mutual grace, and establishes connection.

Respect views relationship as safe only if behavior permits. Honor deems relationship sacred because value is inherent.

Honor is Heaven's remedy for earth's rejection. It sees design where respect sees dysfunction and future where respect sees failure.

Transition

At this point, it becomes clear: respect can be withdrawn, but honor carries permanence.

Section 6 – Respect Can Be Withheld; Honor Cannot

A man can say, *"I don't respect him anymore,"* because respect was earned through performance. But no one can rightly say, *"I refuse to honor him,"* because honor was never based on behavior, it was based on identity.

Even when a person acts dishonorably, their God-assigned value does not change. Honor is not an **endorsement of behavior**; it is a **recognition of divine intention**. Honor refuses to strip away dignity even when addressing failure. It confronts with clarity but without contempt. Respect reacts. Honor responds. Respect is conditional; honor is covenantal.

Transition

With this in mind, we must now look beyond refusal and into divine replacement, what Heaven asks instead of respect.

Section 7 – Honor: The Divine Replacement for Respect

When Scripture says, *"Honor all men,"* it eliminates the notion of selective value. God does not ask you to honor only the agreeable, the mature, the consistent, or the familiar. He commands honor because all carry His image, His intention, and His purpose.

Respect looks backward and weighs worthiness.
Honor looks upward and acknowledges origin.
Respect asks, *"What did you do?"*
Honor asks, *"Who did God make you to be?"*

Respect deals with history.
Honor deals with identity.

Respect is determined by man.
Honor is released by Heaven.

Conclusion – *Honor: The Culture of Sons*

If you live by respect, you will govern people by judgment. But if you live by honor, you will govern relationships by redemption.

Respect protects your own comfort. Honor protects your own character. Respect imitates fairness. Honor imitates Christ. Respect can change with emotion. Honor anchors you in truth.

Honor is the language of sons, the culture of the Kingdom, and the only posture that Heaven authorizes.

Respect may be practiced socially, but it is not upheld spiritually. Honor is the divine alternative to respect, and the only response that aligns with the nature of God Himself.

Chapter 7 Review & Reflection

Honor vs Respect

Core Revelation

Respect is built on judgment and past performance; honor is built on identity and divine intention. Respect evaluates history. Honor recognizes design.

Kingdom Principle

Honor is the culture of Heaven; respect is the culture of earth.

Scripture Focus

- 1 Peter 2:17 – *"Honor all men."*
- Proverbs 3:9 – *"Honor the Lord with your possessions…"*
- Exodus 20:12 – *"Honor your father and your mother…"*
- 1 Timothy 5:17 – *"Let the elders who rule well be counted worthy of double honor."*
- Proverbs 24:23 – *"It is not good to have respect of persons in judgment."*

Truths to Remember

1. Respect depends on the receiver; honor depends on the giver.
2. Respect is earned; honor is commanded.
3. Respect looks backward at behavior; honor looks upward to God's intention.
4. Respect imitates human fairness; honor imitates Christ.
5. Respect can change with seasons; honor anchors you in truth.
6. When you live by respect, you will live judgmentally. When you live by honor, you will live redemptively.

Application

- Ask the Holy Spirit to show you where you've substituted respect for honor in relationships.
- Intentionally speak to identity, not just to behavior, when dealing with others.
- Refuse to let someone's past become your standard for their present value.
- Practice seeing people as image-bearers first, not performers.
- Consciously choose Kingdom culture (honor) over earth's culture (respect) in conflict and disappointment.

Reflection Questions

1. Who have I withheld honor from because I disapproved of their past or present behavior?
2. Do I treat people more according to their history or God's intention for them?
3. Where have I allowed respect (judgment) to replace honor (value) in my heart?
4. How might my relationships change if I saw every person as an image-bearer rather than a performer?
5. Is my treatment of others shaped more by Heaven's culture or earth's culture?

Declaration

"Father, I renounce the world's system of respect, the judgment of people according to their past. I embrace the culture of Heaven, the honor of people according to their identity in You. I choose to:
- *Honor all men because You created all men.*
- *Recognize value where flesh sees failure.*
- *Treat others as You treat me, through mercy, not memory.*
- *See design, not dysfunction.*
- *Look at purpose, not performance.*
- *Respond by the Spirit, not by history.*

Honor: The Language Of Sons

I refuse to relate through respect when You have called me to honor. I honor because You honor. I value because You value. I see because You saw me first. Honor will be my posture, my language, and my identity, because honor is the culture of the King, and I am a son of the Kingdom. Amen."

CHAPTER 8

THE HONOR OF OBEDIENCE: WHEN SUBMISSION BECOMES STRENGTH

Section 1 – The Posture of Submission

Submission is not subjugation; it is synchronization. It is not the loss of identity; it is the alignment of it. In the Kingdom, obedience is not the posture of slaves but the privilege of sons. Where rebellion says, *"I will,"* obedience says, *"Thy will."* One builds Babel; the other builds Zion.

When God invites you into obedience, He's not testing your willpower; He's tuning your heart. He's bringing your rhythm into harmony with Heaven's melody. True obedience doesn't begin in action, it begins in affection. We obey whom we love. Jesus said, *"If you love Me, keep My commandments."* He was not demanding proof; He was describing flow. Love naturally listens.

Obedience as Honor

Obedience is the tangible form of honor. It is the visible evidence that you value God's voice above your own reasoning. In Eden, dishonor entered not through hatred, but through independence, man deciding to act apart from divine order. That single act fractured harmony between Heaven and earth.

When Jesus came, He restored honor by restoring obedience. He said, *"I do only what I see My Father doing."* His submission was not servitude, it was shared sovereignty. Heaven trusted Him with authority because He never stepped outside alignment. This is the secret of Kingdom power: authority flows where submission is established.

The centurion understood this mystery when he said, *"I am a man under authority."* He recognized that Jesus' miracles were not rebellion against natural law but results of divine order. Obedience connects earth to Heaven's circuitry.

The Freedom Hidden in Surrender

The world teaches that freedom means doing whatever you want. Heaven teaches that freedom means being restored to what you were created for. Disobedience creates bondage disguised as autonomy; obedience restores liberty through alignment. You were never meant to be the source, only the vessel. When you surrender to God's design, you stop carrying the weight of outcomes.

Obedience releases rest. You no longer strive to control; you yield to flow. That's why Jesus said, *"My yoke is easy and My burden is light."* The yoke of obedience fits because it was custom-made for sons. When you wear His will, you move without friction. Submission is not loss of freedom, it's entrance into divine ease.

Submission to God's Order

To honor God is to honor His order. Everything in creation responds to divine sequence: the sun rises when He says, tides shift at His command, seasons change at His signal. Only man questions the order that sustains him. Rebellion is resistance to rhythm. But when you return to obedience, peace returns to your soul.

That's why Paul taught, *"Let every soul be subject to the higher powers, for there is no authority except from God."* He wasn't giving political advice; he was reminding believers that divine order is not bondage, it's balance. Where submission reigns, chaos ceases. Submission restores alignment so that power can flow unhindered through the body.

Obedience and Relationship

You can't have relationship without obedience because relationship requires trust. Obedience is trust translated into action. When you delay obedience, you delay destiny. Partial obedience is just rebellion wearing robes of religion. The moment you obey fully, grace floods the atmosphere.

Abraham proved this when he offered Isaac. He didn't understand, but he trusted. And in his obedience, he discovered provision, the ram caught in the thicket. Provision always hides behind obedience. God's miracles are often waiting at the intersection of instruction and surrender.

Transition

Submission is not silence, it's alignment. It empowers, protects, and multiplies. In the next section, we'll explore how submission to authority, both divine and delegated, releases divine protection and power, and how rebellion short-circuits Kingdom flow.

Section 2 – The Chain of Honor: Authority, Alignment, and Protection

Heaven operates through order. Power without order is chaos, and freedom without alignment becomes anarchy. From the beginning, creation moved in synchronized response to God's voice, light, land, life, all arranged by sequence. The same principle governs the Kingdom: honor maintains alignment, and alignment maintains authority.

When you honor divine structure, you place yourself inside Heaven's protection system. To rebel against it is to step outside the covering that keeps you safe. That's why submission isn't punishment, it's preservation. The moment you come out from under authority, you become exposed to what that authority was shielding you from.

Heaven's Structure of Order

The Father, Son, and Spirit show us that authority is relational, not hierarchical. The Son is not inferior to the Father, yet He submits in perfect honor. The Spirit is not lesser than the Son, yet He glorifies Him continually. Each yields, each honors, and each functions perfectly within divine unity. This is the *"chain of honor"* at its purest, the circulation of love, not the enforcement of rank.

When the Church reflects that same pattern, authority becomes beautiful. Husbands lead through love, wives partner through strength, children obey through trust, and spiritual sons and daughters submit through faith. Honor connects every relationship like arteries in one body. Remove one, and circulation stops.

Authority as Covering, Not Control

The devil has spent centuries distorting authority. He makes people associate submission with suppression. But true authority doesn't crush; it covers. It doesn't take freedom; it guards it.

Think of an umbrella in a storm. You're not weaker for standing beneath it, you're wiser. Covering doesn't mean you lose individuality; it means you gain immunity. When you honor the leaders, parents, and mentors God has set over you, you stand inside their shield of grace. Their victories become your victories; their warfare deflects what would have reached you alone.

Authority is God's delegated protection system. When we dishonor it, we don't merely reject a person, we step outside a provision.

Rebellion as Exposure

Rebellion is not always loud. Sometimes it looks like quiet independence, the subtle belief that we can navigate life without accountability. But the enemy knows: isolation is vulnerability.

He hunts the disconnected. Lucifer's rebellion was not against God's existence but against His **order**. He wanted position without submission. The moment he dishonored divine structure, he lost access to divine strength.

That's why the spirit of rebellion still seeks to separate sons from fathers, sheep from shepherds, believers from body. Disconnection is always the first stage of deception. But alignment restores discernment. When you walk under authority, you see through clarity.

The Power of Delegated Authority

God moves through delegated authority because He honors His own system. When Jesus healed the centurion's servant, He marveled at the man's understanding: *"I also am a man under authority."* That centurion recognized that Jesus' words carried power because He was perfectly submitted to the Father. Heaven backs whatever flows in alignment.

In the same way, when you serve faithfully under authority, Heaven amplifies your voice. Submission multiplies strength; rebellion isolates it. David honored Saul's position even when Saul dishonored him. Because of that, Heaven preserved David while Saul perished in his own pride. You cannot dishonor order and inherit destiny.

Honor Protects the Flow

Every relationship that God ordains carries a specific flow of grace. Honor is what keeps that flow unbroken. Dishonor creates leaks. You can be in the right place but out of alignment if your heart is dishonoring. When murmuring, jealousy, or comparison enter, the flow slows and eventually stops. That's why Paul said, *"Let all things be done decently and in order."*

Honor is Heaven's plumbing; it keeps the flow of the Spirit unobstructed. The moment you honor again, the pipes clear and the oil runs freely. Alignment doesn't just bring blessing; it sustains it.

Honor in Leadership and Submission

Every believer must learn to **lead** and to **follow**. You cannot lead well if you have not followed well. Honor trains you for both. When you serve faithfully under authority, you learn how authority feels from the inside. When God raises you, you lead from empathy rather than ego. That's how the Kingdom reproduces safe leaders, sons who understand covering because they've lived under it.

In Heaven's eyes, submission is not a season; it's a spirit. Even when you are in authority, you remain under it. Jesus is still submitted to the Father, even seated on the throne. That's why His reign is eternal, honor sustains it.

Transition

Submission restores what rebellion destroys, trust, flow, and safety. But obedience doesn't stop with alignment under leadership; it must also govern how we respond to divine instruction in our daily walk. The next section will explore the obedience of faith, how hearing and heeding God's voice becomes the highest demonstration of trust.

Section 3 – The Obedience of Faith: Trusting the Voice Beyond Understanding

Faith begins where understanding ends. Obedience becomes powerful when logic runs out. God often gives instruction before explanation, because obedience is not about information, it's about transformation. When He speaks, He's not testing your hearing; He's training your trust.

Abraham's story proves it: *"Go to a land I will show you."* No map. No timeline. Just voice. Obedience to that voice birthed a nation. The Kingdom moves through people who say yes before they know why.

When Trust Is the Only a Compass

The obedience of faith doesn't always look strategic. It often looks senseless until seen from the other side. Noah built an ark before rain existed. Moses lifted a rod over water before the wind began to blow. Peter cast a net in daylight when fish normally hid. Each miracle was born from obedience that preceded understanding.

Faith obeys not because it comprehends, but because it's convinced. When the Word is enough, you no longer need guarantees. You realize that every step of trust builds a bridge you couldn't see before. This is how Heaven teaches sons to walk, step by step, voice by voice.

Obedience Unlocks Revelation

Understanding often comes after obedience, not before. Revelation follows response. When you obey what you do know, God reveals what you don't. Many believers remain stagnant not because Heaven is silent, but because they haven't moved on the last word.

Jesus said, *"If anyone wills to do His will, he shall know of the doctrine."* Knowledge follows willingness. When your heart says yes, light increases. Obedience is the **on-switch** for revelation. It's why disobedience darkens discernment, you can't hear clearly when you're holding back.

Faith That Acts

Real faith moves. It's not mental agreement; it's motion toward divine instruction. James said, *"Faith without works is dead."* That doesn't mean salvation by performance; it means trust always takes form. Every *"yes"* to God's prompting, whether to forgive, to give, to go, or to wait, is an act of worship that alters the spiritual atmosphere.

Sometimes the smallest steps carry the greatest significance. Naaman's dip in the Jordan looked ridiculous, but obedience restored his flesh. Obedience is the currency that converts Heaven's promise into earth's reality.

When Obedience Hurts

Faithful obedience doesn't always feel peaceful at first. Some instructions cut deep, leave, let go, be still. But pain is often the doorway to peace. God isn't trying to harm you; He's pruning for fruitfulness. Every act of surrender trims what hinders growth. When you yield without resistance, you discover new dimensions of His goodness.

Obedience is not supposed to be easy, it's supposed to be eternal. Each yes strengthens your spirit until obedience becomes instinct. You stop negotiating with God and start partnering with Him.

Hearing and Heeding

Faith comes by hearing, but breakthrough comes by heeding. Many hear God's word but never harvest it. The difference lies in immediate response. Delayed obedience creates spiritual interference, it gives doubt time to argue. Prompt obedience silences confusion before it starts.

The more you act on what He says, the clearer His voice becomes. Obedience trains spiritual hearing: disobedience dulls it. That's why sons live responsive lives, listening hearts that translate revelation into movement.

The Peace of Obedience

Every act of obedience carries peace within it. It may not bring comfort, but it brings confirmation. Peace is Heaven's signature that you're in alignment. Even when outcomes are unclear, there's an inner stillness that says, *"You're walking with Me."* That's how Jesus could sleep through storms, He was never out of sync with His Father.

Peace doesn't mean absence of trouble; it means presence of trust. When you obey, Heaven's rhythm becomes your rest.

Transition

The obedience of faith births revelation, rest, and reward. But obedience is not only personal, it also governs how we walk in community and leadership. The next section explores corporate obedience, how collective alignment releases Kingdom authority in families, ministries, and nations.

Section 4 – Corporate Obedience: The Power of Collective Alignment

Heaven moves fastest through agreement. One person in alignment carries weight, but an entire community in alignment carries government. Personal obedience builds character; corporate obedience builds culture. When a people respond together to the voice of God, Heaven finds a place to rest, not just to visit.

That's why the Book of Acts begins not with a miracle, but with obedience. *"They were all together in one place and in one accord."* That unity was not merely emotional, it was positional. Their obedience created an atmosphere strong enough to host the Holy Spirit. Fire fell where alignment had gathered.

The Sound of Agreement

Obedience has a sound. When hearts synchronize, Heaven hears harmony. God told Israel, *"If you diligently obey My voice, blessings will overtake you."* That wasn't an individual promise, it was a national invitation. Obedience unites sound and spirit until Heaven's word finds echo on earth.

Corporate obedience sounds like worship that's not performance but posture. It sounds like intercession that doesn't compete but completes. It's the rhythm of sons moving as one body, many members, one mind. That's the Ekklesia, Heaven's embassy made audible.

Obedience Builds Atmosphere

When people obey collectively, the unseen shifts visibly. Atmosphere thickens with presence, miracles multiply in shared submission. Disorder drains anointing, but unity attracts it. That's why Psalm 133 links unity to oil, it describes a corporate environment so aligned that Heaven's fragrance flows from head to hem.

Wherever I've seen lasting revival, it was never just a gifted leader, it was a people who obeyed the same rhythm. When God says move, and a church moves as one, demons lose jurisdiction. When He says wait, and they wait in patience rather than panic, Heaven deepens its well among them. Corporate obedience turns gatherings into gateways.

When One Disobeys

Disobedience affects more than the disobedient. When Achan hid forbidden treasure in his tent, Israel's entire army suffered defeat. One man's secrecy broke the nation's synergy. God doesn't punish collective obedience for individual sin; He highlights the power of shared consequence. The body suffers when one member withdraws alignment. Honor among the people keeps the flow pure.

In the same way, obedience repairs what dishonor broke. When Israel repented, victory returned. Collective repentance restores corporate authority.

Leadership and the People

True leaders cultivate obedience through example, not demand. They model submission to God's word until their followers see that obedience is safety, not subservience. When leadership honors Heaven's timing, the people naturally follow. The Church becomes synchronized like an orchestra under one Conductor.

Moses lifted his rod, and Israel crossed the sea because the people obeyed the command, not the personality. When leaders and people align in mutual honor, the Red Seas of impossibility part again.

National Alignment

Every great move of God in history began with a remnant of obedient hearts. When Nineveh obeyed Jonah's warning, judgment was reversed. When Josiah obeyed the rediscovered Word, a nation was renewed. When the early Church obeyed the Great Commission, the world was turned upside down. Obedience doesn't just bless individuals, it redeems territories.

That's why the Spirit keeps calling for alignment in this generation, not more noise, but more yes. Nations bow when the Church walks in obedience, because obedience restores authority. We lose influence not because of persecution, but because of disunity. Corporate obedience reclaims it.

The Kingdom Principle of *"One Accord"*

Heaven's government rests on *"one accord."* This phrase is more than harmony; it means *"same passion, same pursuit."* When hearts burn for the same purpose, power multiplies exponentially. That's why Jesus sent His disciples two by two, not because one wasn't enough, but because agreement magnifies impact. When multitudes obey, darkness collapses over regions. Collective obedience is how the Kingdom colonizes earth.

Transition

Corporate obedience creates an atmosphere for authority and breakthrough. But it also reveals something deeper: obedience as worship. In the next section, we'll explore how obedience itself becomes the fragrance that pleases God, the worship that outweighs words.

Section 5 – Obedience as Worship: The Fragrance of Honor

Let me preface this section with the reality that worship far transcends music and song. Worship is a life lived not a song sung! With that understanding let's continue on.

Worship begins where obedience continues. The truest songs are sung with surrendered lives. Before there was an altar with fire, there was a garden with a command. Obedience was, and still is, God's favorite sound.

Many can lift their hands in worship, but only the obedient lift their hearts. In Heaven, incense rises from yielded will. Obedience is not music for the ear; it's fragrance for the throne. It carries the scent of love proven through trust. That's why Samuel told Saul, *"To obey is better than sacrifice."* Sacrifice without submission is noise; obedience without performance is perfume.

The Scent of Submission

When Jesus knelt in Gethsemane and said, *"Nevertheless, not My will but Yours be done,"* He filled eternity with the aroma of pure worship. That one sentence carried more power than a thousand songs. Heaven recorded not just His words but His posture. In that moment, all creation smelled redemption.

Obedience always carries fragrance because it releases agreement between Heaven and earth. When the human will bows to divine will, the atmosphere changes. Hell loses jurisdiction wherever someone says yes to God.

The Weight of Disobedience

Disobedience is costly because it breaks harmony. When Saul disobeyed, he lost the kingdom, not because God despised him, but because disobedience carries a different scent. Rebellion pollutes what worship purifies. The moment Saul prioritized image over instruction, he chose presentation over presence.

This is the tragedy of much modern religion; it sings loudly but listens little. We measure worship by volume instead of by obedience. But Heaven's measure is still the same: Did you do what I said?

The Sound Heaven Recognizes

Heaven doesn't respond to emotional noise; it responds to familiar frequency. When Abraham raised the knife over Isaac, Heaven heard the pitch of obedience and intervened. When Mary said, *"Be it unto me according to Your word,"* Heaven heard the same tone and overshadowed her. When Jesus said, *"It is finished,"* that sound shook hell itself.

Every act of obedience reverberates in eternity. It's how sons sing without instruments, through yielded choices, through unseen surrender.

Your yes is worship.
Your obedience is melody.
Your alignment is incense.

Obedience Outlasts Emotion

Emotion fades: devotion remains. There will be days when you don't feel His presence, when silence tests your loyalty. That's when obedience becomes your offering. Worship is not always euphoria; sometimes it's endurance. Faithful obedience in dry seasons is the sweetest fragrance Heaven knows.

When you obey without reward, you remind Hell that your love isn't for sale. That aroma fills Heaven with delight. Even angels can smell the steadfast heart that keeps saying yes.

When Worship and Obedience Meet

When obedience and worship meet, glory appears. Moses built the tabernacle exactly as the Lord commanded, and when he finished, the glory filled the tent. Precision invites presence. God will always fill what is formed in obedience.

Likewise, when your life becomes an altar built to His specifications, He inhabits it. Worship without obedience is empty ritual; obedience without worship is rigid religion. But when the two embrace, Heaven kisses earth.

The Joy of the Father

Nothing delights the Father more than a son or daughter who trusts Him enough to obey. That obedience becomes the Father's inheritance in you, the evidence that His nature has taken root. When Jesus obeyed unto death, the Father's pleasure thundered: *"This is My beloved Son, in whom I am well pleased."* That same approval still echoes over every act of surrendered faith.

Every time you say yes, Heaven hears family resemblance. Obedience is how sons sound like their Father.

Transition

Obedience as worship reveals that honor is not only about behavior, but also about alignment of heart, sound, and submission. The next and final section of this chapter will explore the reward of obedience, how submission becomes strength and how those who honor authority walk in divine authority.

Section 6 – The Reward of Obedience: Authority Born from Alignment

Every *"yes"* carries inheritance. Obedience is not only the expression of honor, it's the qualification for authority. Before God gives dominion, He tests disposition. If you can be trusted to submit, you can be trusted to rule. Heaven never promotes rebels; it commissions the yielded.

Jesus' authority was not inherited by title but entrusted through obedience.

"He became obedient unto death, even death on a cross. Therefore God has highly exalted Him."

The cross was not His demotion, it was His coronation. Heaven enthrones those who bow first.

Authority Flows From Alignment

Power doesn't come from position, it comes from posture. When you align yourself under divine order, Heaven flows through you effortlessly. This is why Jesus marveled at the centurion's understanding: *"I also am a man under authority."* The centurion knew that to command, one must first be commanded. Authority flows through those who remain under authority.

You don't have to demand influence when you dwell in alignment; it follows you naturally. People sense the weight of Heaven on those who have learned to yield. Obedience anchors glory, it's what makes anointing sustainable.

Submission Produces Strength

The world sees submission as weakness, but in the Kingdom it's strength under control. Like a river contained by banks, obedience channels power. A river without boundaries floods and destroys; a river within its course nourishes and transforms. God doesn't restrain you to limit you; He aligns you to release you safely.

When your will becomes one with His, resistance becomes irrelevant. The devil can't intimidate a man who no longer argues with Heaven. Such a person carries quiet strength, the authority that needs no announcement. That's what Jesus meant when He said, *"Learn of Me, for I am meek and lowly in heart, and you will find rest for your souls."* Meekness isn't weakness, it's mastery.

Obedience and Anointing

Anointing is Heaven's endorsement on obedience. Oil never falls on rebellion. When Samuel anointed David, the Spirit rushed upon him because his heart was already yielded. Obedience prepared the vessel before oil filled it.

Every time you obey a divine instruction, you make space for new grace. That's why miracles often follow motion. Naaman wasn't healed because of the water; he was healed because of the word. The water had no power until obedience activated it. When obedience moves, anointing manifests.

The Weight of Divine Trust

God doesn't trust titles; He trusts temperaments. When you prove faithful in private obedience, He entrusts you with public authority. David learned to honor God by tending sheep before he ever faced giants. He ruled quietly long before he ruled visibly. Heaven tests sons in secret so that power never spoils purity.

When authority comes through honor, it never becomes arrogance. True authority doesn't shout; it simply stands. It carries the stillness of someone who knows Heaven is backing them.

Obedience Releases Dominion

Dominion is delegated, not demanded. It's the overflow of consistent obedience. Adam lost authority through disobedience; Christ restored it through submission. Every time you obey, you recover ground Adam forfeited. Your alignment reactivates Heaven's government in the earth.

That's why obedience isn't optional for Kingdom people, it's governmental. You're not just obeying a command; you're enforcing a covenant. Each act of submission widens Heaven's reach through your life.

The Joy of Alignment

Obedience doesn't end in exhaustion; it ends in joy. Jesus endured the cross *"for the joy set before Him."* Joy is the final fruit of obedience because you're walking in harmony with divine intention. When your will and God's will become indistinguishable, peace becomes perpetual.

That's when strength feels like serenity. You're no longer striving for authority; you're living from it. You've entered the rest reserved for the aligned.

Conclusion: The Crown of the Submitted

Obedience ends where authority begins. Every crown in Heaven was once a yoke on earth. The sons that God is raising now will not wear crowns they haven't carried as crosses. Their influence will not come from charisma but from consecration.

Heaven will entrust the next measure of Kingdom rule to those who have learned the language of honor through obedience. They will govern not by command, but by compassion. Not by force, but by flow. For when submission becomes strength, Heaven has truly found a son.

Chapter 8 Review & Reflection

The Honor of Obedience: When Submission Becomes Strength

Core Revelation

Obedience is not the loss of will but the alignment of it. It is not about control, it's about connection. Submission does not suppress identity; it synchronizes it with divine intention. When we obey God and the authorities He ordains, we position ourselves in the same posture as Christ, one of yielded strength.

Obedience is the visible language of honor. It brings Heaven's order to earth, releases authority through alignment, and transforms worship from mere expression into embodiment.

Kingdom Principle

Obedience is Heaven's power protocol. Authority flows through alignment, protection rests beneath covering, and strength is born in submission.

Scripture Focus

- Philippians 2:8–9 – *"He became obedient unto death... therefore God highly exalted Him."*
- 1 Samuel 15:22 – *"To obey is better than sacrifice."*
- Romans 13:1 – *"Let every soul be subject to the higher powers..."*
- Matthew 8:9–10 – *"I also am a man under authority."*
- John 14:15 – *"If you love Me, keep My commandments."*
- Hebrews 5:8 – *"Though He was a Son, yet He learned obedience by the things He suffered."*

Truths to Remember

1. Obedience is the fragrance of honor, Heaven smells submission before it sees service.
2. Alignment precedes authority. You cannot lead effectively until you have learned to follow faithfully.
3. Submission is protection, not punishment. Authority covers, not controls.
4. Faithful obedience births revelation; delayed obedience delays destiny.
5. Corporate obedience creates collective authority. One accord produces one anointing.
6. Obedience is the sound Heaven recognizes, every *"yes"* becomes a frequency of favor.
7. True worship is obedience in motion. Songs reach Heaven when lives match lyrics.
8. Obedience brings rest because it ends resistance.
9. The world crowns rebellion; Heaven crowns reverence.
10. Every crown of authority begins with a cross of obedience.

Application

- Respond quickly to the promptings of the Holy Spirit. Don't wait to understand fully, faith moves first.
- Honor leadership by seeing covering as protection rather than limitation.
- Practice corporate obedience, move in unity with your church, family, or team when God gives instruction.
- Check your posture. Ask, "Am I aligned or simply active?"
- Worship through obedience. Make every yes, an offering.
- Submit joyfully. Submission without joy becomes servitude; submission with joy becomes strength.
- Guard the flow of honor. When disagreement arises, keep reverence intact.

Reflection Questions

1. In what areas has obedience become optional rather than essential in my life?
2. Am I living under authority that I trust, and do I honor it from the heart, not just in appearance?
3. Have I confused submission with weakness, or do I see it as Heaven's strength?
4. How can I turn my worship into obedience beyond the platform or service?
5. What "yes" have I delayed that Heaven is waiting on?

Declaration

"Father, I yield to Your rhythm. Align my will with Yours until obedience becomes my delight. Teach me to honor Your voice, Your order, and Your timing. I renounce rebellion and embrace divine alignment. Let submission become my strength and obedience my worship. Through yielded authority, may Your Kingdom flow through me in power, peace, and presence."

CHAPTER 9

HONOR IN LEADERSHIP: SERVING FROM THE SEAT OF SONSHIP

Section 1 – Leadership Reimagined

Leadership was never God's idea of dominance; it was His design for demonstration. When Heaven entrusts leadership, it is giving someone permission to show what the Father looks like. Jesus said, *"He who has seen Me has seen the Father."* That is leadership's definition in a single sentence, representation, not replacement.

The world measures leadership by position; the Kingdom measures it by posture. In the world, leaders climb ladders; in the Kingdom, they build tables. Earth promotes talent; Heaven promotes trust. Real authority is not grasped, it's granted to those who can carry others without controlling them.

Leadership is not a destination; it's a disposition. When you lead from sonship, you don't rule over people, you serve on behalf of the Father. You stop striving to be significant because you've already been named beloved. From that security flows the strength to lift, to build, to release.

The Model of the King

Every Kingdom leader begins with the pattern of Christ, the Son who led as a servant and served as a King. Philippians 2 says He *"made Himself of no reputation... and took on the form of a servant."* He emptied Himself not because He was powerless, but because He was trusted. Power unused for self is the hallmark of mature leadership.

When Jesus washed His disciples' feet, He wasn't performing humility; He was revealing government. The basin and towel were symbols of throne and scepter. Leadership in the Kingdom doesn't sit higher, it kneels deeper. That posture released authority greater than any crown could hold.

Leadership Born of Honor

Honor is the soil from which righteous leadership grows. Dishonorable hearts may achieve influence, but they cannot sustain it. When ambition outruns honor, anointing turns to manipulation. God resists the proud because pride refuses alignment, it wants inheritance without intimacy.

A leader who honors God's voice before their own vision becomes a conduit of Heaven's clarity. Such leaders don't use people to build ministry, they use ministry to build people. They understand that success in the Kingdom is not crowds gathered, but sons and daughters matured. Their authority is measured not in how many obey them, but in how many resemble Christ because of them.

The Seat of Sonship

Leadership without sonship becomes performance. Sonship gives leadership its identity, it anchors assignment in affection. Before Jesus ever preached a sermon or healed the sick, the Father declared, *"This is My beloved Son."* That affirmation came before achievement, proving that **approval precedes activity**.

The *"seat of sonship"* is not a throne you earn, it's a position you inherit. From that seat, you lead without insecurity because you're not proving anything, you're reproducing Someone. Sons don't compete; they complete. Their leadership style is rest, not rush. They govern through grace, not grind.

Stewardship, Not Ownership

A Kingdom leader never says, *"my people"* or *"my church."* Those words reveal ownership, not stewardship. Everything entrusted to you is the Lord's. The moment you forget that, pressure replaces peace.

When you realize the sheep belong to the Shepherd, you stop controlling outcomes and start cultivating growth. You lead with open hands, not clenched fists. Stewardship keeps your heart light and your motives pure; it allows God to move resources, people, and seasons as He pleases. Leaders who steward faithfully never fear subtraction; they trust multiplication through obedience.

Transition

The foundation of leadership is honor expressed as service. The next section will explore how honor flows through servant leadership, the practical rhythm of leading like Christ, carrying towels rather than titles.

Section 2 – Servant Leadership: Towels, Not Titles

In the Kingdom, greatness doesn't climb, it bows. The path to influence is not a ladder but a basin. Jesus didn't just redefine leadership; He reintroduced Heaven's culture of service.

He told His disciples, *"The greatest among you shall be your servant."* That statement wasn't poetic, it was prophetic. He was establishing the blueprint for how power must operate among sons: through humility. If authority is the weight of Heaven, then humility is the handle that carries it safely.

The Towel and the Table

On the night of His betrayal, Jesus took a towel. He could have taken a throne, but He chose a towel instead. And in that moment, He turned the room into revelation. He washed the feet of the very ones who would soon scatter, and He called it leadership.

The towel was His symbol of government. Every foot He washed represented dirt He didn't create but chose to carry. That's what true leaders do, they handle the humanity of those they lead without humiliation. They wash where others judge. They serve where others seek status.

The table He served at wasn't a stage; it was a circle. Servant leaders draw circles, not ladders. They bring others into proximity rather than forcing them into position. Their goal is not to be admired but to be multiplied.

The Test of the Towel

Every leader must pass the towel test. It's not whether you can hold a microphone, it's whether you can wash feet without recognition. Can you serve faithfully when applause fades? Can you bless those who betray you and still call them *"friend"*?

Heaven measures leaders by how low they're willing to go for love's sake. The kingdom isn't built by performers but by polishers, those who clean what others step over. Service is the currency of leadership, and humility is the proof of true authority.

If you ever outgrow serving, you've outgrown the Kingdom.

Servanthood Is Not Subservience

C.S. Lewis pointed us in the general direction of "Serving doesn't mean thinking less of yourself, it means thinking of yourself less". True servanthood flows from identity, not insecurity. You don't serve because you're unworthy; you serve because you're trusted. The Father entrusts towels only to those who know they're sons. A slave serves for approval; a son serves from it.

Servant leadership is not being everyone's doormat; it's being Heaven's doorway. People step through your humility into God's heart. Your service creates access for others to encounter the King you represent.

The Anointing of the Servant

There's an anointing that only comes through service. Elisha didn't receive Elijah's mantle because he prophesied well, he received it because he poured water on Elijah's hands. Before he became prophet, he became servant. The oil flows down, if you stay low enough, you catch it.

That's why some never walk in lasting power; they won't kneel long enough to receive it. Heaven only anoints those who understand the honor of serving. Towels are Heaven's training ground for mantles.

The Discipline of Discretion

Servant leaders protect the dignity of those they serve. When Jesus washed feet, He didn't announce whose were dirtiest. He covered what others would have exposed. That's what makes service sacred, it preserves worth even in weakness.

You will know a servant leader by their silence. They don't weaponize people's flaws; they wash them in love. They carry secrets, not scandals. They guard the wounded without gossip, and Heaven trusts them with greater grace.

Greatness Through Gentleness

Gentleness is not frailty; it's strength that refuses to bruise. The world calls leaders to assert dominance; Heaven calls them to distribute gentleness. Paul wrote, *"We were gentle among you, like a nursing mother caring for her children."* That is leadership language in the Kingdom, nurture, not noise. Gentleness wins hearts that authority alone could never reach.

When the Spirit shapes a leader's heart, people don't just follow their words, they rest under their care. That's the essence of Kingdom leadership: people flourish where honor is practiced.

Transition

Servant leadership is Heaven's architecture for authority, towels before thrones, humility before honor. In the next section, we'll explore how leaders cultivate honor in those they lead, how to raise people who respond, not react, who serve willingly, not wearily.

Section 3 – Cultivating Honor in Others: Raising Sons, Not Servants

The true legacy of a leader is not what they build, it's who they become through those they've raised. Jesus didn't leave behind buildings or systems; He left behind sons. Honor multiplies when it's modeled, not mandated. Culture isn't created by commands; it's transmitted by consistency. When leaders live honorably long enough, those around them begin to speak Heaven's language without needing translation.

Leadership, in its truest form, is fathering, imparting nature, not enforcing behavior. Fathers don't just teach principles; they transfer presence. Servants perform from obligation; sons function from likeness. That's why Jesus told His disciples, *"No longer do I call you servants... I have called you friends."* He was raising sons who would represent His heart, not just repeat His orders.

From Compliance to Conviction

Servant-minded followers need supervision; sons carry conviction. One requires monitoring; the other self-governs. You can train servants through rules, but you form sons through relationship. Rules maintain order, but love maintains honor.

A culture of honor emerges when people obey out of revelation, not regulation. They don't follow because they're afraid, they follow because they're aligned. You can sense the shift in an atmosphere when obedience turns into joy. That's when the Kingdom has truly taken root.

Reproducing the Heart, Not the Hustle

If followers imitate your methods without inheriting your heart, you've raised workers, not sons. You can reproduce labor without reproducing likeness. Many ministries collapse under the weight of imitation because they multiplied what they did instead of who they were.

Paul told the Corinthians, *"You have ten thousand instructors in Christ, but not many fathers."* Instructors replicate lessons; fathers reproduce lives. That's why Paul called Timothy his *"true son in the faith."* He wasn't merely training a preacher; he was cultivating a nature, a heart that honors.

When people catch your heart, not just your habits, they become extensions of Heaven's DNA through you.

Creating a Culture of Mutual Honor

Honor flows in two directions, upward and downward. A leader who only expects honor but never gives it creates fear, not family. But when honor circulates both ways, love becomes the ecosystem. In such an atmosphere, correction doesn't feel like rejection, and accountability feels like safety.

Leaders who honor those they lead create teams that thrive instead of survive. They listen, affirm, and empower without losing authority. The highest form of leadership is making room for others to shine. When you delight in another's success, you prove that the Kingdom has taken hold of your ego.

How to Instill Honor Practically

1. **Model Consistency:**
   Honor is caught before it's taught. Be the example you wish to multiply.
2. **Celebrate Faithfulness, Not Fame:**
   Publicly affirm character more than performance.
3. **Guard Conversations:**
   Never dishonor someone behind their back; your team will imitate your tone.
4. **Create Covenant, Not Contract:**
   Build relationships around purpose and trust, not benefit and control.
5. **Correct with Compassion:**
   When discipline is needed, preserve dignity. Rebuke should heal, not humiliate.
6. **Release Responsibility Gradually:**
   Trust develops maturity. Give people opportunity, not entitlement.
7. **Stay Approachable:**
   Honor thrives where fear dies. Let transparency be the language of your leadership.

The Reward of Raising Sons

When you raise sons, you multiply legacy instead of labor. Sons extend what servants execute. They become carriers of the same DNA in new territories, ensuring that the sound of honor continues beyond your years. Jesus' ministry multiplied after His ascension because He had reproduced His Spirit in those He trained. The goal of Kingdom leadership isn't control, it's continuation. Legacy is not about how long you lead but how well you reproduce.

When the culture of honor is sown into hearts, it outlives structures. Buildings may crumble, organizations may shift, but sons remain. That is eternal fruit.

Transition

Leaders reproduce what they reveal, and they reveal most what they honor. In the next section, we'll explore how honor governs correction and confrontation, how to handle disagreement, failure, and discipline without losing dignity or unity.

Section 4 – Honor in Correction: Confronting Without Crushing

Correction is one of the greatest tests of honor, for both the leader giving it and the person receiving it. Many can love when there's agreement, but few can love when truth confronts. Yet in the Kingdom, confrontation isn't conflict, it's care. If love covers sin, honor heals it. Correction is Heaven's hand of restoration disguised as rebuke.

When Paul told Timothy to reprove, rebuke, and exhort, he added this essential phrase: *"with all longsuffering and doctrine."* In other words, correction without compassion becomes condemnation. Honor is what keeps truth redemptive.

The Heart Behind Correction

Correction is never punishment; it's protection. It's the Father's way of keeping sons aligned with destiny. Proverbs says, *"Whom the Lord loves, He corrects."* Love does not stay silent while destruction develops. If you won't confront, you don't care enough. But how you confront determines whether honor remains intact.

Leaders correct not to control, but to cultivate. They see beyond behavior to potential. The goal of correction is not to expose sin, but to restore sight, to remind people of who they really are. Jesus' question to Peter after his failure, *"Do you love Me?"*, was not interrogation; it was reinstallation.

The Tone of Heaven

The tone of correction determines its outcome. Truth spoken harshly wounds, but truth spoken honorably heals. Heaven's tone always carries invitation, never humiliation. That's why Jesus could tell the woman caught in adultery, *"Go, and sin no more,"* yet she left freed, not shamed. Honor corrects with dignity intact.

Leaders who learn Heaven's tone build disciples instead of defensiveness. They speak truth in love, which is not softness, it's precision. Truth by itself can cut; love applies the healing balm.

Correction That Builds, Not Breaks

You can recognize correction born from honor by its fruit:
- It convicts without condemning.
- It exposes error without erasing value.
- It leads to repentance, not resentment.
- It leaves the person grateful, not guilty.

When correction is dishonorable, it leaves people broken and bitter. When it's honorable, it produces humility and growth. Even strong rebuke, when rooted in love, leaves behind peace. That's the mark of Kingdom discipline, it restores the image of the Father, not the image of fear.

How to Correct with Honor

1. **Pray First**.
   Never correct from irritation. Speak only when you've regained Heaven's heart.
2. **Address Privately Before Publicly**.
   Protect dignity before protecting image. Correction in secret preserves honor in public.
3. **Affirm Identity Before Addressing Behavior.**
   Start by reminding them who they are, a son, not a failure.
4. **Speak Truth Without Targeting.**

Focus on the action, not the person. *"This decision is dangerous,"* not *"You are a disappointment."*
5. **Provide a Path Forward.**
   Correction without direction is cruelty. Always show how restoration can begin.
6. **End with Grace.**
   Let mercy have the last word. Leave no wound open for shame to speak through.

The Honor of Being Corrected

Correction received with humility is a mark of maturity. Wise sons invite discipline because they recognize it as investment. Proverbs 9:8 says, *"Rebuke a wise man, and he will love you."* The immature resist correction because pride resists mirrors, it can't stand to see itself honestly. But the mature know mirrors are mercy.

Every correction carries an opportunity for promotion. Those who receive instruction without offense qualify for new levels of trust. Heaven can only entrust authority to those who remain teachable.

Restoring Fallen Leaders

Honor must also govern how we treat those who fail in leadership. Restoration doesn't mean ignoring sin; it means walking someone back to wholeness. Galatians 6:1 says, *"If anyone is overtaken in a fault, you who are spiritual restore such a one in a spirit of meekness."* That word *"restore"* is a medical term, it means *"to reset a broken bone."* The goal isn't **removal**, it's **realignment**. When we restore fallen leaders with humility, we mirror the mercy that kept us standing.

Honor covers the fallen the way Noah's sons covered their father, with their faces turned away, moving backward, refusing to dishonor what God had anointed. The covering wasn't denial, it was devotion. Such honor releases healing and reaffirms Heaven's design: redemption always outruns disgrace.

The Cost of Avoiding Correction

Avoiding correction for fear of offense is dishonor in disguise. Silence in the face of destruction is not love, it's abandonment. Leaders who withhold truth to preserve comfort will eventually lose credibility. But those who love enough to confront in grace will earn eternal trust.

A culture without correction is a culture without direction. Honor and truth must walk hand in hand, or both will lose meaning.

Transition

Correction reveals the Father's nature and protects the future of those being led. But even with correction, leaders must also understand how to balance authority and vulnerability, how to lead transparently without losing reverence. The next section will explore *"The Vulnerability of Leaders: Transparency Without Loss of Authority."*

Section 5 – *The Vulnerability of Leaders: Transparency Without Loss of Authority*

Leadership in the Kingdom is not about perfection, it's about surrender. True authority is not weakened by vulnerability; it is strengthened by it. The world teaches that leaders must hide flaws to maintain respect, but Heaven teaches that transparency builds trust. Jesus ruled by revelation, not reputation. He let people see His tears, His fatigue, and His anguish, and through that honesty, they learned to follow His heart, not just His hand.

Vulnerability doesn't remove authority; hypocrisy does. People will forgive weakness when they can see humility, but they withdraw trust when they smell pretense. Authenticity carries a weight that position never can.

The Strength of Being Seen

When Jesus wept at Lazarus' tomb, He showed that leadership doesn't mean emotional detachment. When He sweat drops of blood in Gethsemane, He showed that even divine assignment doesn't silence human struggle. Those moments didn't diminish His authority, they revealed His intimacy.

Great leaders aren't those who hide pain; they're those who handle it honorably. Vulnerability tells your followers, *"You can be real and still be righteous."* It opens doors for healing in others because it proves that holiness doesn't mean hardness. Transparency becomes testimony when carried with wisdom.

The Difference Between Transparency and Exposure

Transparency is controlled revelation; exposure is careless revelation. One builds trust; the other blurs boundaries. A wise leader knows when to open their heart and when to guard it. Jesus shared everything with the Father, much with the twelve, and only revelation with the crowd. He modeled levels of access, each defined by purpose, not favoritism.

You don't owe everyone your details, but you owe everyone your integrity. Transparency doesn't mean telling all, it means hiding nothing false. Truthfulness is what keeps vulnerability pure. When leaders discern who to confide in, transparency becomes strength instead of scandal.

The Healing Power of Honest Leadership

When a leader admits weakness, it gives permission for others to be healed. Pretending to be untouchable isolates people in shame. But when you share how God met you in frailty, it builds faith that He'll meet them too. Paul did this when he said, *"We were pressed beyond measure... that we might not trust in ourselves but in God who raises the dead."* He wasn't boasting of strength, he was revealing dependence. Dependence is Heaven's definition of maturity.

Honest leadership tears down the illusion that anointing means immunity. People stop idolizing you and start imitating your trust. That shift keeps Christ at the center and the culture of honor intact.

Guarding the Sacred While Remaining Sincere

Being transparent doesn't mean being careless. Leaders must protect the sacred while remaining sincere. Some details belong only before the Lord; others belong in trusted circles. The key is motive: share for the sake of healing, not attention.

Vulnerability offered from wholeness invites grace; vulnerability offered from woundedness seeks validation. Before you share pain, ensure it has been processed in prayer. Once healed, your story becomes a seed that others can grow from instead of a wound they must bandage.

The Spirit of wisdom always partners with the spirit of truth. Together, they keep authenticity holy.

Authority That Flows From Authenticity

People follow confidence, but they connect to authenticity. Confidence tells them you can lead; authenticity tells them you can understand and are trustworthy. Jesus was both, the Lion and the Lamb. Authority rooted in authenticity carries rest; it doesn't need to prove itself.

When your followers can see your humanity and still sense His divinity through you, they know Heaven is near. That's what made Jesus irresistible, He was holy yet human, exalted yet approachable. True leaders reflect that same paradox.

The balance of transparency and strength becomes a living invitation: *"Follow me as I follow Christ, not because I'm flawless, but because I'm faithful."*

Transition

Vulnerability keeps leadership real; humility keeps it righteous. The next and final section of this chapter will reveal how leaders lead with leaders, the principle of mutual honor and shared authority that keeps Kingdom structures from becoming empires.

Section 6 – Mutual Honor: Leading With, Not Just Over

The greatest test of maturity in leadership is how you handle power when you are surrounded by peers, not subordinates. Anyone can lead from above; few can lead alongside. Mutual honor is Heaven's pattern for shared authority. The Kingdom isn't a pyramid, it's a body. Every joint supplies, and every member matters.

When Jesus sent His disciples two by two, He was teaching partnership, not pecking order. Heaven's government flows through relational agreement. There are no lone kings in the Kingdom, only co-laborers in Christ.

The Circle of Authority

Human systems build towers, but Heaven builds tables. Towers reach upward for recognition; tables reach outward for relationship. When leaders sit at tables together, they trade ego for equity. Each voice adds perspective, and honor keeps conversation holy.

The early Church didn't operate through one dominant figure but through apostles, prophets, and elders who submitted to one another in reverence for Christ. Mutual submission was not a loss of power, it was the source of it. When authority circulates through humility, no one gets glory except God.

Honor as the Language of Leadership Teams

Honor among leaders is the difference between synergy and sabotage. A team that competes cannot complete. Competition breeds insecurity; collaboration breeds increase. When you celebrate the grace on another leader, you expand your own capacity.

Paul modeled this beautifully with Barnabas, Silas, Timothy, and Titus. He didn't need to be the loudest voice; he was the listening one. He made room for their gifts to grow, even when they surpassed his shadow. That is the confidence of a father and the humility of a son.

Honor recognizes the strength in another without feeling diminished by it.

The Death of the Lone Leader

The *"one-man show"* mentality is the death of Kingdom government. God never called one person to carry the whole weight of His work. Moses learned this when Jethro told him, *"What you are doing is not good... appoint others."* True wisdom is not holding more; it's trusting more.

When leaders delegate through honor, they empower through trust. Delegation isn't about distributing tasks; it's about sharing identity. Those who lead with others reflect the Trinity more than those who lead alone. The Father, Son, and Spirit have always ruled through relationship, never rivalry.

If Heaven functions through shared honor, how could earth's leadership function any other way?

Submission Among Equals

Mutual honor means recognizing grace, even when positions differ. Peter and Paul corrected each other without dishonor. Paul rebuked

Peter publicly, yet Peter later called Paul's writings *"Scripture."* Why? Because their correction never canceled covenant.

When mature leaders walk in honor, disagreement doesn't destroy unity, it refines it. Honor keeps correction from becoming competition. You can submit to another's grace without surrendering your calling. Honor doesn't shrink you; it synchronizes you. The orchestra plays best when every instrument stays tuned to the same key.

The Sound of Agreement

The sound of Heaven is unity in diversity, many voices, one Spirit. When leaders honor each other, that sound fills the earth. Acts 4 says the early believers were *"of one heart and one soul,"* and great grace was upon them all. Grace follows agreement, and agreement is born of honor.

Mutual honor silences jealousy and amplifies joy. It removes striving and invites synergy. Every time leaders choose unity over ego, Heaven gains ground on earth. When honor governs leadership, the Body governs nations.

The Legacy of Shared Leadership

Leaders who honor one another multiply longevity. Empires die with their founder; families live through generations. The apostolic model was never about building names, it was about birthing nature. Shared leadership ensures the sound of Heaven continues beyond one man's voice.

Jesus left a council of apostles, not a crown prince. That council birthed an unshakable Kingdom community that outlived persecution, division, and time. Such is the strength of mutual honor, it outlasts personality.

Leaders who refuse to compete will always complete Heaven's commission together.

Conclusion: Leading From Sonship

To lead in the Kingdom is to represent the Father. To represent the Father is to honor His image in others. That is the secret of sustained authority, leading with, not just over. Servants may obey orders, but sons share burdens. Sons honor the family name by lifting together.

The world will always be fascinated by powerful individuals. Heaven is impressed only by unified sons. True leadership doesn't echo culture, it establishes Kingdom. And in Heaven's Kingdom, the highest seat is the one that leaves room for others.

Chapter 9 Review & Reflection

Honor in Leadership: Serving from the Seat of Sonship

Core Revelation

Kingdom leadership is not about control but representation. Leaders are not called to be served but to serve, to carry the Father's heart into every sphere of influence. Authority in the Kingdom is relational, not positional born from alignment, not ambition. To lead from sonship is to lead from rest, because identity precedes assignment. The highest demonstration of authority is not dominance but devotion. Leaders lead best when they love most.

Honor transforms leadership from a platform into a posture. It moves us from *"what I build"* to *"who I build."* It replaces competition with collaboration, and insecurity with identity.

Kingdom Principle

Leadership is stewardship, not ownership; service, not status; alignment, not advancement. When leaders honor God's order and one another's grace, the Kingdom flows without friction.

Scripture Focus

- John 13:14–15 – *"If I then, your Lord and Master, have washed your feet; ye also ought to wash one another's feet."*
- Philippians 2:5–9 – *"He made Himself of no reputation… therefore God highly exalted Him."*
- Matthew 23:11 – *"The greatest among you shall be your servant."*
- Romans 12:10 – *"In honor preferring one another."*
- 1 Peter 5:2–3 – *"Feed the flock of God… not lording it over those entrusted to you."*

- Ephesians 4:16 – *"From whom the whole body, joined and held together by every joint, grows as each part does its work."*

Truths to Remember

1. The towel is greater than the throne. Service reveals true sovereignty.
2. Identity must precede influence. Sonship anchors leadership.
3. Honor multiplies what pride diminishes.
4. Correction with compassion restores more than it rebukes.
5. Transparency builds trust; hypocrisy breaks it.
6. Delegation is not distancing, it's discipleship in motion.
7. Shared authority strengthens stability.
8. Mutual honor turns teams into families.
9. Vulnerability is not weakness; it's wisdom wrapped in humility.
10. Empires fade when egos lead; Kingdoms rise when sons serve.

Application

- Lead with a towel. Begin every assignment as an act of service, not superiority.
- Guard your heart from hierarchy. Replace *"my"* language with *"His."*
- Model correction in love. Train others to confront with care and speak truth without shame.
- Be transparent wisely. Let people see Christ through your humanity, not your image.
- Cultivate teams, not followers. Empower others to carry grace equal to their calling.
- Honor across, not just above. Show the same reverence to peers and partners that you expect from those who follow.
- Submit mutually. Accountability keeps authority holy.
- Celebrate others' success. It keeps jealousy from finding a foothold.

- Remain approachable. People thrive when leadership feels safe.
- Multiply sons, not servants. Legacy is measured in likeness, not numbers.

Reflection Questions

1. How have I defined leadership in my own life, by service or by status?
2. Do I model honor toward those I lead as much as I expect it from them?
3. When I correct, does love lead my tone?
4. Have I learned to share authority without insecurity?
5. Where is God calling me to serve with greater humility right now?
6. Do I celebrate other leaders or secretly compare myself to them?
7. How can I lead from the "seat of sonship" rather than from striving for validation?

Declaration

"Father, I receive the call to lead as Your Son led, with humility, honor, and heart. Teach me to govern from grace, to build from rest, and to serve from love. Let my leadership reflect Your likeness, washing feet, lifting hearts, and multiplying sons. Deliver me from pride, competition, and control. I will lead with a towel in my hand, not a title on my mind. May every decision I make reveal the King I represent."

CHAPTER 10
THE ORDERED LIFE: THE TRUE ROOT OF HONOR

Introduction – Why Honor Requires Order

Honor is impossible without order. Not because honor is inherently difficult, but because honor is divine, and the divine cannot flow through a life that is disordered, fractured, or divided. Honor is a Kingdom commodity. It is the culture of Heaven revealed through the character of a man. But no man can release what he does not first possess, and no man can truly possess honor without internal order.

Most people treat honor as an action. Scripture treats honor as an alignment. Honor is not simply something a man does; it is something a man is. It is a manifestation of his internal governance, his reverence for God, and his alignment with truth. Honor is the fragrance of order. Disorder has a smell, honor has a sound, and order has a posture. To understand honor rightly, we must first understand order.

Section 1 – Honor Begins Where Order Begins

The first commands concerning honor in Scripture are not horizontal, they are vertical. They follow divine sequence:

"Honor the Lord..." (Proverbs 3:9)
"Honor your father and mother..." (Exodus 20:12)
"Honor all men..." (1 Peter 2:17)

The order is intentional:
1. Honor God.
2. Honor origin and authority.
3. Honor people.

Honor flows in this divine pattern because order is its source. You cannot bypass God and genuinely honor man. You cannot dishonor authority and claim to honor relationships. You cannot truly honor all men unless you first honor the God who created them.

Where there is no internal order, honor becomes performance.

Honor must begin with God, flow through divine order, and manifest through every relational expression. Without that sequence, honor is merely behavior management, not a fruit of transformation.

Transition

To understand this more deeply, we must examine the heart posture that fuels honor and why honor cannot be manufactured, it must be overflow.

Section 2 – Honor as Overflow, Not Effort

Jesus exposed a generation fluent in the language of honor but bankrupt in the reality of it:

"This people honors Me with their lips, but their heart is far from Me." Matthew 15:8

Their words were correct, but their inner world was disordered. Their lips spoke reverence, but their spirit resisted righteousness. Honor without order becomes hypocrisy.

True honor is revealed when the heart and life are aligned. It is never the result of trying harder, it is always the fruit of living deeper. A man can give respect without order, but he cannot give honor without order. Respect is external behavior; honor is internal posture. Respect is learned; honor is revealed. Respect is intellectual; honor is spiritual.

Respect can be given by a broken man.

Honor can only flow from a whole one.

Honor is not effort, it is evidence of alignment.

Transition

And where alignment is missing, dishonor will arise. Disorder is not just the absence of structure; it is the birthplace of dishonor.

Section 3 – Disorder: The Enemy of Honor

Proverbs paints a sobering image of a disordered man:

"A man without rule over his own spirit is like a city broken down, without walls." Proverbs 25:28

Walls symbolize protection, strength, boundaries, identity. A man without internal governance is exposed, reactive, restless, vulnerable, easily influenced, easily offended, and easily redirected. Such a person cannot express honor because there is no internal governance from which honor can flow.

This is why Paul instructed Timothy that leaders must have their homes in order:

"If a man cannot rule his own house, how will he take care of the church of God?" 1 Timothy 3:5

The principle is universal.

You cannot export honor beyond the borders of your own order.

A disordered home will always produce a disordered ministry. A disordered heart produces disordered relationships. A disordered soul produces disordered loyalties. A disordered mind produces disordered decisions.

Honor is impossible in the presence of internal chaos.

Transition

Dishonor does not enter through the mouth first, it begins in the breakdown of the heart.

Section 4 – Dishonor Is Born in Disorder

Dishonor never begins with speech, it begins with the misalignment of the soul. It is the natural language of disorder.

When a man is out of order, he begins to see inaccurately and interpret incorrectly. His perception becomes clouded, his motives become misaligned, and he begins to project fear and elevate self. He lowers others, resists authority, disconnects from covering, gravitates toward flatterers, and becomes vulnerable to false influence.

Disorder invites strange voices.
Honor recognizes the right ones.

Jesus declared:
"My sheep know My voice... and a stranger they will not follow."
John 10:4–5

Disordered sheep follow strange shepherds. Order preserves alignment.

Transition

This leads us to a profound truth: the presence of order is always the prerequisite for the manifestation of glory.

Section 5 – Order Precedes Glory

Honor is the antidote to shame because honor restores the soul to divine order. Shame disfigures identity; honor restores it. Shame fractures: honor unites. Shame silences destiny: honor unlocks glory.

Honor is the opposite of shame because honor is rooted in glory, and glory only flows where there is divine order. Where there is no order, there can be no glory. Where there is no glory, there can be no honor.

Paul declared:
"To the King, eternal, immortal, invisible... be honor and glory." 1 Timothy 1:17

The two are inseparable. Glory is revealed order; honor is the recognition of that order. To live in honor is to live aligned with the glory of God.

Transition

The implications of order extend beyond personal life, they influence every direction honor must flow.

Section 6 – Order Establishes Honor in Every Direction

Honor flows in three divine directions:
1. **Upward** — toward God and authority.
   Only an ordered heart can sincerely honor those above them.
2. **Outward** — toward peers and people.
   Only a stable and whole soul can offer consistent, fair, and generous honor.
3. **Downward** — toward those we steward.
   Only a governed life can father, mentor, lead, and raise others.

A man who cannot govern himself cannot honor others. And a man who cannot honor others cannot steward them. Order secures the channels through which honor flows.

Transition

Thus, the goal is not merely to give honor, it is to become honor.

Section 7 – Honor as Identity, Not Conduct

Paul exhorted the Church:
"Outdo one another in showing honor." Romans 12:10

That exhortation was not given in isolation, but after teachings on renewing the mind, surrendering the body, living sacrificially, discerning God's will, and walking in humility.

Order → Transformation → Honor.

Honor is the expression of a transformed life. A transformed life is the result of an ordered heart. Honor is not a performance of will power, it is the manifestation of identity. It is who you reveal yourself to be when God restructures your internal world according to divine pattern.

Honor is not what you do.
It is what you become
when your inner world is aligned with the order of the King.

Conclusion – Honor Is Order Made Visible

Honor cannot be expressed until it is established. It cannot be spoken until it is structured. It cannot be bestowed until it is embodied.

Honor begins in hidden places, in the decisions no one sees, in the heart's surrender, and in the soul's realignment to truth. When a man is rightly ordered, governed internally, aligned spiritually, submitted humbly, and rooted in Kingdom reality, honor flows naturally and powerfully.

Honor is the fragrance of divine order. Where honor flows, shame breaks, glory manifests, and relationships flourish.

Honor is not the behavior of man but the expression of alignment with God. Because honor is not merely what you do, Honor is what you become when your life is ordered around the King.

Chapter 10 Review & Reflection

The Ordered Life: The True Root of Honor

Core Revelation

Honor does not begin on your lips; it begins in your inner world. Honor is the fragrance of divine order, where God's government rules within, honor flows effortlessly without.

Kingdom Principle

Honor is not first expressed; it is first established in a life brought into divine order.

Scripture Focus

- 1 Corinthians 14:40 – *"Let all things be done decently and in order."*
- Psalm 37:23 – *"The steps of a good man are ordered by the Lord..."*
- Romans 12:2 – *"Be transformed by the renewing of your mind..."*
- Colossians 3:15 – *"Let the peace of God rule in your hearts..."*

Truths to Remember

1. Honor is not what you do; it is what you become when your life aligns with the King's order.
2. Disorder in the inner world will eventually distort your outer relationships.
3. Where order is restored, honor becomes natural, not forced.
4. God does not ask you to manufacture honor, but to make room for it by entering His government.

5. Where honor flows, glory follows; where glory dwells, shame dies.

Application

- Identify one area of internal disorder (thoughts, habits, rhythms) and invite the Holy Spirit to realign it.
- Re-establish disciplines (Word, prayer, stillness) that support divine order in your inner life.
- Refuse to ignore areas of chaos, see confronting disorder as an act of honor to God.
- Ask trusted spiritual leadership to help you discern blind spots in your internal government.
- Practice decisions that prioritize peace, clarity, and alignment over impulse and reaction.

Reflection Questions

1. What area of my life is most disordered right now?
2. How has this disorder affected my relationships, perception, or leadership?
3. What *"strange voices"* have I followed because my heart was misaligned?
4. Where is God calling me to re-establish boundaries, governance, or discipline?
5. What would honor look like if it flowed from a place of internal order rather than effort?

Declaration

"Father, I surrender every disordered place within me. I renounce confusion, chaos, and compromise. I align my heart with Your government, my mind with Your truth, and my spirit with Your voice.

I declare that:
- *My life comes into divine order.*
- *My inner world is governed by the Spirit.*

- *My relationships are shaped by honor.*
- *My decisions flow from clarity.*
- *My posture reflects humility.*
- *My voice carries integrity.*

I receive the grace to walk in internal order, the courage to confront disorder, and the strength to embody honor from the inside out. Honor is my identity because order is my foundation, and the King is my alignment. Amen."

CHAPTER 11
WORTH AND THE GIFT:
WHY HONOR FUELED THE CROSS

Introduction – *Every Gift Carries a Valuation*

Every gift reveals a valuation. Every sacrifice reveals a worth. No giver pours out more than the receiver is worth unless the giver is foolish, unstable, or reckless. But God is none of these. He is perfectly ordered. His decisions are flawless. His actions are intentional. His sacrifices are strategic.

Therefore, the Cross was not a reaction to sin; it was an expression of value. Love motivated it. Honor justified it. The Cross is not proof of human depravity, it is proof of divine honor.

God did not give His Son because humanity was worthless. He gave His Son because humanity was worth what He gave.

Transition

To grasp the full impact of this revelation, we must understand the principle that governs all true giving: worth always justifies the gift.

Section 1 – *Worth Always Justifies the Gift*

Jesus said, *"Where your treasure is, there your heart will be also"* (Matthew 6:21). Treasures migrate toward what the giver considers valuable.

If a man gives cheaply, he values little. If he gives sacrificially, he values greatly. If he gives his best, he believes the receiver is worthy of his best.

The Father gave His Son, His treasure, His Word in flesh, His express image, His heir, His delight. To give the Son is to reveal the worth of what He came to redeem.

No wise investor bankrupts himself for junk. No intelligent purchaser pays premium for refuse. No ordered God offers His absolute best for what He considers worthless.

The Gift (Christ) reveals the worth.

The Price(The Blood) reveals the value.

You were bought with a price, not merely to redeem sin, but to reveal worth.

Transition

This revelation is embedded in the most quoted verse of Scripture. What many consider a love verse is also a divine valuation statement.

Section 2 – John 3:16: Heaven's Valuation of Creation

We quote it often as a love verse, but it is equally a Kingdom economics verse.

"For God so loved the cosmos…"

Cosmos refers to ordered creation, the intended arrangement, the divine design. God loved what He arranged and refused to abandon it to disorder.

"…that He gave His only begotten Son."

Love motivated the giving.

Honor evaluated its worth.

Value justified the sacrifice.

Order enabled the redemption.

The Cross was not random. It was a calculated act of divine honor. God did not simply rescue creation, He redeemed His own investment.

Transition

This logically leads to a crucial truth: God did not give recklessly. He gave strategically.

Section 3 – God Is Never a Reckless Giver: He Is a Perfect Investor

God never wastes, He does not waste words, breath, power, resources, days, movements, angels, or blood. Foolishness wastes. Love invests. Honor assigns worth. Everything God does is intentional, strategic, aligned, purposeful, and ordered.

Therefore, the Son was given because creation was worthy of the Son, not morally worthy, but intrinsically worthy because it originated in Him. The worth of anything is tied to the worth of its origin. You came from God; therefore, your worth is divine.

Transition

And this is possible for one profound reason: God's internal order makes perfect honor possible.

Section 4 – Divine Order Makes Divine Honor Possible

I once asked, *"Isn't the fact that God is perfectly ordered the reason He could do such a thing?"* The answer is undeniably yes.

Perfect love flows only from perfect order. Where there is internal disorder, love becomes unstable, inconsistent, selective, and reactive. But God is one, whole, undivided, stable, self-governed, eternally aligned.

Therefore, His love is perfect, and His honor never fluctuates. He does not evaluate your worth based on behavior but based on original intention. Honor recognizes design, not dysfunction.

God does not love emotionally.

He loves positionally.

He loves intentionally.

He loves governmentally.

He loves eternally.

Transition

And the ultimate revelation of what God believes you are worth is found at the Cross.

Section 5 – The Cross Reveals What You Are Worth

If something is worthless, one discards it. If broken, one replaces it. If cheap, one ignores it. But if something is valuable, one redeems it. Only treasure is redeemed, trash is thrown away. The Cross was an act of valuation. A public disclosure of worth. A proclamation of divine honor.

Heaven's greatest gift was given to earth because earth possessed Heaven's greatest value.

The giving of the Son is the highest economic declaration ever made:
"You are worth this to Me."

Transition

But what moved God to act was not only love, it was honor.

Section 6 – *Love Reaches, but Honor Pays*

Love moved God toward the world.
Honor revealed the value of the world.
Worth justified the sacrifice.
Order enabled the redemption.

Love says, *"I desire you."*
Honor says, *"You are valuable."*
The Cross says, *"You are worth the highest price."*

Transition

And God paid the price based not on what we had done, but on who He made us to be.

Section 7 – *Redemption Was Based on Worth, Not Behavior*

If God redeemed based on behavior, no one would have qualified. If based on merit, the price would have been minimal. If based only on potential, He might have postponed redemption.

But He redeemed based on identity, design, image, intention, inheritance, and worth. Value is whatever someone is willing to pay. God paid everything. Therefore, creation is worth everything.

Transition

This is why honor, and the Cross are inseparable. They are the same language.

Section 8 – *The Cross Speaks the Language of Honor*

At the Cross, we see more than love displayed, we see honor revealed.

Honor for His image-bearers.

Honor for His creation.

Honor for His name.

Honor for His promise.

Honor for His covenant with Himself.

Honor for His eternal purpose.

God honored humanity because humanity came from Him.

He honored the cosmos because He ordered the cosmos.

He honored His own glory by redeeming what bore His signature.

Conclusion – *Honor Is the Logic Behind Redemption*

God did not rescue worthless sinners. He redeemed valuable sons. He honored His own creation. He invested in His own design. He acted from order, not impulse. He paid based on worth, not pity. He gave based on valuation, not emotion.

The Cross is Heaven's eternal declaration:

"You are worth My Son."

This is honor at its highest expression.

Because honor is love wearing its crown.

Chapter 11 Review & Reflection

Worth and the Gift: Why Honor Fueled the Cross

Core Revelation

The Cross is not primarily proof of how sinful you were, it is proof of how valuable you are. God did not redeem trash; He redeemed treasure. Love moved Him, but honor evaluated and justified the price.

Kingdom Principle

The price reveals the worth: God paid everything; therefore creation is worth everything.

Scripture Focus

- John 3:16 – *"For God so loved the world that He gave His only begotten Son…"*
- Matthew 6:21 – *"Where your treasure is, there your heart will be also."*
- 1 Corinthians 6:20 – *"For you were bought at a price…"*
- Romans 5:8 – *"While we were still sinners, Christ died for us."*

Truths to Remember

1. Every gift reveals valuation; every sacrifice reveals worth.
2. God is not impulsive, wasteful, or reckless, He never overpays.
3. The Cross was not a reaction to sin; it was an expression of value.
4. Religion says, *"You were so sinful that Jesus had to die."* The Kingdom says, *"You were so valuable that Jesus chose to die."*

5. God redeemed you based on identity, design, and intention, not on behavior or merit.
6. The Cross is Heaven's eternal declaration: *"You are worth My Son."*

Application

- Renounce internal narratives of worthlessness, shame, and "barely tolerated" identity.
- Meditate on the Cross as a valuation event, let it reframe how you see yourself.
- Allow this revelation of worth to reshape how you treat others, they were paid for by the same blood.
- In worship, thank God specifically for the value He placed on you, not just for forgiveness.
- Let your view of your worth inform your boundaries, decisions, and relationships.

Reflection Questions

1. What have I believed about myself that contradicts the value God declared at the Cross?
2. Have I confused love with pity instead of honor with valuation?
3. Do I live as someone constantly trying to prove worth, or as someone purchased at the highest price?
4. What parts of my identity need to be redefined in the light of my redeemed value?
5. How does knowing my worth reshape the way I honor other people?

Declaration

"Father, I receive the revelation that I am worth what You paid. You are not a wasteful giver. You do not invest in junk, overspend on refuse, or bankrupt Yourself for the worthless.

You gave Your Son because You judged me, by origin, not behavior, worthy of the Son. I renounce every lie of shame, inferiority, self-hatred, and worthlessness. I agree with Heaven's valuation:

- *I am valued, not tolerated.*
- *Chosen, not pitied.*
- *Selected, not merely spared.*
- *Honored, not overlooked.*

The Cross is the receipt of my value. Redemption is Your honor placed upon my existence. Let this truth reshape how I see myself and how I honor others. In Jesus' name, amen."

CHAPTER 12

THE HONOR OF UNITY: THE STRENGTH OF ONE SOUND

Section 1 – The Sound of Oneness

Heaven has a sound, and it is the sound of agreement. Before creation ever echoed with light, Heaven already vibrated with unity, the Father, the Word, and the Spirit moving as one. Nothing in Heaven competes; everything completes. And what makes completion possible is honor. Honor is the glue of divine relationships, the governing posture that keeps each Person of the Godhead aligned in functional distinction yet united in eternal purpose.

The Kingdom's power is not found in hierarchy, it is found in harmony. And harmony is only possible where honor is established.

Harmony is not the absence of difference; it is the **honoring** of it. Honor recognizes that every tone carries divine intention. Uniformity silences distinction: honor celebrates it. Without honor, difference becomes division. With honor, difference becomes design.

Unity, therefore, is not sameness. Uniformity demands conformity, but unity is diversity aligned through honor. Each note has a distinct tone, but when tuned to the same key, a symphony emerges. That is the sound of Heaven, not one sound by replication, but one sound by agreement.

It is what Jesus prayed in John 17: *"That they may be one, even as We are one."* He was not asking them to look alike, think alike, or sound alike, but to honor alike. Because honor produces the love that makes unity possible.

True unity is the result of honor.

Harmony is the expression of honor.
Glory is the manifestation of honor.

In music, harmony does not emerge from identical notes, but from unique tones aligned to a higher composition. So, it is in the Kingdom. The moment diversity submits through honor to divine order, harmony forms, and where harmony forms, glory responds.

"Honor is not one part of unity; it is the power that makes unity possible."

The Sound That Shook the House

Acts 2 reveals that when the disciples were *"in one accord and in one place,"* the Spirit came with a sound from Heaven. Before tongues were given, a sound was heard. That sound wasn't just noise, it was the evidence of harmony. Heaven had found resonance on earth, and power rushed through it like wind through a corridor.

Pentecost was not only an outpouring of power; it was a restoration of sound. Babel divided language; Pentecost united it. Where pride once produced confusion, honor produced clarity. The Spirit didn't just fill individuals, He filled a body. They weren't gathered around personality; they were joined around purpose. Unity always precedes outpouring. When Heaven hears its sound reproduced on earth, glory follows.

The Weight of Honor in Unity

Unity cannot exist where honor is absent. Honor is the glue that holds diversity together. It allows difference without division, conversation without competition. Where there is no honor, unity becomes impossible because dishonor fractures trust.

We see this in the process of creation. In Genesis, the Spirit's presence hovered over the chaos. But order did not manifest until the Word spoke in unity with the Spirit under the Father's authority. Presence was brooding. Glory was waiting for agreement.

Honor produced that agreement. Honor is what allowed divine roles, Father (intention), Son/Word (expression), and Spirit (activation), to align and manifest creation.

David wrote, *"How good and pleasant it is for brethren to dwell together in unity."* He described it like oil, running down Aaron's beard, saturating the garments. Unity flows like oil because honor is the anointing's conduit. It starts at the head and runs through the body, if the body stays connected.

When you dishonor leadership, you disconnect from flow. When you dishonor one another, you dam the river. But when honor circulates freely, every part receives its portion. That's why corporate anointing is always greater than personal anointing, because unity multiplies what individuality limits.

Heaven's Resistance to Division

Division is not just a relational issue, it's a spiritual resistance to Heaven's government. God's Kingdom operates in perfect harmony; therefore, anything divided cannot host His glory. Jesus said, *"A kingdom divided against itself cannot stand."* That applies to homes, churches, teams, and nations alike. Disunity doesn't just weaken structure, it evicts presence.

The Holy Spirit does not dwell in chaos, He hovers over it in anticipation of order. At creation, He brooded over the formless void, not in agreement with disorder, but waiting for divine order to be spoken. Likewise, He waits for the sound of unity before He moves in power again.

The Spirit's presence was not an endorsement of chaos, but a prophetic posture. He hovered, not to sustain the disorder, but to activate creation when the Word aligned the atmosphere.

He does not manifest in confusion, but He positions Himself over it, ready to move the moment order speaks. If Heaven is waiting to move, perhaps it's waiting for agreement.

The Law of Resonance

When two frequencies vibrate in harmony, their combined amplitude increases exponentially. That's resonance, a principle both scientific and spiritual. When two believers walk in honor and unity, their agreement amplifies Heaven's power. That's why Jesus said, *"If two of you agree on earth as touching anything, it shall be done."*

Agreement is more than consent, it's covenant. It's not just *"I like your idea"*; it's *"I align with your spirit."* You can't have true agreement with someone you secretly compete with. Unity demands heart posture, not verbal assent.

Wherever people choose honor over ego, Heaven finds resonance. When sons move in one sound, hell loses its frequency.

Transition

Unity is not a goal to reach, it's a culture to sustain. The next section will explore how honor cultivates relational harmony, the practice of walking together without comparison or control.

Section 2 – Harmony in Diversity: The Practice of Walking Together

The Kingdom was never meant to sound monotone. Heaven's harmony depends on difference, each voice, each gift, each grace expressing a unique tone that, when honored, reveals a fuller picture of the King. Diversity is not Heaven's challenge; it is Heaven's chorus. But only honor can turn difference into harmony. Without honor, diversity creates tension; with honor, tension becomes melody.

Unity without diversity is imitation; diversity without unity is chaos. The Father designed both to exist in tension and in beauty. Where honor is present, tension becomes melody. Where dishonor enters, difference becomes division.

The Glory of Difference

God never intended sameness to equal strength. In the natural body, strength comes from coordinated difference, eyes see, hands touch, feet walk. No single member can claim independence; each depends on the others to express life. Paul said, *"The body is one, and has many members, and all the members of that one body, being many, are one body in Christ."*

Unity does not erase individuality; it sanctifies it. When we honor each member's grace, the full glory of Christ becomes visible. To dismiss another's function is to dishonor the God who designed it. To envy another's role is to distrust His wisdom in assigning ours.

Heaven calls this cooperation, not competition. Every gift reveals part of His nature, every grace releases part of His sound.

Comparison: The Thief of Harmony

The quickest way to silence Heaven's sound is to compare your note to another's. Comparison is the language of **orphans**; confidence is the **song of sons**. When you know your note, you no longer compete, you contribute. In the orchestra of the Kingdom, every instrument matters. The danger is not playing small, it's refusing to play at all because someone else's sound seems louder.

David could honor Saul even while knowing he carried greater anointing. Joseph could serve Pharaoh without envying his throne. Jesus could wash Judas' feet while aware of betrayal. Honor keeps the heart free from comparison because it sees difference as design, not threat.

Walking Together Without Control

Honor is what allows people to walk closely without crossing boundaries. Control masquerades as unity, but it's really fear of difference. Some leaders demand agreement because they fear diversity; others avoid accountability because they fear correction.

True unity requires both courage and humility, courage to walk with those who challenge you, and humility to learn from those who differ from you.

Amos 3:3 asks, *"Can two walk together unless they be agreed?"* Agreement here doesn't mean identical, it means aligned. Walking together doesn't require uniform perspective; it requires shared purpose. You can walk in agreement with someone whose method differs, as long as your mission is the same.

That's the miracle of the Kingdom: alignment without assimilation. Heaven isn't looking for copies; it's forming community.

Honor as the Tuning Fork

Every musician knows that before a performance, instruments must be tuned to the same standard. In the Kingdom, that tuning fork is honor. Honor calibrates hearts to Heaven's pitch, humility. When pride enters, tones clash; when honor reigns, melodies blend.

Honoring others keeps your spirit in tune with Heaven. You can't stay in harmony while harboring offense. Forgiveness is not a feeling; it's spiritual tuning.

Each time you forgive, you return your heart to Heaven's frequency. Unity is not sustained by agreement but by continual re-tuning through honor. That's why humility and repentance must remain constant rhythms in any community seeking God's presence.

Walking in the Light Together

The apostle John wrote, *"If we walk in the light as He is in the light, we have fellowship one with another."* Walking in the light means walking in truth, with transparency, trust, and tenderness. Light reveals difference without shame. It exposes not to humiliate, but to harmonize.

When communities walk in the light, gossip dies, and grace thrives. People stop defending appearances and start cultivating authenticity. Honor turns relationships into safe places for correction and growth. The light doesn't divide, it defines. It clarifies motives, cleanses misunderstandings, and keeps hearts clear of hidden agendas.

To walk in the light together means you value relationship more than image, truth more than titles, and connection more than control. It is a continual decision to stay uncovered before God and unoffended before people.

Where light rules, darkness loses dominion. And where honor reigns, unity becomes effortless. The sound of Heaven flows best through hearts that are clean and uncovered.

Harmony in Practice
1. **Celebrate Variety**: Thank God for voices, styles, and perspectives unlike yours.
2. **Listen Intentionally**: Don't just wait to speak; seek to understand.
3. **Stay Curious**: Ask, "What part of God's nature do you reveal that I need to see?"
4. **Repent Quickly**: Dishonor begins where apology ends.
5. **Pray Together Often**: Prayer synchronizes hearts faster than discussion.
6. **Speak Well Publicly and Privately**: Unity thrives in consistent honor.

These are the simple, sacred habits that preserve harmony and silence hell's agenda of division.

Transition

Harmony is Heaven's power in motion. When people of difference choose honor, the Kingdom's culture becomes visible on earth. The next section will explore how unity releases supernatural power, how one sound in Heaven's frequency shakes cities and transforms nations.

Section 3 – *The Power of Agreement: When One Sound Shakes the Earth*

Heaven is drawn to agreement. Agreement not based in sameness but born of honor. Honor is what makes agreement spiritual rather than institutional.

God's throne is surrounded by voices that cry, *"Holy, holy, holy,"* not in competition but in perfect synchronization. It's not repetition, it's **resonance**. Every time the redeemed lift their voices together in oneness, the sound echoes that eternal song, and Heaven responds with glory.

Agreement is not just a principle, it's a power. It's the multiplying law of the Spirit. When individuals agree through honor, they create a portal of authority through which Heaven invades earth. That's why Jesus said, *"If two of you shall agree on earth as touching anything that they shall ask, it shall be done of my Father which is in heaven."* Heaven doesn't move because of numbers; it moves because of unity. Ten thousand voices out of tune cannot move God like two hearts in alignment.

The Mathematics of the Kingdom

In the natural, one plus one equals two. But in the Kingdom, one plus one can release exponential power, not because of human strategy, but because of divine unity.

Deuteronomy 32:30 speaks of enemies overpowering Israel because God withdrew His covering due to their misalignment, not because of unity:

"How could one chase a thousand, and two put ten thousand to flight, unless their Rock had sold them?"

That verse reveals what happens when unity is absent and honor is abandoned, God steps back.

But the opposite is also true:
- When honor aligns hearts, Heaven steps in.
- When unity is established under divine order, authority is multiplied, not diminished.

Jesus revealed this principle correctly:
"If two of you agree on earth as touching anything... it shall be done." (Matthew 18:19)

Agreement is more than mutual preference; it is spiritual alignment. Honor is the force that fuses individuals into one sound Heaven can empower.

Unity doesn't merely add strength, when born of honor, it compounds it. That is why hell fights agreement more than anointing... Because an anointed individual is powerful, but an anointed unified people are unstoppable.

Deuteronomy 32:30 shows what happens when God steps back due to dishonor; Matthew 18:19 reveals what happens when God steps in because of it. Hell, fears unity not because of numbers, but because of honor.

Agreement as a Weapon

Unity is not just worship, it is relational alignment that disarms the adversary's influence. This is not spiritual warfare directed at a devil in the air; it is the protection of covenant against division, which is how the adversary attempts to work through people.

When we walk in honor, accusation loses its access. Dishonor gives the adversary vocabulary; honor takes it away. Agreement is not powerful on its own, it is powerful because it is the echo of honor. Unity is what you hear; honor is what sustains it.

The enemy's oldest strategy has never been direct confrontation, it has been relational disruption. If he can separate hearts, he can weaken authority. But when a community remains aligned through honor expressed as love and humility, every scheme collapses under its own confusion.

The Church's greatest weapon is not its preaching, its singing, or its programs, it is its honoring posture that keeps oneness intact.

The early Ekklesia did not overthrow Rome with protest or persuasion, but through a relational oneness birthed in honor. Their unity did not produce authority, it revealed it. Honor positioned them under Heaven's government, and no empire could withstand that alignment.

Agreement doesn't lock hell out, honor does. Agreement is simply what harmony sounds like when honor has done its work.

"Unity doesn't fight the adversary; honor starves him of a voice."

The Sound That Governs

The Kingdom does not advance through noise; it advances through sound, one frequency of faith, hope, and love vibrating together in honor. That sound governs atmospheres. It causes demons to flee, hearts to open, and entire regions to shift.

When you walk into a place where people love one another purely, you feel Heaven's authority. That's why Jesus said, *"By this shall all men know you are My disciples, if you have love one for another."* Love is Heaven's proof of government because love never divides, it always unites.

The Church that walks in honor releases more than revival meetings, it releases Kingdom government. That sound doesn't fade when the music stops; it abides, shaping cities and nations. One sound can shake prisons; one heart can shift history.

The Ministry of Agreement

Agreement is more than shared opinion; it's spiritual harmony.

It requires three dimensions:
1. Agreement with God's will – Honoring His Word.
2. Agreement with God's order – Honoring divine authority.
3. Agreement with one another – Honoring (Valuing) difference.

When these three are aligned, Heaven's power is fully released. You don't have to manufacture miracles; they manifest naturally in that environment. Every great move of God has begun with simple agreement among hungry hearts who refused to let offense or ego divide them.

Honor builds the bridge that keeps that agreement intact.

Transition

When unity becomes sound and sound becomes power, Heaven's government invades earth. The next section will explore how disunity destroys destiny, why dishonor is the enemy's silent weapon and how to guard the sound of oneness.

Section 4 – The Enemy of Unity: How Dishonor Destroys Destiny

Unity is Heaven's sound; dishonor is hell's silence. Where honor joins hearts, dishonor severs them. Where agreement builds, offense breaks. Hell doesn't have to defeat a church that can't stay together; it only needs to divide it.

The enemy cannot overpower what God has united, so he whispers suspicion, jealousy, and comparison until people willingly separate. Every division begins with dishonor. It is never just a relational issue; it is rebellion against Heaven's order. When you dishonor someone God sent, you disconnect from the flow of what they carry.

The Anatomy of Division

Dishonor begins quietly:
- A thought unguarded.
- A word unmeasured.
- A conversation uncorrected.

Eve didn't fall because of a sword but because of a sentence: *"Has God really said?"* That one whisper fractured unity between God and man. Dishonor always begins as doubt. When you question the integrity of authority or the intention of a brother, you invite separation.

If honor builds bridges, dishonor burns them. Offense never travels alone, it brings accusation, pride, and eventually isolation. It turns family into factions and converts conversation into competition.

That's why Paul pleaded, *"Mark those who cause divisions... and avoid them."* Division is not discernment; it's disobedience disguised as revelation.

How Dishonor Silences Heaven's Sound

When dishonor enters, Heaven goes silent, not because God stops speaking, but because the atmosphere becomes uninhabitable for His presence. God speaks through order, not chaos. When Miriam dishonored Moses, the entire camp halted until she was restored. Dishonor delays destiny because Heaven won't advance in disorder.

When the people of Nazareth dishonored Jesus, He could do no mighty works there. Their disbelief wasn't intellectual, it was relational. They couldn't receive from the one they refused to honor. Dishonor closes Heaven's flow; honor reopens it. Power never departs because God is unwilling; it departs because people become unreceiving.

The Spirit Behind Dishonor

The spirit of dishonor is the spirit of Lucifer. It refuses to submit, rejects alignment, and seeks recognition apart from order. Lucifer didn't stop worshiping, he just wanted the glory for himself. Dishonor always wants the benefits of Heaven without the boundaries of it. That's why rebellion is compared to witchcraft, it manipulates through pride instead of yielding through trust.

Where Lucifer said, *"I will ascend,"* Jesus said, *"I will descend."* One lost the throne; the other inherited it. Heaven crowns humility, not ambition. Every time we choose honor over ego, we silence Lucifer's language.

The Subtle Forms of Dishonor

Dishonor doesn't always shout. Sometimes it whispers through sarcasm, delayed obedience, or selective submission. It's not always rebellion in action, it can be rebellion in attitude. Refusing to celebrate another's success or listen to correction are small leaks that sink great ships.

Gossip is dishonor spoken; cynicism is dishonor thought. Silent resentment is dishonor felt. If you want to keep Heaven's flow in your relationships and ministry, you must starve every form of dishonor. Don't entertain the whispers that wound unity, confront them with truth, forgiveness, and gratitude.

The Price of Division

Every divided house pays a cost:
- Vision loses focus.
- Presence loses power.
- People lose protection.

Again, that's why Jesus prayed in John 17 not for miracles, but for unity: *"Father, make them one."* He knew miracles would follow unity, but division would destroy destiny. No church can outgrow dishonor, and no movement can outlast pride. The sound of Heaven only fills what remains in one accord.

Restoring What Dishonor Damaged

Dishonor can be healed, but only through repentance and restoration. Unity cannot be **negotiated**; it must be **renewed through humility**. Confession rebuilds bridges faster than conversation. If you've been dishonored, forgive quickly. If you've dishonored, repent publicly when necessary. Restoration isn't weakness, it's wisdom. It proves that honor is greater than ego.

The prodigal son's restoration began with one phrase: *"Father, I have sinned against Heaven and before you."* When confession met compassion, the robe, ring, and relationship were restored. Repentance always reopens Heaven's flow.

Guarding the Gate of Unity

Every community needs gatekeepers, men and women who protect the culture of honor. They watch for gossip, pride, or division, not to police behavior but to preserve presence. Guarding unity isn't controlling people; it's contending for atmosphere. If you lose the sound of one accord, you lose the sound of Heaven.

Choose silence over slander, prayer over pride, reconciliation over resistance. Honor is the only language hell cannot counterfeit. Keep it alive and the sound will remain pure.

Transition

Dishonor divides; honor unites. When honor governs relationships, Heaven finds a home on earth. Honor is the highway upon which the Kingdom travels into the earth, answering the prayer of Jesus: *"Thy Kingdom come, Thy will be done on earth as it is in Heaven"* (Matthew 6:10).

At Nazareth, Jesus could do no mighty works, not because power was absent, but because dishonor broke alignment (Matthew 13:57–58). The Kingdom could not manifest where honor was withheld. Likewise, Jesus declared, *"He who receives you receives Me, and he who receives Me receives Him who sent Me"* (Matthew 10:40), revealing that Kingdom transfer flows through honor, not preference.

Honor creates alignment; alignment invites government; government establishes the Kingdom.

Moments of passion may stir presence, but only honor establishes the throne of His rule. In the next and final section of this chapter, we'll explore how unity is maintained as a lifestyle, how one sound is preserved through growth, transition, and even generational change.

"Honor is the highway of the Kingdom."

Section 5 – *Sustaining One Sound: The Lifestyle of Unity*

Unity is not a feeling to be chased; it is a covenant to be kept. Moments of great harmony can happen suddenly but sustaining them requires intentionality. The early church didn't remain in one accord because of personality, they did so because of posture. They cultivated unity as a lifestyle, not an event.

The sound of Heaven on earth is maintained the same way it is made: through honor. Unity fades when honor fades, because unity is not a personality agreement, it is an honor posture.

It is honor that protects the frequency of fellowship. The devil cannot destroy a praying people, but he can divide a proud one. Prayer without honor may create noise, but prayer with honor creates sound. Pride scatters what honor gathers. That is why humility must remain the ongoing rhythm of a united people.

Unity Is Daily, Not Occasional

The strength of the early believers in Acts 2 wasn't their upper-room experience, it was their daily devotion. They continued *"daily with one accord."* Unity was a rhythm, not a reaction. They ate together, prayed together, and gave together, and as a result, the Lord added to the church daily.

Unity fades where fellowship becomes optional. When we isolate, suspicion grows; when we gather, grace flows. Community is Heaven's strategy for consistency. When people walk together long enough in honor, unity becomes instinct.

Guarding the Sound

Sustaining one sound requires protecting it from three subtle enemies:
1. **Neglect**.
   Unity withers when we stop tending relationships.
   Don't assume connection; nurture it intentionally.
2. **Offense**.
   Unforgiveness detunes hearts.
   Keep short accounts. Release quickly. Refuse bitterness.
3. **Familiarity**.
   When honor turns to commonness, the flow diminishes.
   Remember who people are in God, not just what they are to you.

The sound of Heaven must be guarded like a sacred fire, it burns bright when fed by humility and fades when starved by pride.

Building Bridges Across Generations

Unity is incomplete if it ends with one generation. The God of Abraham, Isaac, and Jacob is the God of legacy. Each generation carries a part of the same sound, and the only way to preserve it is through honor between the old and the new.

Elders must honor emerging voices by making space; sons must honor fathers by remembering source. The next move of God will not come from youth or age alone, it will come from agreement between them. When generations honor one another, the sound becomes unbroken.

Legacy is sustained harmony.

Maintaining Unity Through Growth

Growth tests unity because multiplication magnifies difference. As new people enter a community, the temptation to divide by preference increases. But the mark of maturity is learning to expand without fragmenting. True unity doesn't mean everyone fits your comfort zone; it means everyone finds their covenant.

Growth requires new levels of humility. You can't maintain yesterday's unity with tomorrow's numbers unless you increase capacity for honor. Every revival becomes a reformation only when honor scales with growth. Heaven trusts enlargement only to people who guard the sound.

Living as One

Unity sustained looks like this:
- We speak one language - love.
- We carry one goal - the King's glory.
- We share one rhythm - obedience to the Spirit.

It's not sameness of expression, but sameness of essence. That essence is honor, because only honor can sustain unity without suppressing identity. When you live in that flow, jealousy dies, offense loses its voice, and joy becomes the common sound. Heaven calls that atmosphere peace.

Peace is not the absence of conflict, it's the presence of order. It's the stability that allows creativity, healing, and growth to flourish. That is the Kingdom made visible.

The Eternal Echo

The sound of unity will not end when time ends, it will echo into eternity. Revelation describes multitudes from every nation and tongue singing as one: *"Worthy is the Lamb!"* That is the final fulfillment of Jesus' prayer, *"That they may be one."* Every time we choose honor over offense, humility over pride, and covenant over convenience, we are rehearsing for eternity's song.

Unity begins in worship but ends in dominion. It turns gatherings into governments and moments into movements. One sound; born of one Spirit, sustained by one heart; will shake the earth until the kingdoms of this world become the Kingdom of our Lord and of His Christ.

Unity is not the climax, honor is. Unity is merely the evidence that honor has taken root.

Conclusion

Unity is Heaven's echo in human hearts. It is the sound that signals maturity, the fragrance that proves honor, and the evidence that sons have become one with the Father's will. When we live as one, the Kingdom becomes visible and the King becomes irresistible.

Unity is what people hear; honor is what Heaven sees. The one sound that shakes the earth is not made by many voices; it is made by many voices honoring One.

Honor sustains the sound.
Humility protects it.
Love perfects it.

Chapter 12 Review & Reflection

The Honor of Unity: The Strength of One Sound

Core Revelation

Unity is the sound of Heaven made visible on earth. It is not uniformity or the absence of difference, it is the blending of distinct tones under one Spirit. Honor is what makes unity possible; humility is what keeps it pure. When hearts are aligned in love and submission, Heaven's government finds expression through people.

The greatest proof of maturity is not gifts, miracles, or revelation, it is honor. Unity is simply the visible evidence of an honoring culture. Where there is honor, the flow of God never stops; where there is dishonor, the sound goes silent. The Kingdom advances at the speed of alignment through honor.

Kingdom Principle

Unity releases authority: honor preserves it. The Holy Spirit moves freely where honor, love and humility sustain one sound.

Scripture Focus

- John 17:21–23 – *"That they may be one, as We are one."*
- Psalm 133:1–3 – *"How good and pleasant it is when brethren dwell together in unity... there the Lord commands the blessing."*
- Acts 2:1–2 – *"They were all in one accord in one place... and suddenly there came a sound from Heaven."*
- Matthew 18:19 – *"If two of you agree on earth as touching anything... it shall be done."*
- Philippians 2:2–3 – *"Being of one accord, of one mind; in lowliness of mind let each esteem others better than themselves."*

- Ephesians 4:3 – *"Endeavor to keep the unity of the Spirit in the bond of peace."*

Truths to Remember

1. Unity is Heaven's sound; division is hell's silence.
2. Honor is the tuning fork of the Kingdom; it keeps hearts in harmony.
3. Diversity is not opposition to unity, it's its orchestra.
4. Comparison detunes; celebration aligns.
5. Forgiveness keeps the melody pure.
6. Dishonor disconnects you from the grace you criticize.
7. Honor multiplies authority exponentially, agreement reveals it
8. Humility sustains what passion begins.
9. Generational honor keeps the sound unbroken.
10. Legacy is sustained harmony, one Spirit across time.

Application

- Practice daily fellowship. Unity grows through consistent connection, not occasional gathering.
- Guard relationships from offense. Don't let pride or gossip distort the sound.
- Value diversity. See others' differences as design, not defect.
- Stay in tune through repentance. Quick forgiveness keeps the Spirit's flow clear.
- Pray corporately. Shared prayer synchronizes hearts faster than shared ideas.
- Bridge generations. Honor the fathers while empowering the sons.
- Correct with compassion. Keep truth and tenderness united.
- Refuse comparison. Celebrate another's grace without diminishing your own.
- Rehearse Heaven's sound. Every time you choose love over pride, you echo eternity.

Reflection Questions

1. Do I treat unity as sacred or situational?
2. What relationships in my life need to be retuned through forgiveness or humility?
3. Am I contributing to the sound of harmony or the noise of division?
4. How can I honor difference without feeling diminished by it?
5. Is my community producing one sound, or multiple agendas?
6. What practical steps can I take to keep the sound of Heaven alive in my home, church, or team?

Declaration

"Father, tune my heart to Your frequency. Teach me to honor beyond preference and to love beyond difference. Let my words, worship, and relationships release one sound, the sound of Heaven on earth. I renounce every spirit of dishonor that leads to division, pride, and competition. I receive the grace to walk in harmony with Your people. Make us one, Lord, that the world may know You have sent us. Let the sound of unity shake the earth again."

CHAPTER 13

HONORING LIFE SOURCES: THE WELLS THAT GOD APPOINTS

Before God sends people into purpose, He sends them to a well.

Unity sustains the sound (as we discovered in the last chapter), but wells sustain the flow that empowers the sound. The Kingdom moves at the speed of agreement, but it grows at the depth of its supply. Even the greatest revelation requires nourishment, and that nourishment always comes through vessels, life sources intentionally placed by God.

There are voices that teach you, voices that inspire you, and voices that inform you... and then there are voices that birth you. Those voices are not merely influential; they are instrumental. They do not just help you improve; they awaken who you truly are. They do not just speak to you; they speak into you. These are what Scripture reveals as wells.

A life source is a God-ordained well in the earth, through which identity, nourishment, and direction are drawn. It is not something we select by affinity but something we discover by alignment. Life sources do not arrive by preference; they are recognized by revelation. And once recognized, the only correct Kingdom response is honor.

Years ago, before I fully understood the weight of it, Bishop Tudor Bismarck released this revelation. He spoke of honoring the voices, vessels, and wells through which God chooses to channel His life. At the time, I understood it as gratitude. Later, I learned it was government. Honor was not merely thankfulness, it was alignment. It was not about courtesy; it was about capacity. I began to realize:

Life sources do not merely inspire, they impart.
They do not simply instruct, they awaken.
They do not just speak, they shape.

And I have lived long enough now to know: honor keeps the flow open, and dishonor shuts it down.

Section 1 – What Is a Life Source?

Before God gives us platforms, He gives us patterns. Before He entrusts us with ministry, He introduces us to alignment. The Kingdom does not begin with opportunity; it begins with order. And one of the first orders God establishes is the recognition of the life source He appoints to us.

A life source is not simply someone we respect; it is someone by whom God reveals us. They do not merely influence growth; they initiate it. They are more than teachers, mentors, or friends; they are wells dug by God in the earth to establish flow.

A life source is a person, place, or relationship through which God supplies identity, revelation, spiritual nutrients, alignment, covering, government, direction, and inheritance.

Life sources are origins. They are the first point of divine release concerning identity and assignment. You do not begin in purpose, you begin in a source God appoints. Before calling is activated, origin must be honored. To dishonor the origin is to dilute the outcome.

This includes those through whom our lives were originated naturally and those through whom our purpose was originated spiritually.

Biological parents are life sources because without them, we would not exist in the earth. Regardless of how well or how poorly they stewarded our upbringing, Scripture requires honor, not because they were perfect, but because they were God's chosen gateway for our arrival (Exodus 20:12).

Spiritual fathers and mothers are life sources because without their voice, covering, and obedience to divine assignment, we may not have discovered ours (1 Corinthians 4:15).

Founding pastors, apostles, or ministry pioneers are life sources because without their yes to God, the very platform we stand upon would not exist. To dishonor a founder is to dishonor origin. Even when invited, we must speak from alignment, not contradiction, recognizing that we stand within their well, not beside it.

Life sources are origins. Honor is stewardship of beginnings.

Life sources are not merely influential, they are foundational. They represent where God chose to begin your formation. What begins in a life source flows into purpose, so what is not honored at the origin cannot be fully inherited in destiny.

These are not casual connections; they are covenant conduits, vessels God chooses to transfer life into us. You don't get to choose them. You only get to recognize them.

That recognition is a spiritual experience, not an emotional response
- A preference identifies what you like;
- A life source reveals who you are.
- A preference is comfort-based;
- A life source is purpose-based.

You don't choose a life source like you choose a restaurant or a friend. You discover them by discernment. And once discovered, you are responsible before Heaven to honor that well, lest the flow be diminished.

"A life source is not a preference; it is a placement. It is not based on comfort; it is based on assignment. It is less about comfort and more about covenant."

When God sends a life source, He is sending an extension of His intention. The connection is prophetic before it is personal. That is why many miss their well, because they are looking for familiarity instead of divinity. What feeds your spirit may not always match your preferences. Kingdom wells are not dug for convenience but for covenant.

This is the pattern seen throughout Scripture. Before God fully establishes a man or woman into their identity, He places them under a life source, a God-ordained well, so that what is in them can be drawn out of them.

Just as water does not come from the soil until it is dug from the earth, what is planted within you does not emerge until you find the well God has appointed to draw it forth. Honor is the bucket that draws from the well, and without it, even deep sources remain undrunk.

A well may rest beneath your feet, but without honor, the water remains unseen.

Let me say it clearly:
"You do not access life from a life source because they are gifted, you access it because you honor what they carry."

Gifts attract talent; honor opens inheritance.

This is why dishonor disconnects even while proximity remains. You can be seated in the house where your life source dwells and still miss the well if familiarity replaces reverence. Honor is the key that unlocks the supply.

And once unlocked:
- flow begins,
- identity awakens,
- grace activates,
- and fruit becomes evident.

Honor is not merely a **Kingdom courtesy**; it is the **Kingdom currency** through which spiritual transactions take place. Honor is Heaven's protocol for receiving what God has already made available.

Transition

If life sources are divine placements, then they cannot be measured by preference or proximity, but by purpose. They are not selected by people; they are assigned by God. To understand the power and responsibility of recognizing a life source, we must next examine how God establishes these wells, not out of human convenience, but sovereign design.

Section 2 – Life Sources Are God's Design, Not Man's Convenience

Life sources are not the invention of leadership models or ministry structure, they are the manifestation of divine order. They do not appear because a person desires mentorship or chooses spiritual connection. They are assigned because Heaven has established a pattern that identity and inheritance are transferred through relationship, not merely through revelation.

In Scripture, God never matured a leader in isolation. He always connected destiny to a person prepared ahead of them. Every well precedes the one who drinks from it. This is not accidental; it is intentional. God appoints life sources because He honors the pattern of transference, He plants life in one and draws it out through another.

This is why Jesus told His disciples, *"I have come to send you"* before *"Go ye therefore."* One cannot truly be sent until they have first been formed. And that formation nearly always comes through a life source, someone who carries an element of what God has already spoken concerning you.

Let us walk through the scriptural pattern:
- **Abraham & Melchizedek** – before Abraham is fully revealed as father of nations, he encounters a priest-king who reveals divine order, blessing, and covenant. Not mentorship, alignment.

- **Moses & Jethro** – Moses had seen miracles but had no model for government until God used Jethro to reveal structure. Jethro did not teach Moses ministry; he preserved Moses from collapse.
- **Joshua & Moses** – Joshua carried military gifting, but Moses imparted movement. Without honor for Moses, Joshua may have fought battles but never led a generation into promise.
- **Elisha & Elijah** – Elisha had the plow, but Elijah held the pattern. When Elisha honored the well, he inherited not just Elijah's mantle, but double portion, proving the law of honor reproduces with increase.
- **Timothy & Paul** – Paul did not merely instruct Timothy; he fathered his identity. That is why Paul says, *"My son in the faith."* Honor gave Timothy what information could not impart.
- **John & Jesus** – John was not just a disciple; he became the only apostle referenced as *"the one whom Jesus loved"*. John didn't just learn the Word, he leaned into it. That posture of honor gave him access to the heart of Jesus in a way others did not receive.
- **Ruth & Naomi** – Naomi could not give Ruth a throne, but she gave her alignment. Ruth honored the well that had no blessing, and God turned it into lineage. Naomi did not look like a future; she looked like a widow. But honor sees divine placement beyond human situation.
- **Ananias & Paul** – Paul was called by Christ Himself, yet before his preaching began, God sent him to a man no one knew. It wasn't convenience, it was order.

None of these life sources would have been selected by preference. In fact, by preference, most would have been rejected.
- Elijah was volatile.
- Moses was complicated.
- Paul was confrontational.
- Naomi was bitter.
- Jethro was not Hebrew.
- Ananias was obscure.
- Melchizedek offered bread and wine, not a strategy.

This confirms one truth:
God often hides life sources behind what tests your honor. He will not hide water from you, but He may hide it within someone you would overlook if pride is present. Life sources are not assigned based on compatibility; they are given based on capacity, to draw out what is in you and to sustain what God deposits.

Let this be clearly stated:
"You do not honor a life source because they are perfect, you honor them because they are placed."

Their authority over your formation is not human appointment, it is Kingdom design.

And design demands honor. Where honor meets placement, inheritance flows.

Transition

Now that we understand that life sources are assigned by divine design, we must explore the impact of our response to that assignment. If the well is appointed by God, then the purity of our heart toward that well determines the purity of what flows from it.

This leads us directly into the next truth: Honor protects the flow. Dishonor pollutes the well.

Section 3 – Honor Protects the Flow: Dishonor Pollutes the Well

If life sources are God-appointed wells, then honor is the bucket by which we draw from them. The well can be full, but without honor, you cannot access what it carries. Dishonor does not change the well's supply, it changes your capacity to receive from it.

Spiritual Fathers: Wells That Carry What Sons Will One Day Walk In

When Proverbs 20:5 says,

"The purposes of a man's heart are deep waters, but a man of understanding draws them out,"

we often interpret that to mean that wisdom pulls potential from within a person. While this is true in part, in the context of Kingdom order and spiritual fathering, something even more profound is revealed:

- Those *"deep waters"* frequently reside first in the father, not the son.
- God deposits portions of a son's future inside the father so they may be drawn out in the right season.
- Honor is the drawing mechanism that gives sons access to what fathers carry.

For years, I believed my spiritual father was drawing potential out of me. Now I understand, he was not simply extracting identity from me. He was releasing what God had already placed in him for me, before the foundation of the world. My destiny was hidden like a well inside my spiritual father, and through honor, I was able to draw from waters that carried my identity in his assignment.

This is the mystery of generational grace:
Spiritual fathers carry water their sons are destined to drink from.

Abraham dug wells that Isaac later re-dug (Genesis 26:18). Isaac did not have to create the water source, he simply reopened what his father had already accessed. Likewise, Elisha did not create the prophetic mantle he received; he aligned with Elijah until it flowed freely (2 Kings 2:9–15). Joshua inherited not just leadership but the blueprint from Moses. Paul did not just instruct Timothy, he imparted what he carried (Philippians 2:22). Jesus did not merely model identity for His disciples, He released it into them.

This is why Scripture says:
"The glory of children are their fathers." (Proverbs 17:6)

A true father carries spiritual identity for his sons long before they mature into it. The child grows into what the father held for him. That is why dishonor towards a spiritual father does more than break relationship, it blocks the flow of identity and interrupts purpose.

Fathers dig wells. Sons drink from them.

Honor does not give a son depth; it gives him access to the depth the father already carries. A spiritual father is not merely someone who recognizes potential; he often contains it prophetically. What the son will one day walk in is often already alive in the father, awaiting transference through alignment, service, and honor.

Therefore, as sons, we must understand that discovering our identity is not an act of self-extraction or self-sufficiency. We are not waiting for something to be drawn out of ourselves alone. Without life sources, spiritual fathers appointed by God, we may never fully come into the revelation of who we are or why we were sent.

This is why Paul, even in a church filled with many instructors, insisted that they still needed fathers (1 Corinthians 4:15). Teachers can inform potential, but only a father can unlock it. Without fathers, our potency may never be activated, and our purpose may remain hidden beneath the surface.

"Sons don't drink from their own wells first. They drink from the wells their fathers dug."

Summary Thought

The purposes of the son are deep waters, but God often stores those waters first within the father. Honor draws them forth. Destiny is transferred before it is discovered.

Life sources are origins. What God intends to fulfill in you often begins in someone before you. Without honoring origin, discovery becomes delayed. Sons do not create wells; they inherit them. They do not originate the source, they recognize it. Honor is how the son acknowledges that what God is doing began before he arrived.

The principle is simple, but profound:

"What you dishonor cannot feed you. What you dishonor cannot bless you. What you dishonor you cannot receive from."

— Bishop Tudor Bismarck

Dishonor is not merely bad behavior, it is a breach in divine order, and anytime order is disrupted, flow is interrupted. God designed His Kingdom to move through people, so dishonor toward the vessel becomes a filter over the flow of Heaven.

When Life Sources Are Rejected: A Generational Diagnosis

"There is a generation that curses its father, And does not bless its mother." Proverbs 30:11

Scripture often reveals generational conditions not through commands, but through observation. Proverbs 30 is one such passage. Attributed to Agur, this chapter does not function as moral instruction as much as it does a prophetic diagnosis. Agur identifies patterns that emerge when wisdom is absent and honor is severed from its source.

The phrase *"there is a generation"* carries more weight than a reference to age. The Hebrew word dor speaks of continuity, an order, a cycle, a relay of life intended to pass from one to another without interruption. What Agur observes is not a momentary rebellion, but a fractured transmission.

To curse one's father does not simply mean to speak harshly. The Hebrew word qalal means to make light of, to diminish, or to strip weight. In Scripture, honor (kabod) is always associated with weight, substance, and value. To curse the father, then, is to reduce the perceived weight of authority, instruction, and identity. It is not merely rejection, it is redefinition. A father's voice is no longer treated as a source, but as an obstacle.

Likewise, the phrase *"does not bless its mother"* reveals more than neglect. The Hebrew word barak means to speak life, to invoke increase, and to authorize continuation. Mothers in Scripture represent nurture, formation, and environment, the shaping context in which life matures. To withhold blessing is not neutrality; it is the refusal to affirm the very process by which life is sustained and developed.

Together, these two actions describe a generation that rejects both identity and formation. The father is dismissed as a source of instruction and authority, and the mother is denied as a source of nurture and development. The result is not independence, but disconnection, sons and daughters who desire outcomes without origins, fruit without roots, and authority without lineage.

This is why honor is not a social virtue but a spiritual conduit. Life does not merely originate with God; it flows through God-ordained sources. When those sources are dishonored, life flow is disrupted. What remains is often mistaken for strength but is, in reality, a refined form of orphanhood, self-directed, self-affirmed, and increasingly isolated from the very structures designed to sustain life.

Agur's observation is not a condemnation; it is a warning. Where honor collapses, continuity collapses. And where continuity is broken, identity must be reconstructed artificially. The language of sons is lost not in open rebellion, but in the quiet dismissal of life sources that were never meant to be optional.

This is why honor is not taught as etiquette in the Kingdom, but as alignment, because sons do not merely receive life; they remain connected to its source.

Honor Opens Inheritance

Jesus taught this clearly:
"He who receives a prophet in the name of a prophet shall receive a prophet's reward." Matthew 10:41

The reward is not based on proximity to the prophet, nor on the prophet's gifting, it is based entirely on honor.

Proximity gives access.
Honor enables transfer.
Dishonor blocks inheritance.
Many stand near wells yet remain thirsty, not because the well is empty, but because honor is absent.

Dishonor Restricts Grace

When Jesus ministered in Nazareth, the Scripture says:
"He could do no mighty works there… because of their unbelief."

- Matthew 13:58

This unbelief was not intellectual, it was relational. They dishonored His humanity (*"Is this not the carpenter's son?"*), and therefore disqualified themselves from His divinity. They did not reject His ability, they denied His identity.

Dishonor always diminishes identity in the eyes of the dishonoring. It is why Elisha had to tear his garment before receiving Elijah's mantle. He had to remove what represented the old posture before he could step into what honor prepared for him.

Dishonor sees through the lens of familiarity. Honor looks through the eyes of revelation.

Dishonor Pollutes the Water

Genesis 26:15 describes how the Philistines treated the wells Abraham dug:
"They stopped them and filled them with earth."

Every time dishonor enters a relationship, conversation, or community, it throws dirt into the flow, stones of complaint, soil of offense, sand of comparison. What was life-giving becomes contaminated. Honor keeps the well clean. Dishonor makes the water bitter.

This is why Hebrews warns us:
"That no root of bitterness springing up cause trouble, and by this many become defiled." Hebrews 12:15

Bitterness does not only contaminate the soul that carries it, it defiles those connected to it. Dishonor is transmissible, so is honor. One spreads infection, the other spreads impartation.

Honor Protects What Feeds You

Honor isn't passive gratitude, it's active protection.

"One of the greatest dishonors a son can commit is allowing others to dishonor their life source in their presence."

Honor does not stay silent when the well is attacked. It speaks up, stands up, and shields.
- Isaac fought to dig again the wells his father dug (Genesis 26:18).
- David defended Saul's honor even after Saul tried to kill him (1 Samuel 24:6).
- Jesus restored Peter publicly because He protected Peter's dignity privately (John 21:15–17).

Dishonor occurs in absence of protection. Honor is revealed in presence of it.

Dishonor Never Destroys the Well, Only the Drinker

Miriam spoke against Moses. Moses remained anointed. Miriam became leprous. (Numbers 12) The well continued flowing; she lost access. Dishonor never dethrones the well, only disconnects the one dishonoring. The tragedy of dishonor is not what it does to the life source, it is what it does in the one dishonoring. It shifts posture from receiving to resisting.

Transition

Honor doesn't just preserve access to revelation, it protects identity. Life sources are not simply wells of wisdom; they are wells of who you are becoming.

In Section 4, we will uncover how honor unlocks identity, and why those who fail to honor their life source often struggle with confidence, clarity, and calling. If honor protects the flow, it also protects what is being formed. Without honor, identity remains dormant.

Section 4 – Life Sources as Wells of Identity

Every life source carries water, but not just for your nourishment, for your becoming. What they pour into you does not merely strengthen you; it shapes you. Life sources do not only deliver teaching; they deliver identity.

Life sources don't just feed you; they name you.
They do not merely inform, they impart.
They don't inspire, they awaken.

Where information trains the mind, impartation transforms the heart. A teacher can communicate knowledge, but a father releases identity. It is the difference between instruction and formation, between learning and becoming.

Jesus asked His disciples, *"Who do men say that I am?"* (Matthew 16:13). They answered with information, prophet, rabbi, teacher. Then He asked, *"But who do you say that I am?"* Peter responded by revelation. Jesus immediately replied:

"Blessed are you, Simon, son of Jonah… And I say to you that you are Peter." Matthew 16:17–18

Honor is what makes identity transferable. Revelation of Him released revelation of Peter. Peter did not identify Jesus correctly because he first knew himself; he identified Jesus correctly because Heaven revealed what the life source had already seen in him. Jesus was not waiting to discover Peter, He had already called him at *"Follow Me."*

Revelation did not create Peter's identity, it awakened what Christ, his life source, had already declared prophetically.

Peter first sensed who Jesus was on the water *("If it is You…"* Matthew 14:28). When the storm shook him, his uncertainty turned into recognition *"Lord, save me."* What began in desperation was completed in revelation.

But it was in Matthew 16, when Peter declared, *"You are the Christ, the Son of the living God"*, that Jesus, the life source, could now release identity: *"And I say to you, that you are Peter."*

Calling begins in the voice of the life source, but identity is received in the moment of revelation. A man may walk with his life source and still say *"if,"* but the moment Christ is truly revealed, he becomes what Christ always saw.

Honor is what postures the heart to receive identity from the life source when revelation arrives. Revelation is God's confirmation of what the life source has already spoken.

You cannot call someone what Heaven calls them if dishonor is in your heart toward them. Likewise, you cannot truly know who you are if dishonor is active toward the one God assigned to draw identity out of you.

Identity Is Hidden in Honor

- Elijah didn't just train Elisha, he shaped him, and Elisha called him *"My father, my father!"* as the chariot of fire took him (2 Kings 2:12).
- Paul didn't merely instruct Timothy, he fathered him, calling him *"My true son in the faith"* (1 Timothy 1:2).
- Jesus didn't just disciple John, He stabilized him, changing the *"Son of Thunder"* into the apostle of love (John 13:23; 1 John 4:8).

Elisha never received Elijah's mantle until he responded to him as father. Timothy never received apostolic authority until he embraced Paul as father. John never became an apostle of love until he rested upon love Himself.

Identity flows where honor goes. What you refuse to honor, you cannot become.

Wells Only Pour for Those Who Draw

Just because a source carries what you need does not mean you will receive it. James teaches:
"You have not because you ask not... you ask amiss."

- James 4:2–3

Asking **precedes receiving**, but honor **precedes asking**. You cannot draw from someone you internally resist. Dishonor shuts down your capacity to request and heaven's willingness to release.

Life sources are not convenience, they are covenant appointments. You don't choose them, you discern them. Once discerned, honor maintains the flow. You cannot extract identity from a well you secretly compete with. You will only draw deeply from where you kneel humbly.

Dishonor Paralyzes Identity

This is why orphans struggle with identity, they resist the very sources God sends to help define them. Without honor, development becomes delayed.

- Saul dishonored Samuel and lost kingship.
- Absalom dishonored David and lost legacy.
- Judas dishonored Jesus and lost destiny.

Dishonor disconnects you from the very voice heaven intended to clarify who you are becoming.

Dishonor is identity abandonment.
Honor is identity acceleration.

Life Sources Carry Your Future

To honor a life source is to honor who God is shaping you to become. You are not honoring a person, you are honoring the future God placed inside them for you.

This is why Elisha cried,
"My father, my father, the chariot of Israel and its horsemen!" (2 Kings 2:12)

He understood:
Elijah's departure was not his loss, it was his moment of inheritance.

Honor is the unlocking of what you are next.
The well you honor is the future you drink from.

Transition

Honor gives access to identity, but identity alone is not enough. Wells must be protected, not only so they can continue supplying life, but so they remain pure for those following us.

The next section will explore how to guard your life sources, why spiritual theft happens when protection is absent, and how honor safeguards the atmosphere from which destiny is drawn. If honor unlocks identity, it must also protect the voices that define it.

Section 5 – *Protecting Life Sources: Guarding the Wells*

Identifying your life source is only the beginning; honoring them sustains the flow and protecting them preserves it. Wells do not just release life, they must be shielded so life continues uninterrupted. What feeds you must not be left vulnerable.

You do not guard wells out of fear; you guard them out of honor. You protect what God used to shape you because it is part of your future, not just your past.

In biblical times, wells represented not only life but inheritance. To poison a well was an act of war, because it disrupted the survival and destiny of generations. Likewise, to allow dishonor toward your life source is not merely relational negligence, it is spiritual sabotage.

Wells Are Targets of the Enemy

Genesis 26 records that after Abraham died, the Philistines stopped up the wells out of envy and hostility (Genesis 26:15). They were not fighting Isaac; they were fighting his supply. Isaac did not argue or retaliate; he simply dug them open again.

Life sources must be protected, and when attacked, defended, not abandoned. Honor makes you a steward, not a spectator. Those who drink from the well must stand watch over it.

Honor is expressed not only toward spiritual fathers but also toward natural parents and founding voices. Biological parents are life sources of existence; spiritual fathers are life sources of assignment; founding leaders are life sources of environment.

In ministry, to enter someone's pulpit without honoring the founder is to drink from their well while questioning the one who dug it. Honor acknowledges that if they had not said yes, we would not be standing where we stand. Likewise, children must recognize that their biological parents carried the seed God used to position them in time.

What God originates through a life source must be protected through honor, or we risk consuming what we dishonor. You are not honoring a person; you are honoring the future God placed inside them for you.

This is equally true of biological origins and pioneering assignments. You cannot fully inherit what God prepared through spiritual fathers if you cannot first recognize the grace that came through your natural parents. You cannot carry forward the grace of a ministry house while disregarding the one who founded it.

Honor reaches backward before it reaches forward. What you refuse to honor behind you, you cannot steward ahead of you.

Not Everyone Should Have Access to Your Well

Honoring life sources includes protecting them from those who do not value what they carry. Some people will:
- Throw stones into the well (Genesis 26:15) – through criticism or slander
- Pollute it with bitterness – insinuating wrong motives
- Steal from it – taking without submitting

- Devalue it – treating the sacred as common
- Exploit it – using access for personal advancement
- Ignore it – receiving casually instead of covenantally

Honor is not silent when others dishonor what God appointed. Silence in the presence of dishonor is consent to sabotage. A true son or steward speaks up when life sources are attacked, not to defend ego but to protect flow.

The Responsibility of Honor

When Miriam spoke against Moses, God Himself responded, calling her dishonor not just misalignment with Moses but rebellion against divine order (Numbers 12:1–9). Moses didn't defend himself; God defended the well.

Honor provokes divine protection.
Dishonor provokes divine delay.

Just as wells were covered to preserve their purity, so must your heart cover those God has used to pour into you.

A Case Study in Life Sources: Noah, Ham, and the Power of Honor

One of the clearest biblical pictures of honoring a life source is found in Genesis 9. After the flood, Noah, God's appointed source for repopulation and covenant, became vulnerable and lay uncovered in his tent.

"Ham... saw the nakedness of his father and told his two brothers outside." Genesis 9:22

Ham exposed what he should have covered. Instead of guarding the well, he broadcast its weakness.

"But Shem and Japheth took a garment, laid it on both their shoulders, and walked backward and covered the nakedness of their father." Genesis 9:23

The difference was simple:
- Ham looked and spoke.
- Shem and Japheth looked away and covered.

Ham responded with dishonor. Shem and Japheth responded with covenant.

Noah's reaction was prophetic:
"Cursed be Canaan...Blessed be the Lord, the God of Shem; may God enlarge Japheth." Genesis 9:25–27

Dishonor cost Ham's lineage their inheritance. Honor secured Shem and Japheth's legacy. The curse didn't fall because Noah was flawed, it fell because Ham violated divine order around a life source.

Honor protects flow, even in the presence of weakness.
Dishonor magnifies weakness and disrupts destiny.

Transition

Honor not only identifies and draws from a life source, it shields them so the flow remains clean and unbroken. But honoring a source is also about understanding the spiritual implications of receiving from them, for what flows through them becomes part of your inheritance.

The next section will explore how honoring a life source honors God Himself, how receiving from a vessel aligns you with Heaven's order, and how dishonor toward a source is rejection of divine supply.

If a life source is a well, then honor is both the bucket that draws and the gate that guards. Let's now see how receiving from them is receiving from God.

Section 6 – *Honoring a Life Source Is Honoring God*

Honor does not end with the vessel, it rises to the One who sent the vessel.

Jesus Himself made this clear:
"He who receives you receives Me, and he who receives Me receives Him who sent Me." Matthew 10:40

To honor a life source is to recognize that God, not our preference, chose them as a channel of grace. To dishonor them is not merely a relational offense; it is a rejection of divine arrangement.

You are not honoring the **man;** you are honoring the **mandate.** You are not submitting to the personality; you are aligning with the purpose. The vessel is human, but the flow is heavenly.

Honor is not given because a vessel is flawless, it is given because God is faithful. You are not honoring perfection; you are honoring selection.

God Moves Through Vessels by Design, Not by Default

Throughout Scripture, God used flawed men to deliver flawless grace:
- Moses stuttered yet delivered the law.
- Elijah struggled with despair yet released prophetic fire.
- Peter was unstable yet held the keys of the Kingdom.
- Paul was once a persecutor yet became an apostolic pillar.

Their imperfections did not disqualify the flow, dishonor would have.

"We have this treasure in earthen vessels…". 2 Corinthians 4:7

The treasure should never be dismissed because of the vessel that carries it.

Dishonor Rejects God's Choice

When Korah and his followers dishonored Moses and Aaron, they weren't fighting them, they were resisting God's structure (Numbers 16). Scripture notes their rebellion as against the Lord, not against men.

When Miriam dishonored Moses, her punishment delayed the entire nation (Numbers 12:15). Dishonor toward a life source doesn't merely affect relationship, it halts destiny.

Dishonor is not disagreement, it is disconnection.
And you cannot receive from what you are disconnected from.

Honor Activates Heaven's Reward

Jesus taught:
"He who honors a prophet in the name of a prophet receives a prophet's reward." Matthew 10:41

The reward is not access to the person, but to what Heaven placed on the person. You do not receive from gifting alone; you receive through alignment with grace. A son can sit under brilliant teaching and still remain unchanged if he does not carry posture. Revelation does not flow to gifted ears; it flows through honoring hearts.

Honor is the hand that receives what Heaven gave through a vessel. Honor turns teaching into impartation. Honor converts information into transformation.

You Cannot Extract From a Well You Privately Disrespect

It is possible to sit physically under a voice you are spiritually withdrawn from. Distance doesn't begin in geography; it begins in honor.

When Jesus returned to Nazareth, He could do no mighty works (Mark 6:5). Not because He lacked power, but because they lacked honor. Dishonor didn't diminish Jesus; it diminished their ability to receive. His power remained; their hearts rejected it. Heaven does not withhold from dishonor; dishonor withholds from Heaven.

Honor Is Alignment With God's Government

In the Kingdom:
- God chooses the source
- You recognize the source
- Honor activates the flow
- Alignment sustains the flow

The purpose of honor is not emotional, it is governmental. It positions your heart correctly inside God's arrangement so that grace can move unhindered. Honor is not flattery; it is spiritual positioning. To honor the vessel is to trust the sending.

This is why honor is non-negotiable in the Kingdom: it affirms that God is Lord not just over blessing, but also over channel.

Transition

A life source is not meant to be admired, it is meant to be honored, guarded, and continued. If honor aligns us with the source, then impartation ensures that what flowed into us now flows through us. Honor kept the well open; impartation ensures the well multiplies.

The next section will explore the transformational nature of life sources, how impartation turns recipients into vessels, and how stewardship of a well becomes legacy.

Section 7 – My Life and Bishop Clowers: From Impartation to Continuation

Revelation can be taught, but impartation must be caught.

The first time I heard the term life source was through Bishop Tudor Bismarck. His teaching planted the seed of this understanding in me long before I had the maturity to fully steward it. He articulated a truth that stirred something in my spirit: that God moves through wells, men and women chosen to transfer divine life.

But while Bishop Tudor introduced me to this revelation, it was my spiritual father, Bishop Gary Clowers, who incarnated it before my eyes. He did not simply teach me about honor, he fathered honor into me.

If Bishop Tudor gave language to the revelation,
Bishop Clowers gave life to it within me.

Through years of walking under his voice, I did not just gain information, I encountered transformation. Bishop Clowers exemplified honor in word, posture, and presence. His life became the well God used to stabilize my identity, shape my ministry, and unlock what revelation alone could not.

Teaching brought understanding. Fathering brought formation.

Fathering Is the Highest Form of Life Source

Life sources inspire and instruct, but spiritual fathers impart identity and alignment.
- Bishop Clowers did not merely speak to my gift; he spoke to my core.
- He didn't pull on my potential; he prioritized my becoming.
- He did not push me, it was his voice that located and launched me.

Like Paul to Timothy, he did not just provide perspective, he provided posture.

"For though you have ten thousand instructors in Christ, yet you do not have many fathers." 1 Corinthians 4:15

Mentors teach information.

Fathers transfer inheritance.

Honor Was Imparted, Not Imposed

Honor did not become my message simply because I studied it, it became my message because I lived under it.

Bishop Clowers taught me that:
- Honor is not protocol; it is posture.
- Authority is not enforced; it is entrusted where honor is first observed.
- Legacy is not built through gifting; it is transferred through living alignment.

He never demanded honor, he demonstrated it, both upward and downward. Watching him honor his own spiritual fathers gave me the blueprint to honor mine. The impartation I carry today is not imitation, it is continuation.

Impartation Produces Multiplication

When a life source is honored, the grace carried becomes **transferable**.
- Elisha didn't inherit Elijah's mantle by proximity, but by posture.
- Timothy didn't step into apostolic assignment by ambition, but by alignment.
- I did not begin teaching honor because it was trending, but because it was transforming.

The message is not from academic pursuit, it is from apostolic impartation. The well I now dig for others was first dug in me through honor.

This chapter is not just **tribute**, it is **testimony**.

The grace that flowed to me must now flow through me. The honor that shaped me must now be multiplied in sons and daughters.

Inheritance is not what you **leave behind**, it is what you **live ahead** through honor.

Transition

Life sources introduce assignment. Fathers activate alignment. Honor keeps the well open, and legacy keeps it flowing.

Now that we understand what life sources are, how honor activates flow, and how impartation shapes identity, we arrive at the heart of this chapter:

Honor is the mechanism of inheritance. If you steward the well you receive from, you become the well others draw from. The Conclusion will bring this together with clarity, revelatory synthesis, and prophetic charge.

Conclusion - Life Flows Through Honor

Life does not spread through information; it spreads through impartation. A man may grow through teaching, but he is transformed through alignment. Honor is what makes that alignment possible.

Life sources are not incidental, they are intentional. God appoints wells in every generation, and those wells do not just provide sustenance, they release identity, direction, and formation. They do not simply fill a man, they frame him. Honor is not courtesy. Honor is covenant. It is the posture that recognizes divine placement and protects divine flow.

You do not honor a life source because they are flawless, you honor them because God chose them. You do not protect them because they are fragile, you protect them because the flow is sacred. Their value is not measured by preference but by purpose.

When honor is present, inheritance is released. When dishonor appears, flow dries up, not because God stops giving, but because we stop receiving.

Honor Is the Mechanism of Inheritance

Revelation may bring understanding, but honor opens the well. Impartation may come through encounter, but honor sustains the transfer. Legacy is not built through gifting but through alignment with grace.
- Elisha received Elijah's mantle because he honored the source.
- Timothy inherited Paul's assignment because he honored his spiritual father.
- Joshua stepped into Moses' leadership because he remained in posture.

Inheritance is not earned. It is entrusted where honor has first been proven.

Life sources do not exist to be admired, they exist to be continued. If you drink from the well and do not dig it deeper for those who come after, you have received from it, but you have not stewarded it.

Because life sources are origins, honor is the preservation of where God started His work in you. When origin is honored, inheritance is entrusted. When origin is dishonored, identity becomes unstable. You cannot build securely on a foundation you refuse to value. To honor a life source is to honor God's beginning in you, and Heaven only finishes what it began through honor.

Honor Turns Receivers into Wells

The revelation of Bishop Tudor opened my eyes to the existence of wells. The impartation of Bishop Clowers opened my spirit to become one.

His life did not just shape my message, it shaped my posture. The honor he lived became the honor I now lead with. That is the power of spiritual fathering: it doesn't duplicate, it reproduces what Heaven initiated.

It is not imitation; it is impartation in continuance.
Every chapter of this book is watered by that well.

Honor Is How Heaven Entrusts Regions

When God desires to establish His work in a region, He does not send strategies, He sends stewards. He plants wells and watches the posture of those who drink from them. If honor is present, He multiplies flow. If honor is abandoned, the well becomes a monument instead of a movement.

Honor keeps grace active.
Dishonor turns grace into history.

The Final Revelation

If honor sustains the well, then dishonor abandons it.

If honor increases inheritance, dishonor forfeits it.

If honor keeps you connected to divine supply, dishonor disconnects you from future purpose.

Because life flows through honor,
destiny flows through honor,
and legacy flows through honor.

Final Charge

Honor the well God used to form you.
Defend the voice He trusted to guide you.
Protect the flow that awakened you.
And become a well for those He will send after you.

When sons honor life sources, they become life sources. When generations honor those who poured, they become those who pour. Honor is how the Kingdom travels from one life to another. It is how Heaven's blueprint becomes an earthly legacy. And it is how we ensure that what God began in us is not lost through us but multiplied beyond us.

Where honor flows, life flows.
Where honor is withheld, life dries up.
Honor your source, honor your future.
And through honor, become a source for another's.

Chapter 13 Review & Reflection

Honoring Life Sources: The Wells God Appoints

Core Revelation

Life does not progress through information; it progresses through impartation. God assigns life sources not based on our preference but on His purpose. These sources act as wells, channels of grace, identity, alignment, and direction.

Honor is what keeps the flow open. Dishonor shuts it down.

You do not receive from a life source because they are perfect, but because God chose them. Honor is the mechanism that allows inheritance to pass from vessel to vessel. When you honor your well, you retain the flow and become one for others.

What you honor, you can receive from.
What you dishonor, you are locked out of.

Honor is not a feeling, it is posture. It is not courtesy, it is covenant.

Kingdom Principle

Life flows through honor. Inheritance is passed by alignment, not by ambition. Honor is not about personality; it is about placement. It is the posture that keeps the spiritual well from being polluted, disconnected, or abandoned. God moves through vessels by design, and honor preserves both the flow and the future.

Scripture Focus

- Matthew 10:40–41 – *"He who receives you receives Me... he who honors a prophet receives a prophet's reward."*
- 2 Corinthians 4:7 – *"We have this treasure in earthen vessels."*

- 1 Corinthians 4:15 – *"Though you have ten thousand instructors, yet not many fathers."*
- Numbers 12:1–15 – Miriam's dishonor toward Moses halted the nation's movement.
- Genesis 26:18 – Isaac re-dug the wells his father had dug.
- 2 Kings 2:9 – *"Let a double portion of your spirit be upon me."*
- Hebrews 13:7 – *"Consider those who have spoken God's word to you; imitate their faith."*

Truths to Remember

1. Life sources are discovered, not chosen.
2. Honor opens the well, dishonor buries it.
3. You cannot draw from what you privately disrespect.
4. Identity is often deposited into the father before it awakens in the son. Honor grants access to that identity.
5. The deep waters of Proverbs 20:5 may reside in the spiritual father, drawn out through alignment and honor.
6. Fathers dig wells; sons inherit them. What a father carries may be the future of his son in prophetic form.
7. Revelation informs; fathering transforms.
8. Inheritance is transferred where honor is established.
9. Protect the well from voices that dishonor or pollute.
10. To honor a life source is to honor the God who sent them.
11. Sons multiply what they receive; students only repeat.
12. The measure of impartation is determined by the posture of honor.
13. Where honor flows, legacy begins.

Application

- Identify your life sources. Who has shaped your identity, not just your inspiration?
- Recognize that discovering purpose may require receiving from a life source rather than attempting to extract identity

alone. Ask the Holy Spirit to show you whose well you are called to drink from.
- Guard their voice. Do not allow others to dishonor what feeds you.
- Draw intentionally. Lean in with posture, not entitlement.
- Release gratitude. Appreciation keeps the flow alive.
- Stay aligned even when not in agreement.
- Honor publicly and privately. Silence in dishonor is silent agreement.
- Re-dig wells that past seasons tried to bury.
- Discern who drinks from your well, and who digs holes.
- Impart what was imparted to you.
- Live in such a way that Heaven trusts you to become a well for others.

Reflection Questions

1. Who has functioned as a life source in my journey, and have I treated them as such?
2. Have I been guilty of silent dishonor (neglect, familiarity, casualness)?
3. What wells in my life need to be re-dug through renewed honor?
4. Have I believed my purpose would emerge independently, instead of realizing that it may be imparted through the fathers God has assigned to me?
5. What voices shape me today, and do I guard them intentionally?
6. Am I becoming a well for others, or merely preserving what was given to me?
7. Have I allowed insecurity, offense, or independence to disconnect me from divine supply?
8. How am I preparing sons and daughters to honor their sources, not just access them?

Declaration

"Father, I recognize the voices You have used to shape me. Today I choose honor, deep, intentional, covenantal honor. I repent for any familiarity, silence, or disconnection that has hindered the flow. I honor the well You used to form me, and I declare I will protect what You have entrusted. Let the grace that flowed to me now flow through me. Make me a well for others. I receive my inheritance through honor, and I will release it the same way. I receive identity not through self-reliance but through alignment. I honor the wells God has placed before me, and I recognize that what I may one day walk in lives in those He has assigned to walk before me. Where honor flows, life flows, and I choose life."

CHAPTER 14

THE HONOR OF AUTHORITY: HEAVEN'S GOVERNMENT IN HUMAN FORM

Section 1 – The Divine Order of Authority

Authority is Heaven's structure for stability. It is not man's invention; it is God's idea. From Genesis to Revelation, every act of divine order is expressed through delegated authority. Creation obeyed His Word; angels obey His command; sons obey His Spirit. Heaven itself functions in perfect alignment, Father, Son, and Spirit moving as one will, one nature, one authority.

When God establishes authority on earth, He is not sharing power, He is sharing representation. Authority is not domination; it is delegation. It is Heaven's trust extended to humanity. To honor authority, then, is to honor Heaven's trust. To dishonor it is to resist Heaven's government.

Romans 13:1 says, *"There is no authority except from God, and those that exist have been instituted by God."* This verse doesn't excuse abuse; it explains design. All authority flows from the Throne, pure, holy, protective, and redemptive. When human leadership mirrors that design, Heaven's order manifests visibly on earth.

Authority: Heaven's Currency

Authority is not a badge of superiority; it is the currency of responsibility. Those entrusted with it are called to steward, not to control. Heaven measures authority not by how much power you possess, but by how much obedience you express. Even Jesus said, *"I can do nothing of Myself; as I hear, I judge."*

The Son modeled authority through submission.

In the Kingdom, authority never flows apart from humility. Submission is not weakness; it is the power posture of Heaven. Every level of delegated authority requires an equal measure of surrender. That's why Jesus could cast out demons and calm storms; His authority was pure because His submission was complete. Heaven only backs what Heaven births.

The Purpose of Delegated Authority

God established delegated authority for three primary purposes:
1. **Protection** – Authority guards' purpose. It creates boundaries where growth can occur safely.
2. **Order** – Authority aligns gifts, roles, and callings so that chaos cannot rule.
3. **Representation** – Authority reveals God's character through human leadership.

When these purposes are honored, authority becomes a river of life. When they are corrupted by ego, it becomes a system of control. The difference between order and oppression is the presence of humility.

That's why Paul admonished leaders in 1 Peter 5:2–3 to shepherd *"not as lords over those entrusted to you but being examples to the flock."* Authority in the Kingdom doesn't push people, it pulls them higher through love and example.

The Atmosphere Authority Requires

Authority cannot survive where honor is absent. The moment dishonor enters, authority becomes ineffective. Even Jesus, perfect in holiness, could *"do no mighty works"* in Nazareth because familiarity bred contempt. They saw His humanity and missed His divinity. Honor is what allows Heaven to operate through human imperfection.

You may not agree with everything a leader does, but when you honor the authority they carry, you access the grace attached to them. Honor doesn't endorse wrong; it recognizes order. It looks past personality to perceive placement. Without honor, divine flow becomes dammed by human opinion.

The Weight of Representation

To be entrusted with authority is to carry the weight of Heaven's reputation. That's why James warned, *"Let not many of you become teachers, knowing that we shall receive a stricter judgment."* Leadership is not a platform of privilege; it is a position of pressure. Heaven holds its representatives accountable for the stewardship of influence.

True authority is not loud; it is heavy. The Hebrew word for glory, kabod, literally means *"weight."* When God gives you authority, He is placing His weight on you. How you carry it determines whether people see Him or you. Honor helps both the one leading and the one following bear that weight correctly.

The Two Directions of Honor

Authority and honor always flow in two directions:
- Downward: through leadership, blessing, and covering.
- Upward: through submission, gratitude, and obedience.

If either direction stops, stagnation sets in. When leaders stop honoring those they lead, they lose credibility. When followers stop honoring those who lead, they lose protection. Heaven's government functions like blood flow, constant, reciprocal, and life-giving. Where honor circulates, the body stays healthy. Where it's blocked, the system begins to fail.

Transition

Authority is Heaven's language of order, and honor is the response that keeps it fluent. In the next section, we will explore how to recognize and respond to delegated authority, the posture that opens the flow of Heaven's government in your life.

Section 2 – Recognizing and Responding to Delegated Authority

Every move of God flows through someone God has chosen. Heaven never works without human partnership. Moses parted seas, Elijah shut heavens, Esther saved a nation, Paul planted churches, but behind every act of divine power was the recognition of divine order. The measure of what people received was determined by how they responded to the authority God placed before them.

Recognition Is Revelation

To recognize authority is not to see talent, it's to discern placement. The people of Nazareth saw Jesus as Joseph's son, but Peter saw Him as the Christ. Both looked at the same man, but only one had revelation. Heaven honors revelation because recognition determines reception.

Jesus said, *"He who receives a prophet in the name of a prophet shall receive a prophet's reward."* That statement reveals a law of spiritual exchange: You cannot receive from what you refuse to recognize. Honor is not flattery; it's spiritual sight. It sees the grace on a person and positions itself to draw from it.

Recognition doesn't mean idolization, it means identification. You're not worshiping a vessel; you're acknowledging the God who works through it.

How Heaven Confirms Authority

Heaven confirms true authority through fruit, faithfulness, and fragrance:
1. **Fruit** – Results consistent with God's nature. Authority builds, not breaks.
2. **Faithfulness** – Consistency under pressure. True authority stands when applause fades.
3. **Fragrance** – The invisible presence of humility and holiness that surrounds authentic leadership.

Authority that carries Heaven's DNA smells like peace, not pressure. You don't have to be forced to follow what Heaven has truly appointed; you're drawn to it by spiritual resonance.

The Posture of Response

Your response to authority reveals the maturity of your heart. Submission is not about subordination, it's about synchronization. It means you align your heart with Heaven's structure so that the flow of grace is unbroken.

When the centurion said, *"I also am a man under authority,"* Jesus marveled. Why? Because the centurion understood that true authority is never independent, it's inherited through alignment. He recognized that obedience is not loss of freedom but access to function. Jesus didn't need to come to his house; His word was enough, because alignment had already opened the door.

When you respond with honor, you invite Heaven's government into your circumstances. Submission is not for control, it's for covering.

The Role of Spiritual Fathers and Leaders

In the Kingdom, spiritual authority functions through relationship, not rank. Paul told the Corinthians, *"Though you have ten thousand instructors, you do not have many fathers."*

Teachers inform, but fathers transform. Spiritual fathers carry grace not just to teach you but to form you.

To recognize a spiritual father or leader is to discern the voice that carries Heaven's DNA for your development. It's the voice that unlocks purpose, not the one that feeds preference. You can hear many messages, but there are few voices that mark you. Those voices are divine assignments in human form.

Responding to them with honor doesn't make you lesser, it roots you deeper. Impartation flows through relationship. You can be gifted without guidance, but you cannot be grounded without government.

Receiving Through Imperfect Vessels

The challenge of delegated authority is that it always comes clothed in humanity. God hides divine treasures in earthen vessels to test our discernment. If you require perfection before you can honor, you'll miss every impartation Heaven intends for you. Honor doesn't deny weakness, it decides to look beyond it. When you honor the grace on someone instead of focusing on their flaws, you prove that you trust God's order more than man's performance.

David modeled this when he honored Saul even while Saul sought his life. He refused to strike the Lord's anointed, not because Saul was right, but because the order was still holy. Honor doesn't excuse sin; it preserves structure. The moment David touched the garment of his authority, his heart smote him. That is the conscience of a true son.

Testing Your Response

Ask yourself:
- Do I recognize authority only when I agree with it?
- Do I follow only when convenient, or when convicted?
- Do I pray for those who lead me, or do I critique them privately?

- Do I discern God's grace in others even when it challenges my comfort?

Your answers reveal whether you live under covering or simply around it. Honor is not proven by your words in public, but by your posture in private. When you can submit joyfully, serve faithfully, and support silently, you are walking in Heaven's rhythm.

Transition

Authority is only effective when it's properly recognized and honored. In the next section, we'll explore how authority operates in spiritual warfare and covering, how honor becomes a shield of divine protection and how rebellion opens the door to the adversary.

Section 3 – Authority as Covering: Honor in Warfare and Protection

Authority is not only governmental, but also protective. It is Heaven's umbrella in a storm, a spiritual shield against chaos. When you honor divine order, you remain under divine defense. When you step out of that order, you expose yourself to unnecessary warfare.

The first battle ever fought on earth was not between nations, it was between submission and rebellion. Lucifer's fall and Adam's failure both began with the same seed: independence. Rebellion removes covering; honor restores it. Every victory depends on where you stand, under authority or outside of it.

Covering: The Principle of Protection

Spiritual covering is not control, it's covenant. It means you are part of a divinely arranged flow of grace and protection. Psalm 91 describes it perfectly: *"He who dwells in the secret place of the Most High shall abide under the shadow of the Almighty."* That shadow is the posture of submission.

When you dwell under God's authority, every attack that reaches you has to pass through Him first. Covering doesn't prevent storms; it prevents destruction. Many believers battle storms that were never theirs to fight because they left the shelter of honor. Disorder invites warfare; alignment invites peace.

How Authority Shields Us

When you are properly aligned, the authority above you absorbs what was meant to harm you. Like a roof intercepts rain, leadership intercepts unnecessary warfare. That's why God places shepherds over His people, to watch, guard, and intercede. When Israel fought Amalek, victory didn't depend on the soldiers' strength but on Moses' raised hands. As long as his hands were lifted, Israel prevailed. Their strength on the battlefield was tied to the authority on the hill.

Authority is not just positional; it is spiritual jurisdiction. Every battle you face is fought under a banner. When you're under covering, you fight from Heaven's jurisdiction. When you step outside of it, you fight in your own strength and lose ground that could have been protected through honor.

Rebellion: The Exposure of the Uncovered

Rebellion is spiritual exposure. It disconnects you from the grace that guards you. When Korah rebelled against Moses, the earth opened beneath him. That wasn't God's anger, it was gravity at work. Heavenly order had been rejected, so earthly order responded. The universe itself is built on submission to divine hierarchy; even the stars keep their orbit through obedience.

When rebellion enters, everything around you begins to shake because rebellion breaks rhythm. Honor restores that rhythm, bringing stability back to the soul, the home, and the house of God. Submission, therefore, is not bondage, it's alignment with Heaven's balance.

The Armor of Obedience

Ephesians 6 speaks of the armor of God, truth, righteousness, peace, faith, salvation, and the Word. But before listing the armor, Paul writes, *"Submit yourselves one to another in the fear of God."* Submission is the unseen armor that holds all the others in place. Without it, righteousness becomes self-righteousness, faith becomes presumption, and truth becomes weaponized.

Obedience clothes the believer in spiritual authority. Every *"yes"* to God tightens your armor; every act of rebellion loosens it. You cannot wield authority over darkness while resisting authority in light. The devil only yields to those who themselves have yielded to God. That's why James 4:7 says, *"Submit to God, resist the devil, and he will flee from you."* Submission precedes strength.

When Honor Becomes Warfare

Honor itself is a weapon. When you respond with humility where others expect pride, you disarm the enemy. When you bless instead of retaliate, you shift the atmosphere from natural to supernatural. Satan operates through pride; Heaven operates through honor. Every time you honor leadership, family, or spiritual authority, you reinforce Heaven's government against hell's rebellion.

David's refusal to dishonor Saul was not weakness, it was warfare. He defeated more demons by restraint than by sword. The anointing on his life grew stronger every time he chose submission over retaliation. Honor multiplied his authority while rebellion destroyed Saul's.

Covering in the Modern Church

In today's culture of independence, many have confused accountability with control. But spiritual covering is not manipulation, it's maturity. You can't be both uncovered and unbothered. Those who resist authority in the name of "freedom" often end up fighting battles that a father's voice could have prevented. Elisha's double portion was not the result of greater talent, but greater submission. He followed Elijah through Gilgal, Bethel, Jericho, and Jordan because covering was the key to inheritance.

Authority protects inheritance. When you remain aligned, you don't have to chase blessings, they flow to you by order.

The Test of Covering

God will often test your heart by placing you under imperfect authority. If you can honor flawed leadership, you prove that your submission is to God, not to man. When you can serve faithfully in another man's vision, Heaven prepares your own. You cannot be trusted to lead until you have been proven to follow. Your covering today becomes your credibility tomorrow.

Elisha poured water on Elijah's hands before he parted waters with his own mantle. Those who wash before they wield always carry greater weight in the Spirit.

Transition

Covering provides protection, inheritance, and authority, but it also demands responsibility. In the next section, we will explore the responsibilities of those in authority, how leaders must steward honor without abusing it, and how Heaven measures their governance.

Section 4 – *The Responsibility of Authority: Stewarding Honor Well*

Authority is not ownership, it's stewardship. It is borrowed weight, entrusted for a season to accomplish divine purpose. Those who lead in the Kingdom must never forget: the authority you carry is not yours, it's His. You are not the source of honor; you are the steward of it. How you handle people's reverence determines whether Heaven continues to trust you with influence.

In Matthew 8, Jesus marveled at a man who understood submission. In John 13, He demonstrated leadership through service. In both moments, He revealed Heaven's model: authority only works when humility holds it.

Authority Without Humility Becomes Abuse

Whenever authority forgets its origin, it becomes abusive. Lucifer fell not because he lacked beauty, but because he believed his brightness was self-generated. Authority without humility becomes idolatry, it exalts the vessel above the voice. That's why God often hides true authority inside humility; it's the only container that can hold His glory without cracking.

A leader's greatest danger is beginning to believe honor is admiration. Honor is Heaven's currency, not man's applause. When you start craving what was meant to be redirected to God, your authority becomes corrupted. King Herod learned this when the people cried, "The voice of a god, not of a man!", and immediately he was struck down. Heaven will never share glory with pride.

Servant Leadership: The Weight of the Basin

Jesus didn't protect His reputation; He preserved His representation. When He knelt with a towel, He was showing that the basin is heavier than the crown. True leaders wash feet before they wear mantles. Every level of authority is an opportunity to go lower in love. The higher God lifts you, the more people's dirt you'll be entrusted to wash.

You can identify false authority by what it demands; you recognize true authority by what it serves. If leadership doesn't smell like sacrifice, it's not Kingdom, it's empire.

How Heaven Judges Leadership

God measures authority by stewardship, not success. He doesn't ask, *"How many followed you?"* but *"How many did you serve into freedom?"* When Jesus told Peter, *"Feed My sheep,"* He was assigning care, not celebrity. Leaders are shepherds, not stars. A shepherd carries the scent of the flock, not the perfume of platforms.

When authority becomes self-serving, God withdraws His backing until humility is restored. That's not punishment, it's purification. Heaven will always prune before it promotes. Moses lost access to the Promised Land because he misrepresented God's heart to the people. He struck the rock instead of speaking to it. Leaders must never let frustration fracture representation. You don't just carry God's Word, you carry His tone.

This is why Scripture warns us,
"Let not many of you become teachers, knowing that we shall receive a stricter judgment" (James 3:1). Leadership in the Kingdom is not an elevation of status, it is an increase of accountability. Heaven does not measure how many followed us but how accurately we represented the One we were sent to reveal. *"They watch out for your souls as those who must give account"* (Hebrews 13:17).

We are not permitted to speak in our own tone; we speak as ambassadors. *"Therefore, we are ambassadors for Christ, as though God were pleading through us"* (2 Corinthians 5:20). To misrepresent His heart, even out of frustration, is to deny God His rightful voice in the earth. To lead well is to steward not just His message but His manner. Heaven holds us responsible for both.

We do not carry authority to speak for God, we carry authority to speak as God would. We aren't judged by how many listened to us, but how clearly Heaven spoke through us.

Honor as a Double-Edged Gift

To be honored is both a privilege and a test. Honor magnifies whatever is in you. If humility dwells there, honor will elevate your effectiveness. If pride hides there, honor will expose your motives. This is why some leaders grow purer under honor while others grow toxic.

Honor is not meant to feed ego; it's meant to fuel service. When people honor you, they're offering Heaven's trust. Your job is to redirect that trust upward, never inward. When you deflect glory to God, you protect your own soul.

Leaders as Living Coverings

To lead is to become a covering. When God places people under your care, He expects you to protect them, not possess them. A healthy covering shields: an unhealthy one smothers. The difference lies in motive, protection is motivated by love, control by fear. If your leadership produces dependency instead of development, you're not covering, you're caging.

True authority releases. A father's joy is not in how many stay under him, but how many rise because of him. You have stewarded honor well when those who followed you can now stand in the same authority you once carried for them. Releasing sons and daughters is not loss, it's legacy.

The Discipline of Transparency

Every authority must live with open accountability. Isolation breeds illusion. When leaders remove themselves from counsel, deception enters quietly. That's why Scripture commands, *"In the multitude of counselors there is safety."* Transparency doesn't make you less anointed, it keeps you authentic.

Accountability is how authority remains holy. Submission doesn't end when you begin to lead; it deepens. Even Jesus said, *"I do nothing except what I see the Father do."* If the Son of God stayed submitted, so must every servant of God.

The Reward of Righteous Authority

Heaven delights in righteous leadership. When authority operates in humility and honor, it attracts Heaven's favor. Psalm 45 says of the King, *"You love righteousness and hate wickedness; therefore God has anointed You with the oil of gladness above Your fellows."* Joy follows just authority because Heaven trusts it. Where leaders govern with honor, people flourish.

Families heal. Nations prosper. The Kingdom advances through credibility and compassion.

Transition

Authority is Heaven's expression of trust, but it must remain tethered to humility, accountability, and love. In the next section, we'll look at the relational balance between leaders and those they lead, how mutual honor keeps authority from becoming oppressive and submission from becoming servile.

Section 5 – Mutual Honor in Leadership and Followership

Heaven's design for authority is not one-sided, it is circular. The Kingdom is not built on dominance from above nor defiance from below, but on mutual honor that flows like breath, leaders exhaling grace, followers inhaling trust. When this rhythm is broken, dysfunction begins. When it's restored, Heaven finds expression in the earth again.

Honor is not about hierarchy; it's about harmony. The leader and the follower are partners in purpose, not competitors in position. Each role reveals an aspect of Christ's nature, leadership mirrors His headship; followership reflects His humility. Together, they display His wholeness.

The Circle of Honor

In Kingdom order, honor doesn't start or stop, it circulates. Paul wrote in Romans 12:10, *"In honor, prefer one another."* That command applies to every level of relationship. Leaders honor by serving those who follow; followers honor by supporting those who lead. Both are responsible for protecting the atmosphere of trust.

When honor flows in both directions:
- Leaders lead with compassion, not control.
- Followers serve with devotion, not duty.
- The community thrives in peace, not pressure.

Where the circle breaks, through pride, fear, or suspicion, the entire system suffers. Heaven's authority cannot flow through blocked arteries of dishonor.

Honor from Leaders to Followers

True leaders never demand honor; they demonstrate it. Jesus called His disciples *"friends,"* not *"servants."* He honored them by sharing revelation, *"All that I have heard from My Father I have made known to you."* To honor those who follow is to **communicate**, **include**, and **empower**.

When leaders treat people as co-laborers rather than commodities, loyalty becomes love, not obligation. Honor from a leader says, *"I see you; I trust you, and I need your grace."* Such humility creates ownership in the hearts of those who serve. People rise where they are honored.

A leader's tone sets a congregation's culture. If you speak down, the people shrink; if you lift up, they soar. Honor lifts people into their potential.

Honor from Followers to Leaders

Scripture calls believers to *"remember those who rule over you, who have spoken the Word of God to you."* Honor for leadership is not blind allegiance, it's spiritual recognition. Followers honor by praying, protecting, and partnering. They guard their leader's reputation, not as worshippers of man, but as stewards of God's government.

Moses' arms were held up by Aaron and Hur; their honor secured the entire nation's victory. When followers uphold leadership through intercession and faithfulness, they share in Heaven's reward. A true follower doesn't just agree, they assist. They don't just admire, they align. Their strength sustains what their leader shoulders.

The Exchange of Grace

Honor is Heaven's exchange rate. What flows downward as blessing returns upward as thanksgiving. Paul told the Philippians that their partnership in giving, and prayer caused fruit to *"abound to their account."* Mutual honor keeps the spiritual economy healthy, no one depletes, everyone increases.

When leaders honor followers, they release grace; when followers honor leaders, they multiply it. The result is continual abundance. The Church grows, not because of gifting, but because of gratitude.

The Bond of Love

Mutual honor matures into love. And love, not labor, is what keeps the Kingdom alive. Paul said, *"Through love serve one another."* Love transforms authority into family and submission into joy. It's impossible to love truly and dishonor simultaneously.

The highest compliment in Heaven is not *"You led well"* but *"You loved well."* Every leader and follower will answer for how they loved, not how they ranked. When love governs leadership, structure becomes strength instead of strain.

The Balance of Accountability

Mutual honor doesn't eliminate accountability, it refines it. Followers can confront leaders respectfully; leaders can correct followers redemptively. In the Kingdom, accountability is not confrontation against a person, it's confirmation of purpose. Both sides help each other remain aligned to the voice of God. When accountability is practiced in honor, correction never feels like condemnation, it feels like covenant.

That's how Paul could rebuke Peter in public, yet Peter later call Paul's writings *"Scripture."* Their accountability preserved relationship because honor governed their exchange. Truth spoken in love never divides, it deepens trust.

The Reward of Mutual Honor

When honor circulates freely between leaders and followers, the result is supernatural growth. Acts 9:31 says the Church *"walked in the fear of the Lord and the comfort of the Holy Spirit and multiplied."* Fear speaks of reverence; comfort speaks of relationship. The balance of both is the secret to sustained expansion.

In such environments:
- People feel covered, not controlled.
- Leaders feel trusted, not targeted.
- The Holy Spirit feels welcome, not grieved.

Where mutual honor reigns, Heaven commits long-term residency. That is how the Church becomes unshakable, Heaven's government manifested through human relationship.

Transition

Authority cannot be sustained by titles or charisma; it must be upheld by mutual honor. In the next and final section of this chapter, we will explore the reward and responsibility of representing Heaven's government, what happens when leaders and followers walk together in mature order and divine trust.

Section 6 – The Reward of Divine Order: Representing Heaven on Earth

Heaven's order is not just to be studied, it is to be seen. When divine authority and human honor align, Heaven becomes visible on earth. This was Jesus' prayer: *"Thy Kingdom come, Thy will be done on earth as it is in Heaven."* The Church's call is not to replicate Heaven's worship but to reproduce Heaven's government. That government flows through honor, manifests through obedience, and sustains through love.

Heaven's Government Made Visible

In Heaven, no being resists divine order. Angels don't negotiate assignments; they execute them with joy. The glory that fills Heaven exists because everything there is in perfect alignment with God's throne. When the Church walks in that same order, the same glory manifests.

Glory is not just a feeling; it is the visible evidence of divine alignment. When authority is honored and order is established, the glory of God fills the house. This is what happened in 2 Chronicles 5:13–14: When the priests and singers became one sound, *"the house was filled with a cloud."* Glory always follows government. Where there is divine order, there will be divine presence.

Authority Reflects the King

Every person walking in authority reflects the King they represent. The world reads God through His representatives. That's why Jesus said, "He who receives you receives Me." Authority is the language of representation, not domination.

When you lead with integrity and humility, you are translating Heaven's rule into earth's reality. You become an ambassador of the invisible Kingdom. People don't just see leadership, they encounter the Lordship of Christ expressed through your stewardship.

The greater the submission, the clearer the reflection. That's why Jesus could say, *"He who has seen Me has seen the Father."* The purest authority is transparent, it reveals the One behind it.

Honor Invites Glory

When honor governs relationships, glory governs environments. Dishonor clouds the air with confusion, but honor clears it with clarity. In homes, churches, and nations where authority is honored rightly, the presence of God abides tangibly. Miracles flow without striving; peace reigns without debate.

Honor creates atmosphere. It's the unseen protocol that tells Heaven, *"You are welcome here."* Every time we submit to God's order, we extend an invitation for His weight to dwell among us.

When people honor, God inhabits. That's why Scripture connects reverence to revival, *"The fear of the Lord is the beginning of wisdom."*

The Multiplication of Grace

Peter wrote, *"Grace and peace be multiplied to you through the knowledge of God."* The word *"knowledge"* there implies intimate recognition, honor. In other words, grace multiplies where honor increases. When we properly relate to authority, we position ourselves for multiplied grace. What once came by measure begins to flow without limit.

Honor is Heaven's multiplier. It doesn't just add blessing, it expands capacity. The woman who honored Elisha with a room didn't just receive a prophet's visit; she received a promise that broke barrenness. Honor creates space for the miraculous. Every act of recognition opens a realm of reward.

The Peace of Divine Alignment

Divine order doesn't only produce glory, it produces peace. Paul's benediction in 2 Thessalonians 3:16 says, *"Now the Lord of peace Himself give you peace always by all means."* Peace is not the absence of conflict but the presence of authority. Where God's order is established, chaos has no jurisdiction.

In homes aligned to God's government, tension dissolves. In churches governed by honor, division disappears. In nations led by righteousness, prosperity flows. Divine alignment restores Edenic atmosphere, Heaven on earth.

Representatives of the Throne

Every believer carries a measure of delegated authority. You are Heaven's representative, an ambassador of the King. Your home, your workplace, your church, and your city are all territories of representation. When you walk in honor and submission, you bring Heaven's government wherever you go.

You don't have to announce your authority; you simply demonstrate it through obedience.

Demons recognize it.
Creation responds to it.
People feel it.

Authority that flows from humility carries an unspoken power; it shifts atmospheres without shouting. When your life mirrors Heaven's order, everything around you begins to reorder itself. That is Kingdom dominion.

The Ultimate Reward: Rest

The highest reward of divine order is rest. Authority is exhausting when carried without alignment, but effortless when carried in agreement with Heaven. When you live under covering, you stop striving to prove, defend, or control. Rest is not inactivity, it's confidence in divine structure. The soldier under orders doesn't fear the battle; he trusts the command. Likewise, sons under authority live from peace, not pressure.

Rest is Heaven's confirmation that order has been established. It is the Sabbath of the soul, the evidence that the Kingdom has come.

The Restoration of Representation

The first Adam lost dominion through dishonor; the last Adam restored it through obedience. Through Christ, authority has been purified, and honor has been redefined. Heaven's government is now reinstated in every born-again believer who walks in the Spirit. To live in divine order is to walk again as Adam walked, crowned with glory and honor.

Psalm 8:5 says, *"You crowned him with glory and honor, and set him over the works of Your hands."* That crown is not ornamental it's governmental. Honor restores authority, and authority reveals the Kingdom. When we honor rightly, we reign rightly.

The Sound of Heaven's Order

When authority and honor operate in harmony, the Church releases the same sound that shook Sinai and filled Pentecost. It's the sound of Heaven's government in motion, the vibration of perfect agreement between Creator and creation. Every time believers submit to divine order; Heaven's frequency fills the atmosphere again. That sound is not noise; it's nature returning to its Source.

It's what Paul described in Romans 8: creation groaning for the manifestation of sons, those mature enough to carry authority in honor. When that day fully comes, Heaven and earth will no longer compete, they will cooperate. The sound of rebellion will be silenced by the song of righteousness.

Conclusion

The honor of authority is the revelation of Heaven's trust. To lead with humility and follow with faith is to host the very government of God. Where order is restored, Heaven is revealed. The Kingdom is not a theory, it is the manifestation of divine alignment among sons who mirror their Father's heart.

To honor authority is to host Heaven. To walk in authority is to represent Heaven. Together, they complete the circle of glory that began before the world was.

When Heaven's government finds a home in human hearts, the prayer of Jesus is answered: *"Thy Kingdom come, Thy will be done, on earth as it is in Heaven."*

Chapter 14 Review & Reflection

The Honor of Authority: Heaven's Government in Human Form

Core Revelation

Authority is Heaven's government expressed through human vessels. It is not domination, it is delegation. Every act of true authority mirrors God's heart and functions through humility, not hierarchy. When authority is honored rightly and stewarded righteously, Heaven's government becomes visible on earth.

Honor keeps authority holy; humility keeps it healthy. To resist authority is to resist order. To abuse authority is to misrepresent God. But when both authority and honor flow together, the Kingdom operates without hindrance, just as it does in Heaven.

Kingdom Principle

Honor sustains Heaven's government; humility safeguards it. The measure of your authority is the measure of your submission.

Scripture Focus

- Romans 13:1 – *"There is no authority except from God, and those that exist have been instituted by God."*
- Matthew 8:9–10 – *"I am a man under authority... and Jesus marveled."*
- 1 Peter 5:2–3 – *"Shepherd the flock of God among you... being examples to the flock."*
- Hebrews 13:17 – *"Obey those who rule over you, for they watch for your souls."*
- 1 Samuel 24:6 – *"I will not stretch forth my hand against the Lord's anointed."*
- John 13:14–15 – *"If I, your Lord and Teacher, have washed your feet, you also ought to wash one another's feet."*

- 2 Chronicles 5:13–14 – *"When they were as one, the house was filled with a cloud."*
- James 4:7 – *"Submit to God, resist the devil, and he will flee from you."*

Truths to Remember

1. Authority is Heaven's structure for stability; honor keeps that structure intact.
2. Submission is not subordination; it is synchronization with Heaven.
3. To recognize authority is revelation; to resist it is rebellion.
4. Covering protects, control imprisons.
5. Authority that cannot be questioned is already corrupt.
6. Leaders represent God best through humility, not hierarchy.
7. Followers honor God by honoring His order, even when leaders are imperfect.
8. Mutual honor creates Kingdom flow, each part preferring the other.
9. Rebellion exposes; honor covers.
10. Divine order produces glory, peace, and rest, the visible Kingdom on earth.

Application

- **For Leaders:** Lead from the basin, not the throne.
- Protect, don't possess.
- Model submission to those above you and accountability with those beside you.
- Steward honor humbly; never consume it.
- Let correction flow from compassion, not control.
- **For Followers:** Recognize authority as Heaven's design.
- Pray for your leaders regularly.
- Support with faithfulness, not flattery.
- Guard your heart from offense, offense blinds recognition.
- Receive correction as care, not criticism.
- Keep communication open and honor unbroken.

- Allow accountability to refine, not restrain.
- Remember: authority and submission are not opposites, they are partners.

Reflection Questions

1. Have I ever misrepresented God's tone while correctly delivering His truth, and what was the result?
2. How do I currently respond to authority, resistance, compliance, or honor?
3. Do I see submission as loss of freedom or alignment with Heaven?
4. Am I stewarding influence as a servant or as an owner?
5. Have I ever misused the honor given to me? How can I restore it to God?
6. Who in my life carries authority that I've stopped honoring internally?
7. How can I practice mutual honor with those I lead or follow?
8. Is my environment, home, ministry, or workplace, governed by peace or tension? What does that reveal about order?

Declaration

"Father, I yield to Your divine order. I honor the authority You have placed in my life, and I commit to steward any authority You entrust to me with humility and integrity. Let my leadership reveal Your heart and my submission reflect Your trust. May my home, ministry, and relationships become a visible expression of Heaven's government on earth. I choose honor over independence, obedience over pride, and service over status. Let Your Kingdom come, through me, around me, and within me."

CHAPTER 15

THE HONOR OF CORRECTION:
THE WISDOM THAT GUARDS GROWTH

Section 1 – *Correction: The Language of Love*

Correction is not punishment, it is protection. It is Heaven's mercy disguised as confrontation. Where there is no correction, there can be no growth; where there is no growth, there can be no maturity.

Scripture says, *"Whom the Lord loves, He corrects, even as a father the son in whom he delights"* (Proverbs 3:12). Correction, then, is not the evidence of God's displeasure, it is proof of His delight. He only disciplines those He intends to develop. The absence of correction is not grace; it is neglect.

Every healthy father corrects, not to shame a child, but to shape one. Correction reveals belonging, God only adjusts those He calls His own. That is why Hebrews 12 calls correction *"the discipline of sons."* If you can live in disobedience and never feel conviction, it's not freedom, it's abandonment. Conviction is Heaven's embrace.

Correction Is a Conversation, Not a Condemnation

Religion uses correction to humiliate; relationship uses it to heal. God never corrects through accusation; He corrects through invitation. From the garden to the cross, His first question to fallen man was not *"What did you do?"* but *"Where are you?"* That is the sound of redemptive correction, an invitation back into proximity.

True correction restores fellowship before demanding performance. The tone of Heaven's discipline is always restorative. Even Jesus' harshest rebukes were aimed at hypocrisy, not humanity. He confronted the Pharisees to expose pride but lifted the adulterous woman to redeem purpose. Correction that humiliates does not come from God; correction that heals always leads back to Him.

Correction: Heaven's Guardrail

Correction acts as a guardrail on the path of purpose. Without it, zeal turns into error and gifting becomes dangerous. Many fall not from immorality, but from isolation, no one around them cared enough to correct them.

Correction is not a sign of distrust; it is a safeguard of destiny. When David strayed, Nathan's confrontation saved his kingship. When Peter erred, Paul's rebuke preserved his apostleship. Every relationship ordained by God will include correction, because growth requires friction.

Correction is Heaven's quality control, it ensures that what God builds in you maintains His standard, not yours.

The Culture of Correction

In a culture of honor, correction is not taboo, it is treasured. People don't fear being corrected because they trust the heart of the one correcting. Love makes truth digestible. Correction delivered in honor brings healing; correction delivered in anger brings harm.

A culture that celebrates encouragement but avoids correction will produce gifted infants, talented but immature. The goal of correction is not to control behavior but to cultivate maturity. True sons desire correction because they equate it with growth, not guilt. To reject correction is to reject formation.

When a person resists correction, they stop developing; when they embrace it, they accelerate destiny.

The Honor in Receiving Correction

Receiving correction with humility is one of the highest forms of honor. It proves that you value truth more than pride. Proverbs 9:8–9 says, *"Rebuke a wise man, and he will love you; instruct a just man, and he will increase in learning."* Honor doesn't just agree with truth, it invites it.

When you receive correction without offense, you demonstrate spiritual sonship. Immature believers seek affirmation; mature sons seek alignment. Affirmation makes you feel better; alignment makes you become better. Honor says, *"I would rather be corrected and stay in order than applauded and stay deceived."*

Correction is not an attack, it's an investment.
Heaven spends truth on those it trusts.

Transition

Correction is love expressed in truth. In the next section, we will explore how correction functions as Heaven's pruning process, cutting not to kill, but to cultivate greater fruitfulness.

Section 2 – The Pruning of Purpose: Correction That Cultivates Growth

Jesus said, *"Every branch in Me that bears fruit, My Father prunes, that it may bear more fruit"* (John 15:2). This verse dismantles a common misconception: pruning isn't punishment for failure, it's preparation for increase. Correction doesn't come because something is wrong; it comes because something is working.

Pruning is Heaven's vote of confidence. It's the Father saying, *"I see fruit in you, but I also see potential for more."* The knife of correction is the hand of cultivation. Only fruitful branches qualify for pruning; barren ones are simply removed. That means the more you grow, the more God trims. Maturity welcomes this process rather than resists it.

Pruning Protects the Future

Every gardener knows: unchecked growth becomes unproductive. Branches that grow wild drain nutrients from the fruit-bearing parts of the vine. Likewise, unchecked ambition, distraction, or comfort can drain the vitality of purpose. Correction removes what competes with destiny.

When God prunes, He isn't trying to take away your life, He's preserving it. What you call loss, Heaven calls alignment. Every cut is strategic; every wound has wisdom in it. The knife never touches the branch except through the love of the Vinedresser's hand.

If you feel the sting of correction, it's not rejection, it's refinement. The Father is protecting your future from the weight of unnecessary growth.

Pruning Redirects Flow

In a vine, pruning redirects the flow of sap, life itself. When God cuts away an attitude, habit, or relationship, He's not robbing you; He's rerouting strength to what will last. That's why people and opportunities sometimes fall away after a season of fruitfulness. Heaven will not allow life to flow where fruit cannot remain.

When correction comes, don't ask, *"What am I losing?"*, ask, *"What is God adding to me?"* If you trust His hands, the cut will never be wasted. Every removal is redirection. Every redirection is renewal.

Pruning Reveals Ownership

The branch doesn't choose when or how it's pruned, the Vinedresser does. Correction reminds us that we belong to God. You cannot correct what you don't own. When He corrects you, it's evidence that you are still His.

To resist pruning is to resist belonging. Submission to correction says, *"Father, I trust Your touch even when I don't understand Your timing."* The more you yield, the more you bear. That's why **fruitfulness and faith are inseparable**. Faith trusts that God's cuts are creative, not cruel.

Pruning Clarifies Identity

Pruning not only shapes productivity, but it also clarifies identity. Each cut distinguishes between what is you and what has simply attached to you. Sometimes God will use correction to separate personality from purpose. He refines motives, filters relationships, and removes self-reliance so that your fruit carries only His fingerprint.

Correction cleans the mirror of your soul until Christ's reflection shines through. The goal of pruning is not just more fruit, it's clearer image. You look more like the Vinedresser every time you yield to His hand.

Pruning Produces Purity

The Greek word for *"prune"* (kathairo) means to cleanse. Correction is Heaven's purification system. It washes away attitudes that would contaminate calling. Just as silver is refined by heat until the refiner sees his reflection, so correction burns away dross until Heaven sees its likeness in you.

Purity is not perfection, it's the by-product of surrender. It means nothing foreign interferes with your flow. When correction purifies, presence increases. The more pure the vessel, the stronger the current of glory that can move through it.

Embracing the Knife

To honor correction is to embrace the knife of grace. Those who resist it remain ornamental, appearing healthy but bearing little fruit.

Those who receive it become transformational, producing fruit that feeds generations. You can always tell who has been pruned: their humility carries fragrance, and their fruit remains sweet.

God never prunes to embarrass you; He prunes to entrust you. Every correction is a credential for greater responsibility. Before God multiplies your influence, He purifies your intent.

In Scripture, covenant is not established through comfort but through cutting. The Hebrew word for covenant, berith (בְּרִית), literally means *"to cut."* It signifies that something must be separated for something greater to be sealed.

Cutting is not rejection; it is **covenantal recognition**.

Pruning is not simply God trimming excess; it is God cutting away what cannot carry covenantal weight. Honor receives this cut because it understands what others see as loss, Heaven sees as preparation.

Just as God cut covenant with Abraham through sacrifice (Genesis 15:9–18), so He cuts away at our motives before entrusting us with mantles. Jesus affirmed this when He said, *"Every branch that bears fruit He prunes, that it may bear more fruit"* (John 15:2). Increase is always preceded by incision.

Those who honor correction walk in covenant with their destiny. Those who resist it remain ornamental, seen, but not sent.

Honor always welcomes the cut because it understands that purpose is often released through pain. Those unwilling to be cut will never walk in covenantal depth.

When Jacob wrestled with God, he walked away with both a limp and a new name (Genesis 32:24–28). The cut did not weaken him, it authenticated him.

Honor does not fear the knife. It recognizes it as the instrument of covenant, not the weapon of rejection.

"God doesn't prune to reduce you, He cuts to covenantally commit more to you."

Transition

Pruning is the Father's method for producing mature sons. In the next section, we will explore how correction is administered through spiritual authority and community, how God uses people, not just private conviction, to shape us into His likeness.

Section 3 – *Correction Through Authority: God's Hand in Human Form*

God rarely corrects us in isolation. He corrects us through relationship. From Genesis onward, His pattern has remained the same, He speaks through people. He uses fathers, prophets, friends, and even adversaries to align hearts with Heaven. When you resist correction through human vessels, you are not rejecting man, you are resisting God's chosen method of maturing sons.

Every divine correction passes through human hands. It may come through a mentor's rebuke, a pastor's sermon, or a friend's timely question. When honor recognizes it, Heaven's hand is revealed behind it.

God's Chain of Correction

Hebrews 13:17 reminds us, *"Obey those who rule over you and be submissive, for they watch for your souls."* That phrase, watch for your souls, means guard through guidance. God places authority in our lives to see what we cannot, and to say what we will not. Their correction is not intrusion; it's intercession in motion.

When David was confronted by Nathan, Heaven was speaking through human lips. The prophet's words carried weight because they were birthed from divine concern. David's response determined his restoration. He didn't defend himself, he repented. That moment preserved his throne and lineage. The proof of maturity is not that we never need correction, but that we receive it rightly when it comes.

Correction Through Fathers

Spiritual fathers are Heaven's primary instruments of correction. Their role is not to control behavior, but to cultivate identity. A father corrects because he sees destiny being distorted. When a true father disciplines, it's not anger, it's investment.

Paul modeled this in 1 Corinthians 4:14, *"I do not write these things to shame you, but as my beloved sons I warn you."* Correction from a father doesn't humiliate; it warns. It says, *"You are too valuable to drift."*

If you resist fatherly correction, you reject inheritance. Submission to a father's voice is what gives your calling legitimacy. You can have gifting without guidance, but you cannot have fruit without formation. **Every great son was once a corrected one.**

Correction Through Community

God not only uses leaders, He uses peers. Proverbs 27:17 declares, *"As iron sharpens iron, so one man sharpens another."* Fellowship without friction is fantasy. Correction from those walking beside you helps you grow where pride would otherwise hide.

True community doesn't flatter, it refines. A Kingdom family doesn't say, *"You're fine,"* when you're faltering. They speak the truth in love, trusting relationship enough to risk offense for the sake of your soul.

If you only want friends who agree with you, you'll never grow beyond you. Real covenant requires confrontation. Every healthy community must value correction as much as comfort.

Correction Through Adversity

Sometimes correction doesn't come from mentors or friends, it comes through moments. Circumstances can become classrooms. Jonah learned obedience in a storm; Peter learned humility through failure; Paul learned grace through a thorn. God often allows resistance to reveal where we're still independent. When life's friction intensifies, ask, *"What are You forming in me, Lord?"*

Even enemies can serve as instruments of divine correction. David called Saul *"the Lord's anointed"* even while Saul hunted him. In that tension, God corrected David's heart, not through comfort, but through constraint. Opposition often exposes inner immaturity. The way you respond to unjust authority reveals how much authority you can truly be trusted with.

Recognizing the Hand Behind the Human

Correction is often missed because it's wrapped in humanity. If you require perfect vessels, you'll reject every word God sends. The wisdom is not in the person, it's in the posture behind the person. If the message humbles you, convicts you, and leads you back to righteousness, it's from God, regardless of who delivered it.

Honor looks past personality and perceives placement. When you can hear God through flawed vessels, you have learned the language of maturity. The Pharisees couldn't hear God through Jesus because they expected divinity to come dressed in dignity. They missed correction because they despised familiarity.

Heaven hides correction in humility to expose pride.
Only the meek can receive what the proud resist.

Responding to Correction with Honor

When correction comes, don't defend, discern. Ask the Holy Spirit to show you what truth is hidden in the discomfort. If the rebuke stings, sit with it before you speak. Let humility interpret what pride wants to reject.

Receiving correction honorably looks like this:
1. Listen fully before reacting.
2. Acknowledge the truth, even if partial.
3. Respond with gratitude, not grudge.
4. Pray for the person who corrected you.
5. Make practical changes quickly.

Correction doesn't humiliate, it heals. How you respond to correction determines how Heaven can trust you with authority.

Transition

Correction through authority and community is Heaven's way of keeping us aligned with purpose. In the next section, we will explore how to give correction with honor, how to confront in love without wounding, and to restore without shaming.

Section 4 – Administering Correction: Confrontation with Compassion

To correct someone is to hold their destiny with delicate hands. Correction given in pride crushes; correction given in love cultivates. Both truth and tone matter. Even when God confronts, He does so redemptively. He never corrects to condemn, He corrects to restore alignment with His nature and purpose.

Authority without compassion becomes harsh; compassion without authority becomes compromise. The Kingdom operates in the tension of both: love that tells the truth and truth that sounds like love.

The Spirit Behind the Correction

Galatians 6:1 provides Heaven's protocol:
"If anyone is overtaken in a fault, you who are spiritual restore such a one in a spirit of meekness, considering yourself lest you also be tempted."

Notice that the goal is restoration, not retribution. Correction is not about pointing out failure, it's about pointing back to the Father. The moment correction becomes about being right instead of making things right, it loses Heaven's anointing.

The *"spirit of meekness"* means you correct with full awareness that you, too, could fall. True spiritual authority never forgets its humanity. The more conscious you are of grace, the gentler your hand becomes when extending it to others.

Truth Without Tenderness Becomes Trauma

Words can heal or they can harden. The same sword that divides soul from spirit can also wound when wielded recklessly. Jesus wielded truth like a scalpel, not a sledgehammer. He cut precisely to remove infection, never to mutilate identity.

When correction humiliates, it no longer heals. When it condemns, it ceases to be Christlike. Jesus restored Peter privately before reinstating him publicly. He asked three questions, not to shame him for his denials, but to re-anchor him in love. That is Heaven's way, conviction without condemnation.

If your correction leaves someone hopeless, you've misrepresented the Father.

The Timing of Correction

Even truth has timing. Ecclesiastes 3 reminds us there is a time to speak and a time to be silent. Correction given too soon hardens; correction delayed too long deepens damage. Wisdom listens before it lectures. Pray before you confront. Ask the Holy Spirit when and how to approach.

Correction is most effective when delivered in peace, not passion. Wait until your motive is pure and your tone is steady. Never confront to relieve your frustration; confront to release their freedom.

How to Correct with Honor

1. **Begin with Relationship, Not Reprimand.**
   Affirm identity before addressing behavior. Let them know their worth is not on trial.
2. **Use *"We"* More Than *"You."***
   Correction feels like partnership, not punishment, when spoken inclusively. *"We need to adjust this,"* carries grace that *"You need to fix this,"* does not.
3. **Separate the Person from the Problem.**
   Correct actions, not identity. Say, *"This behavior isn't who you are,"* instead of, *"You've failed."*
4. **Invite Dialogue, Don't Dominate Discussion.**
   Correction that silences rarely transforms. Allow them to speak; listen for the root behind the fruit.
5. **End with Hope, Not Hurt.**
   Leave them with a vision of restoration, not residue of rebuke. Every confrontation should end with a pathway forward.

The Redemptive Goal of Correction

Correction is not the end of relationship, it is the renewal of it. When handled in honor, correction strengthens trust. People are more likely to follow a leader who corrects with compassion than one who avoids confrontation or abuses authority.

Jesus' model with Peter is the gold standard for Kingdom correction: He addressed failure, reaffirmed love, and re-commissioned calling, all in one conversation.

He didn't say, *"You're disqualified."*
He said, *"Feed My sheep."*
Correction should always end with **reactivation**, not **rejection**.

Public Sin, Private Restoration

There are times when public sin demands public address (as Paul did in Galatians 2). But even public correction must be done with redemptive intent. If your goal is to expose rather than restore, you're serving ego, not God. Correction is surgical, only expose what must be exposed to heal what cannot be healed in hiding.

Even church discipline, when handled biblically, is a mercy, not a weapon. It exists to recover, not to ruin. When the Church corrects rightly, it restores credibility to its witness and compassion to its culture.

Confrontation as Proof of Care

Avoiding correction is not kindness, it's cowardice. If love is real, it must eventually confront. You cannot protect people from truth and call it grace. Jesus confronted Peter because He intended to trust him. He corrects those He plans to crown.

Correction says, *"I love you too much to let you stay misaligned."* When delivered with grace, confrontation becomes confirmation, you belong enough to be told the truth.

Transition

Administering correction rightly keeps Heaven's culture pure and relationships redemptive. In the next section, we will explore how correction transforms character, how being corrected and correcting others both shape us into Christ's likeness.

Section 5 – *Correction and Character: Becoming Like the Father*

Correction is not just about behavioral alignment; it's about character formation. Every time God corrects you, He's chiseling His image deeper into your nature. His goal isn't compliance, it's transformation. Obedience without understanding produces servants; obedience with revelation produces sons. Correction transforms obedience into likeness.

The Father's ultimate intent is not to make you behave better, it's to make you become truer. He is shaping your inward world until it mirrors His own. He doesn't simply want submission; He wants reflection.

Correction Shapes Christlikeness

The essence of discipleship is discipline. Without correction, discipleship becomes theory. Every disciple of Jesus was corrected repeatedly, not because they were rebels, but because they were in developmental process. He rebuked their unbelief, redirected their priorities, and realigned their motives. Correction was His classroom for character.

Jesus didn't call perfect followers, He perfected those He called. And the tool He used most consistently was correction. If you are unwilling to be corrected, you forfeit the privilege of being conformed to His image.

To walk in maturity is to invite correction without offense.
A teachable spirit is the soil where Christlikeness grows.

Correction Exposes the Heart

Correction doesn't create offense, it reveals it. Furthermore, it uncovers the depth and degree of honor a person possesses. The way you respond to correction exposes the condition of your heart. Saul and David both sinned, but only David responded rightly to rebuke.

Saul justified himself; David humbled himself. One defended his reputation, the other pursued restoration.

Correction is a mirror. When truth confronts you, it reveals whether pride or purity governs your heart. If correction triggers defensiveness, it means pride is still present. If it provokes repentance, it means humility is active. The difference between Saul and David was not sin, it was softness.

The heart that yields to correction stays tender before God. Tender hearts are moldable hearts, and moldable hearts become glorious vessels.

Correction Builds Resilience

Every correction you endure with humility strengthens your spiritual backbone. People who avoid correction remain fragile. They crave affirmation but collapse under accountability. But those who embrace correction become unshakable.

Resilience is not toughness, it's teachability. When you can hear hard truth and remain in love, you have entered spiritual adulthood. Correction builds the inner architecture that can bear the weight of blessing. Before God enlarges your platform, He strengthens your foundation through correction.

Correction Produces Discernment

The more you yield to correction, the sharper your discernment becomes. Why? Because humility clears perception. A proud heart distorts truth; a humble one perceives it clearly. Correction trains your senses to distinguish right from wrong, pure from impure, and timing from temptation. Hebrews 5:14 says, *"Those who by reason of use have their senses exercised to discern both good and evil."*

Correction is Heaven's exercise routine for discernment. Each adjustment fine-tunes your ability to recognize the Father's voice and intention. Maturity is measured not by revelation received, but by correction retained.

Correction Produces Compassion

Those who have been corrected rightly correct others gently. Grace graduates you from judgment to mercy. Once you've been disciplined without being disowned, you lose the appetite to shame others. You understand that people are often doing the best they can with the light they have.

Correction without compassion becomes cruelty; but compassion without correction becomes compromise. Only those who have walked through both can balance them rightly. That's why seasoned fathers correct with tears, not tones. Correction seasoned by compassion is the sound of Heaven's maturity.

Correction Keeps You Dependable

Heaven only trusts what correction has tested. Before Joseph ruled Egypt, God corrected his immaturity through process. His dreams were divine, but his delivery needed discipline. God corrected his pride through betrayal, false accusation, and prison, until he could handle power without revenge.

Correction doesn't cancel destiny, it calibrates it. It removes the immaturity that would mishandle authority. Uncorrected gifts become dangerous; corrected gifts become dependable. When God can correct you privately, He won't have to expose you publicly. Those who yield to early correction are spared later humiliation.

Correction Reveals Sonship

Hebrews 12:8 says, *"If you are without chastening, then you are illegitimate and not sons."* Correction is Heaven's proof of adoption. God does not discipline orphans, He disciplines heirs. To be corrected is to be trusted with inheritance.

Sons don't run from correction; they recognize it as confirmation: *"The Father still claims me."* Every *"no"* from God is preparation for a greater *"yes."* When you embrace correction as covenant, you enter rest instead of resistance.

The Character of Christ

Ultimately, correction produces the character of Christ
- Humility without humiliation
- Power without pride
- Authority without arrogance
- Grace without compromise

To be corrected by God is to be invited into His likeness. To correct others like God is to represent His heart. In both giving and receiving, correction is the instrument by which love matures.

Transition

Correction doesn't just build individuals, it builds environments. In the next and final section, we'll explore how communities that embrace correction become cultures of safety, strength, and sustained revival.

Section 6 – *The Culture of Correction: Building Safe and Strong Communities*

Correction was never meant to isolate, it was meant to integrate. When a culture honors correction, community becomes the safest place on earth. In such environments, people don't hide, they heal. Leaders don't dominate, they disciple. Sons and daughters don't live in fear, they grow in grace.

A healthy Kingdom community is not one that avoids confrontation but one that administers it in love. Truth spoken in love becomes the language of family. Correction, when honored, builds trust; when resisted, it breeds toxicity. You can measure the maturity of a ministry not by how it worships, but by how it receives correction.

Correction Creates Safety

Correction may feel uncomfortable, but it creates safety. When people know sin, gossip, and disorder will be addressed with love and integrity, they feel secure. Boundaries are not bondage, they are blessings. Children play freely in a fenced yard because they know the limits keep them safe. Likewise, believers flourish when correction establishes holy boundaries around community life.

Where correction is absent, chaos becomes normal.
Where correction is embraced, peace becomes permanent.
Safety is not the absence of error; it's the presence of structure.

Correction Establishes Trust

A church that corrects in love becomes trustworthy to Heaven. When people know that leadership will confront what's wrong while protecting what's right, trust deepens. Correction proves integrity. A leader unwilling to correct is a leader unready to protect.

Trust grows when people witness consistency. If correction is handled privately for the mature and publicly for the immature, bias replaces justice. Heaven's correction is impartial, it is consistent, pure, and rooted in righteousness. A trustworthy culture says, *"Everyone matters, and everyone is accountable."*

Correction Strengthens Honor

Correction is the maintenance system of honor. Without correction, honor becomes flattery; with correction, it becomes formation. People learn that honor isn't blind allegiance but mutual accountability.

When followers can lovingly challenge leaders, and leaders can humbly receive it, the house becomes healthy. Mutual correction, practiced in humility, keeps pride from poisoning honor. In such environments, correction doesn't divide, it deepens trust.

Honor without correction produces hypocrisy; correction without honor produces hostility; but honor with correction produces holiness.

Correction Cultivates Maturity

A culture that honors correction raises mature sons, not emotional servants. People stop chasing affirmation and start pursuing transformation. They measure growth by obedience, not applause. Maturity looks like loving truth even when it hurts and remaining teachable even when successful.

When correction becomes cultural, pride loses its hiding place. The result is humility, unity, and supernatural strength. A mature house doesn't need constant discipline, it self-corrects through shared honor. That's the sign of true apostolic community: correction no longer comes only from leadership, but from love among believers.

Correction Restores the Fear of the Lord

Correction and reverence are inseparable. The fear of the Lord is not terror, it's trembling love. When correction is practiced rightly, it restores awe for God's Word and presence. People stop negotiating truth and start nurturing purity.

A culture of correction births a culture of holiness. When we fear the Lord, we stop fearing each other. Boldness increases because integrity is intact. That atmosphere becomes irresistible to Heaven, it smells like trust.

Correction Protects Legacy

Correction doesn't only shape the present, it preserves the future. Communities that honor correction hand down stability to the next generation. Children raised in such houses grow up knowing that correction is love, not rejection. They become adults who live unoffended, accountable, and fruitful.

Legacy is not secured by charisma; it's sustained by character. Correction ensures that what God builds today remains intact tomorrow. It is the hinge between renewal and reformation, between moments and movements.

Correction Creates Culture, Not Fear

A Kingdom house ruled by correction without grace breeds fear. But when correction flows from relationship, it breeds reverence. People don't fear punishment, they respect order. They stop hiding and start healing because they know discipline is a doorway, not a dungeon.

Correction in honor doesn't silence creativity; it sanctifies it. It doesn't kill freedom; it keeps it holy. Such environments produce disciples who can lead, serve, and build without ego, sons who reflect their Father well.

Conclusion

Correction is the architecture of growth and the language of safety. When a community learns to both give and receive it in love, Heaven's presence lingers. A corrected house becomes a trusted house. A trusted house becomes a dwelling place for God.

Honor may attract presence, but correction sustains it. Love may start reformation, but truth establishes it. When both flow together, the Church becomes unshakable, Heaven's family walking in wisdom, governed by grace, and growing in glory.

Chapter 15 Review & Reflection

The Honor of Correction: The Wisdom That Guards Growth

Core Revelation

Correction is not rejection, it is refinement.

It is Heaven's way of protecting purpose, preserving purity, and perfecting sons. Where there is no correction, love is absent; where correction is received, wisdom abounds. Every act of divine discipline is rooted in delight, not disappointment.

The proof of sonship is not blessing, it's the ability to be corrected without offense. Correction is Heaven's gift to those Heaven intends to trust. It transforms immaturity into integrity and converts zeal into wisdom. Honor receives correction as guidance, not grievance, knowing the Father's heart never cuts to harm but always to heal.

Kingdom Principle

Correction is the scalpel of love, it cuts to heal, not to harm. The humility to receive correction is the hallmark of a true son. It's embracing the essence of covenant, to become what only covenant can make us.

Scripture Focus

- Proverbs 3:11–12 – *"My son, do not despise the Lord's correction... for whom the Lord loves He corrects."*
- Hebrews 12:5–11 – *"He disciplines us for our good, that we may share in His holiness."*
- John 15:2 – *"Every branch that bears fruit He prunes, that it may bear more fruit."*
- Proverbs 9:8–9 – *"Rebuke a wise man, and he will love you."*
- Galatians 6:1 – *"Restore such a one in a spirit of meekness."*

- 2 Timothy 3:16–17 – *"All Scripture is profitable for doctrine, for reproof, for correction, for instruction in righteousness."*
- Psalm 141:5 – *"Let the righteous strike me, it shall be a kindness."*
- Revelation 3:19 – *"As many as I love, I rebuke and chasten; be zealous therefore, and repent."*

Truths to Remember

1. Correction is proof of relationship, not rejection.
2. God corrects to protect what He intends to perfect.
3. Correction reveals heart posture, offense or humility.
4. Pruning is preparation for greater fruit, not punishment for failure.
5. Correction given in love restores identity; correction in pride destroys it.
6. God uses people, fathers, mentors, and friends, as instruments of His correction.
7. Receiving correction builds discernment and resilience.
8. Administering correction rightly proves maturity and compassion.
9. A culture that honors correction becomes a safe, strong, and Spirit-filled house.
10. Correction preserves revival, legacy, and lasting fruit.

Application

- **Personally:** Invite correction as confirmation that you are still being fathered by God.
- When conviction comes, pause, listen, and yield rather than justify.
- Replace defensiveness with discernment, ask what the Lord is forming in you.
- Remember: correction may hurt for a moment, but it heals for a lifetime.
- **Relationally:** Give correction gently and privately; receive it humbly and gratefully.

- Build accountability into your friendships, love that never confronts isn't love.
- Guard your tone when correcting; aim for restoration, not reaction.
- Affirm value before addressing error.
- **Communally:** Help create a culture in your church or team where correction is normalized through love.
- Celebrate growth that comes from pruning.
- Pray for leaders and peers to walk in both truth and tenderness.
- Teach new believers that correction is care, not control.

Reflection Questions

1. How do I personally respond to correction, defensively, fearfully, or gratefully?
2. Have I rejected correction in the past that I now see was God's protection?
3. Who in my life has the right to correct me? Have I given them access with honor?
4. When I correct others, is my motive love or frustration?
5. Does my ministry or family culture celebrate truth-telling in love?
6. What fruit has grown in me because of past pruning?
7. Do I see correction as confrontation or as covenant?

Declaration

"Father, I thank You for loving me enough to correct me.

I receive Your discipline as delight and Your pruning as preparation. Cut away every branch that competes with fruitfulness, and shape me into Your likeness.

Give me wisdom to receive truth with humility and to administer correction with compassion. Let my life, home, and ministry become safe spaces for growth, guided by love and governed by truth. May our culture always honor correction as the wisdom that guards growth and the pathway to glory."

CHAPTER 16
THE HONOR OF GLORY:
THE WEIGHT OF DIVINE RECOGNITION

Section 1 – Glory and Honor: Heaven's Exchange

Glory and honor are inseparable. Scripture says, *"You have crowned him with glory and honor"* (Psalm 8:5). Glory is Heaven's recognition; honor is earth's response. Glory is what God places on you; honor is what you give back to Him. When both move in harmony, Heaven and earth reflect each other perfectly.

Glory (kabod in Hebrew) literally means *"weight"*, the tangible substance of divine essence. When God's presence fills a place or person, it manifests as heaviness, not of burden, but of value. Honor is how we handle that weight. Dishonor treats the sacred as common; honor bears it carefully, recognizing it as holy.

Every time God reveals His glory, He's entrusting weight to someone He can trust not to steal it. That's why humility precedes glory: *"Before honor is humility."* Heaven cannot crown what pride would corrupt. Glory is God's acknowledgment of maturity His recognition that you have learned to carry what once crushed you.

The Weight of Recognition

The true test of maturity is not how you handle rejection, but how you handle recognition. Many survive obscurity but fail under visibility. Fame has destroyed more ministers than failure ever did. When men honor you, Heaven watches your posture. Will you reflect it upward, or absorb it inward?

When the crowd cried, *"Hosanna!"* Jesus rode on, not because He was unmoved, but because He understood who the glory belonged to. He let their praise pass over Him like a mirror toward the Father. That is what it means to carry glory: to become transparent enough that people can see through you to God.

If honor is what opens doors, glory is what fills rooms. But rooms filled with glory collapse under pride. The only safe place for glory to dwell is humility.

Glory Is the Reward of Honor

God never wastes glory. He doesn't place His weight where there's no foundation of reverence. Glory is not given to the gifted; it is entrusted to the trustworthy. Those who live in continual honor create environments where glory can remain.

In 2 Chronicles 5, the priests honored the presence of God through unity and worship, *"For He is good, and His mercy endures forever."* Then, *"the house was filled with a cloud."* Glory is Heaven's *"Amen"* to honor's *"Yes."* It is the manifestation of divine approval upon earthly alignment.

Honor attracts glory.
obedience sustains it.
humility multiplies it.

Glory Is Not for Display

Glory was never meant for display, it was meant for demonstration. When Moses came down from Sinai, his face shone, but he didn't parade the radiance, he veiled it. Glory is not for self-promotion but for revelation. If you must announce it, you probably don't have it. The anointing draws attention to function; glory draws attention to the Father. Anointing empowers what you do; glory transforms who you are.

You can operate under anointing and still be unhealed; but when glory rests, transformation occurs. The anointing visits; the glory dwells.

That's why Jesus prayed in John 17:22, *"The glory You have given Me, I have given them."* He didn't pray for more gifts, He prayed for greater likeness. Glory is the inheritance of sons who have learned to live in honor.

The Stewardship of Glory

When God entrusts you with glory, He expects stewardship. That means protecting presence above performance, intimacy above influence, and purity above popularity. Glory is costly because it cannot coexist with mixture.

To steward glory, you must guard three things:
1. **Your Motives**.
   Why you do something determines whether glory remains or lifts. If attention replaces adoration, the weight will depart.
2. **Your Mouth**.
   Glory thrives in gratitude but dies in grumbling.
   Speak what glorifies God, not what magnifies self.
3. **Your Mind**.
   Keep thoughts anchored in the awareness of His greatness.
   Pride begins in thought long before it manifests in action.

Stewardship of glory means remembering that you are not the source, you are the sanctuary. He dwells in you, but He does not belong to you.

The Progression from Honor to Glory

Honor leads to grace.
Grace leads to obedience.
Obedience leads to glory.

That is Heaven's pattern of transformation. You cannot skip honor and still carry glory. When a person honors God consistently, in private, in purity, and in people, glory begins to manifest visibly.

You don't have to chase glory; you simply create conditions where it feels safe to dwell. God's glory rests where His government is honored. That's why revival is never about visitation, it's about habitation. Glory comes to stay where honor has built a home.

The Weight That Changes You

Glory doesn't just visit rooms, it transforms hearts. Moses didn't just see light; he became luminous. When God's presence rests upon a person, even their countenance changes. Glory is not external glitter, it's internal gravity. It pulls everything in you into alignment with the reality of Heaven.

When glory rests, words become unnecessary. People are healed by presence, convicted by purity, and drawn by love. That's why glory cannot be manipulated or manufactured, it's Heaven's acknowledgment of divine likeness on earth.

Transition

Glory is not God's applause, it is His affirmation. It is Heaven's response to consistent honor, humility, and holiness. In the next section, we'll explore how to become carriers of glory, people who not only encounter His presence but embody His nature everywhere they go.

Section 2 – *Carriers of Glory: The Vessels God Can Trust*

Not everyone can carry glory. Many can host moments of presence, but few can steward the weight of it without collapsing under its holiness.

Glory is not light to the flesh, it's weight to the spirit. It presses out pride, burns away pretense, and exposes motives. That's why glory always begins where self ends.

When Isaiah saw the Lord *"high and lifted up,"* he also saw himself rightly: *"Woe is me, for I am undone!"* The closer you come to glory, the more aware you become of your humanity, and that awareness is not shame; it's safety. Only those who can say *"I am undone"* can be trusted to walk clothed in glory.

Glory Rests Where the Heart Is Ready

Glory does not visit personality, it visits purity. It does not rest on charisma but on character. The presence of God seeks a posture more than a platform. David's psalmist heart prepared him long before his royal position did. He honored presence privately, so he could handle glory publicly.

You cannot prepare for glory in public if you ignore presence in private. The secret place is Heaven's proving ground. When God finds a heart that honors Him in silence, He can trust it with sound.

Glory doesn't rest where there's presentation; it rests where there's representation. That's why Jesus withdrew often to lonely places, to stay aligned with His Source. Isolation isn't always punishment; sometimes it's preparation for greater weight.

The Nature of a Glory Carrier

To carry glory is to live as a mirror of Heaven. A mirror has no light of its own; it only reflects what it faces. When you live turned toward God, His light reflects naturally. When you turn toward man's approval, the reflection fades.

A glory carrier:
- Values presence over platform.
- Prefers obedience over opportunity.
- Pursues holiness over hype.
- Responds in worship rather than self-promotion.
- Protects atmosphere more than image.

Glory carriers are not perfect, they're pure in surrender. They don't have spotless records; they have yielded hearts. What makes them trustworthy is not their strength but their abandonment to His will.

Brokenness: The Prerequisite of Glory

Glory cannot dwell in the unbroken. The alabaster box had to be broken for the fragrance to fill the room. Likewise, the vessel of your life must be yielded before glory can be revealed. Brokenness is not weakness, it's readiness. When your will has been crushed beneath His, the aroma of glory begins to rise.

Every crushing you endure is a prophetic rehearsal for greater capacity. Oil flows where the press is honored. Those who resist the crushing remain decorative vessels; those who yield become carriers of fragrance.

The Fire of Refinement

Before a vessel carries glory, it must pass through fire. Fire refines what pride resists. It removes impurities invisible to the naked eye, selfish ambition, hidden comparison, and silent resentment. The furnace is not punishment; it's preparation.

In 2 Timothy 2:21, Paul writes, *"If anyone purges himself from dishonor, he will be a vessel unto honor, sanctified and meet for the Master's use."* The word purge means to burn away the unnecessary. The same fire that consumes dross illuminates gold. Those who endure refinement become living tabernacles where glory dwells continually.

Glory doesn't rest on comfort; it rests on consecration. When you survive the fire without offense, you emerge radiant, not resentful. You become what Malachi called *"jewels"*; reflectors of divine light.

The Discipline of Hiddenness

Glory carriers learn to love obscurity. God hides His greatest vessels before He reveals them. He shields them from premature exposure because premature glory is deadly. Hidden seasons are not wasted, they are wombs of weight. In secret places, God stretches capacity without applause. He removes the need to be seen so that He alone can be glorified when the light finally shines.

Hiddenness is Heaven's protection from pride. If you can be faithful unseen, you can be trusted visible. The glory of God cannot dwell where ambition still speaks louder than obedience.

Glory Carriers Release Transformation

When glory rests upon a life, it transforms everything it touches. Moses' face shone. Peter's shadow healed. Paul's handkerchiefs delivered. Each became a conduit, not a container. They didn't possess the glory, they participated in it.

The mark of a true glory carrier is transformation in their wake:
Where they walk, people awaken.
Where they serve, hearts soften.
Where they speak, atmospheres shift.
They are not famous, they are fruitful.
Their glory is not their own; it is borrowed brilliance from the King.

Guarding the Glory

The higher the glory, the greater the guard.
To carry it safely, you must protect three realms:
1. **Your Atmosphere**:
   Keep your environment saturated with worship, not worry.
   Glory dwells in clean air, praise purifies the atmosphere.
2. **Your Associations**:
   Glory diminishes when surrounded by dishonor.
   Keep company with those who value purity over popularity.
3. **Your Attention**:

Glory follows focus. Whatever captures your gaze captures your gravity. Stay face-to-face with the King, and His reflection will remain.

Transition

Glory does not make you greater, it makes you gentler. Those who truly carry it become lowly, holy, and luminous. In the next section, we'll explore the manifestation of glory in the earth, how Heaven's weight transforms people, places, and nations when honor creates an atmosphere for it to dwell.

Section 3 – The Manifestation of Glory: When Heaven Fills the Earth

Glory was never meant to remain in Heaven. It was destined to dwell on earth. When God created man, He breathed His glory into dust and called it dominion. When that glory was forfeited through sin, darkness covered the earth, but the prophecy remained: *"The earth shall be filled with the knowledge of the glory of the Lord as the waters cover the sea"* (Habakkuk 2:14).

That prophecy was not poetic exaggeration, it was Heaven's intent. The glory of God is the evidence of His government fully restored in creation through redeemed humanity. When sons walk in honor, glory finds its dwelling again in the visible realm.

Glory Revealed Through Humanity

Glory is not a mist; it is a manifestation of God's nature in man. Romans 8:19 says, *"Creation waits with eager expectation for the manifestation of the sons of God."* Creation isn't groaning for more sermons or songs, it's groaning for sons carrying glory.

When the Spirit of God lives unquenched and unrestricted in human vessels, Heaven and earth meet in perfect resonance. Every act of mercy, every miracle, every moment of reconciliation is a spark of glory bursting through the fabric of creation.

Jesus was the prototype of this manifestation. John wrote, *"We beheld His glory, the glory as of the only begotten of the Father, full of grace and truth."* He revealed that glory is not merely brightness, it's balance. Grace without truth produces sentimentality; truth without grace produces severity. **Glory holds both in perfect tension.**

From Visitation to Habitation

For generations, people have sought visitation, moments when God comes near. But the Kingdom was never meant to host visits; it was meant to host residence. When honor builds a dwelling place, glory stays.

In the wilderness, the tabernacle was filled with glory that came and went. But in the New Covenant, believers are the tabernacle. We are not waiting for glory to fall; glory is waiting for us to function. When the Church matures into oneness with Christ, visitation becomes habitation, and earth begins to look like Heaven.

The glory that once filled the temple now fills the temple of flesh, our bodies, our homes, our gatherings. It is not limited to services but saturates cities through people who carry presence.

Glory in the Marketplace

The manifestation of glory doesn't stop at the sanctuary door. It must spill into the streets, classrooms, boardrooms, and communities. Isaiah 60 commands, *"Arise, shine, for your light has come, and the glory of the Lord is risen upon you."* That light is not for decoration, it's for demonstration.

It illuminates dark systems, unjust practices, and hopeless environments with Heaven's justice, wisdom, and love.

Glory in business looks like integrity. Glory in education looks like revelation. Glory in government looks like righteousness. Glory in family looks like reconciliation. Every domain becomes a stage where God's character is displayed through human conduct.

The Kingdom doesn't need more stages, it needs more stewards of glory who will live the message, not just preach it.

Glory Transforms Environments

Where glory dwells, transformation follows. Glory purges corruption, heals division, and restores order. It doesn't just fill buildings, it redefines them. Jacob called a barren place *"the house of God"* after encountering glory. What was once ordinary became holy because Heaven touched it.

When the glory of God fills an environment:
- Sickness yields to health.
- Division yields to peace.
- Fear yields to faith.
- Oppression yields to liberty.
- Death yields to life.

Glory restores creation's original rhythm, life ruled by light. That's why the ultimate evidence of glory is transformation, not emotion.

Glory Among the Nations

God's desire was never limited to Israel, it was for all nations to see His glory. Isaiah 66:18 declares, *"The time is coming to gather all nations and tongues; and they shall come and see My glory."* This is not a future fantasy, it is an unfolding reality through the global Church.

Every reformation, every missionary movement, every act of reconciliation among believers is another stream flowing toward that prophetic ocean. When nations bow, governments reform, and cultures heal, glory is manifesting. It's not confined to clouds or light, it's seen in justice, compassion, and unity among God's people.

The knowledge of the glory of the Lord will cover the earth, because the sons of glory are filling the earth.

The Earth Responds to Glory

Creation itself recognizes glory.
The sea stills under it.
Mountains tremble before it.
Demons flee from it.
Glory is not passive presence, it's active government.
It doesn't just rest; it reigns.

When Jesus rebuked the storm, it wasn't merely a miracle, it was the glory of God restoring dominion through a man fully aligned with Heaven. When the Church walks in that same authority, even nature will respond again. Romans 8:21 promises that creation itself will be delivered into *"the glorious liberty of the children of God."*

That is the end goal of redemption, not just salvation of souls, but restoration of systems, nature, and nations under the weight of glory.

Transition

The manifestation of glory is Heaven's original dream fulfilled sons and daughters governing creation through love, purity, and wisdom. In the next section, we will explore how to sustain that glory, how to live daily under its weight without losing the wonder or forfeiting the fear of the Lord.

Section 4 – Sustaining the Glory: Living Under the Weight

Glory is easy to encounter. It's far harder to sustain. Visitation requires hunger; habitation requires holiness. The initial manifestation of glory can come suddenly, but the keeping of it is gradual, requiring daily alignment, continual humility, and perpetual awareness of God's presence.

The same God who reveals His glory tests whether we can host it. Sustaining glory is not about emotion but endurance. It's not about how deeply you felt Him once, but how faithfully you walk with Him now.

Sustaining Glory Through Consistency

Glory doesn't remain where inconsistency reigns. It is repelled by dishonor because glory represents God's weight, and weight requires structure. That's why the tabernacle had order before it had glory.

Every time you keep prayer when it's inconvenient, forgive when it's undeserved, or obey when it's uncomfortable, you are strengthening your internal structure to sustain weight.

Glory cannot dwell in lives filled with mixture. Consistency is the quiet proof of consecration. It tells Heaven, *"I can handle more."*

Sustaining Glory Through the Fear of the Lord

The fear of the Lord is not terror, it's tender reverence and honor. It's the continual awareness that God is near, holy, and worthy of honor in every decision. Without the fear of the Lord, glory lifts.

Uzzah's death in 2 Samuel 6 wasn't cruelty, it was consequence. He treated the ark like common cargo and dishonored it. When we handle holy things casually, we lose the consciousness of their weight.

The fear of the Lord keeps familiarity from breeding contempt. It anchors your spirit in humility, ensuring glory remains unhindered. Honor is the soil; the fear of the Lord is the moisture that keeps glory alive.

Sustaining Glory Through Rest

Many lose glory because they try to work for what can only be walked in. Glory is not maintained by striving; it's sustained by abiding. Jesus never rushed to perform; He simply remained in perfect union with the Father.

Rest is not inactivity, it's alignment. It's when the heart ceases to perform for presence and begins to flow from it. Rest keeps glory pure because it silences self-effort and amplifies divine rhythm.

You were never designed to carry the weight of glory alone, you were designed to bear it with Him. His yoke is easy because His presence carries the greater portion.

Sustaining Glory Through Gratitude

Gratitude keeps glory from becoming routine. When you stop thanking God for His presence, you start taking it for granted. Glory fades wherever complaining takes root.

Israel's wilderness was filled with miracles but absent of mindfulness. They saw His power but missed His person. Ingratitude dulled their awareness until the miraculous became mundane.

A grateful heart remains weight-conscious, it never mishandles what Heaven has given. Every moment of thanksgiving resets your awareness of His nearness. Gratitude keeps the oil fresh and the flame burning.

Sustaining Glory Through Accountability

Isolation invites deception.
Even vessels of glory need alignment with others.
Moses had Joshua.
Elijah had Elisha.
Paul had Timothy.
Jesus walked with twelve.

Accountability doesn't reduce anointing; it refines it. When others can correct you, comfort you, and call you higher, glory remains balanced and unpolluted by ego. Unchecked authority breeds contamination, but shared accountability ensures continuity.

Glory thrives in community because humility lives there. Where brothers dwell together in unity, there the Lord commands the blessing.

Sustaining Glory Through Worship

Worship is not a song, it's a stance. It's the daily recognition that every breath, every task, every conversation is unto the Lord. Glory flourishes in atmospheres saturated with adoration.

When worship becomes lifestyle, glory becomes normal. Where there is continual exaltation, there is continual visitation. Worship is the rhythm that keeps glory circulating through the believer's life like oxygen through the body.

When Heaven hears the sound of consistent worship, it recognizes a familiar address, a house that honors the King.

Transcending Worship: From Presence to Glory

True worship goes beyond expression and into transformation. Jesus said, *"These people honor Me with their lips, but their hearts are far from Me"* (Isaiah 29:13; repeated in Matthew 15:8). Honor expressed without heart engagement is noise, not worship. Presence may respond to volume, but glory responds to hearts that honor.

Worship is not simply experiencing His presence, we carry His presence. True worship presses beyond what we already carry to encounter who He is in fullness. Presence is proximity; glory is impact. Presence comforts, glory imprints.

Just as the woman with the issue of blood reached beyond His presence in the crowd to touch the place of virtue (Mark 5:25–34), worship must reach beyond emotional atmosphere to engage His essence. Presence surrounds, but glory saturates. Presence calms, but glory changes.

The objective of worship is not merely divine nearness, it is divine impression.

When worship becomes transcendent, it places a demand on Heaven not only to visit but to manifest. This is why Jesus on the Mount of Transfiguration *"was changed,"* and *"His face shone like the sun"* (Luke 9:29; Matthew 17:2). Worship didn't just attract presence, it caused the glory to break through humanity.

Glory is weight (kabod). The purpose of worship is to receive that weight until it leaves an imprint upon the worshipper. Presence invites God near, but glory engraves God within.

Paul wrote, *"For our light affliction… works for us a far more exceeding and eternal weight of glory"* (2 Corinthians 4:17). Suffering without worship produces despair. Worship in suffering produces weight. When worship rises from pressure, it does not summon comfort, it summons glory.

Worship and suffering are the pathway to glory. When pain becomes praise, it reveals maturity. When worship ascends out of inconvenience or sorrow, Heaven responds not with consolation but with transformation. True glory moments are not emotional, they are formative.

Worship is the journey from presence to glory, from visitation to habitation, from awareness to alteration.

"Presence comforts. Glory imprints."

Sustaining Glory Through the Word

Glory and Word are inseparable. The Word reveals, sustains, and directs glory. Without it, encounters drift into emotion and error.

In 2 Corinthians 3:18, Paul writes that we are transformed *"from glory to glory"* as we behold the Lord through His Word. Each revelation upgrades capacity. Every time you meditate on truth, the mirror of your spirit becomes clearer, and the reflection of Christ becomes brighter.

The Word doesn't just inform you; it conforms you.
That conformity is what keeps glory consistent, not seasonal.

Sustaining Glory Through Love

Love is the highest law of glory. You can prophesy, heal, and preach under anointing, but only love makes glory visible. When love rules, selfish ambition dies and divine nature shines.

Glory thrives in atmospheres of love because love is God's native language. Heaven recognizes itself wherever love leads. When you love purely, you host glory naturally.

The Posture of a Glory Keeper

To sustain glory, you must live both bowed and bold.
Bowed in humility before God, bold in obedience before men.
You become a priest and a king, ministering upward in worship and outward in dominion.

The posture of sustained glory is continual awe:
- Eyes lifted
- Hands clean
- Heart tender
- Will surrendered

Such people don't carry glory for moments, they become environments for it.

Transition

Sustaining glory is not about holding on, it's about becoming one. When the vessel and the presence are indistinguishable, glory no longer visits; it abides. In the next and final section, we'll explore the destiny of glory, when Heaven and earth are one, and sons rule forever in the light of the Lamb.

Section 5 – The Destiny of Glory: When the Earth Is Full of His Light

Glory is not just where the story ends, it's where it began. Before there was sin, there was glory. Before there was rebellion, there was radiance. God clothed man in glory, and man carried that glory through creation. When Adam fell, the Scripture says, *"All have sinned and come short of the glory of God."* Man didn't merely lose a garden, he lost glory. Redemption, therefore, is not God getting man back to Eden; it's God restoring man to glory.

The gospel is not just about forgiveness, it's about reinstatement. We are not saved merely from wrath; we are restored to weight. Jesus didn't die just to cleanse you, He died to crown you. That crown is glory.

The Restoration of Glory

At the cross, Jesus took on the full weight of sin so that the sons of God could again carry the full weight of glory. What Adam forfeited in disobedience, Christ restored through surrender. When He prayed, *"Father, the glory You have given Me, I have given them,"* He declared restoration complete.

From that moment, the potential of Heaven's glory was transferred to the earth through redeemed vessels. The same Spirit that raised Christ from the dead now dwells in us, not visiting, but residing. The glory that once hovered over the Ark now rests within believers, transforming the ordinary into sacred space.

Every miracle, every act of love, every reconciliation is evidence that glory is returning to the earth through us.

Glory and the Lamb

In Revelation 21, John saw the destiny of glory fulfilled: *"The city had no need of the sun or of the moon, for the glory of God illuminated it, and the Lamb is its light."* That light is not borrowed, it's eternal. It emanates from the Lamb who was slain and now reigns.

The Lamb is the final revelation of honor and glory in one person, honor in His humility, glory in His triumph. The One who lowered Himself beneath all men now reigns above all thrones. In Him, we see that glory is not a spotlight, it's the result of perfect surrender.

Heaven is not a distant realm filled with glowing clouds; it is a dimension where glory is visible without hindrance. Every being there honors perfectly and therefore glows perpetually.

Glory in the Saints

When Paul said, *"Christ in you, the hope of glory,"* he wasn't speaking of a distant future, he was revealing an imminent reality. The world's hope is not in another system, revival, or reformer; it is in Christ in you. When that indwelling Christ is honored and obeyed, His light begins to leak out until the knowledge of the glory of the Lord truly fills the earth.

Every believer is a lamp of glory, wired to shine, fueled by the Spirit, and aimed toward nations. The destiny of the saints is not survival; it's radiance. We are not waiting to escape the world; we are assigned to illuminate it.

The Church will not end in weakness but in brightness. Isaiah saw it: *"Arise, shine... His glory shall be seen upon you."* Seen, not imagined, not sung about, but visible in love, unity, and power.

The Glorified Creation

Even creation itself will be transformed under the weight of glory. The curse that warped nature will yield to the light of redemption. Romans 8:21 declares, *"Creation itself shall be delivered from corruption into the glorious liberty of the children of God."* The same Spirit that filled the tabernacle will fill the trees, seas, and skies. The lion will again lie with the lamb because the Lamb reigns from Zion.

In that day, everything will pulse with presence.
Sound will be worship.
Light will be language.
And every nation will walk in the radiance of the Lamb's glory.

Glory as Eternal Communion

The destiny of glory is not just display, it's union. The end of all honor and holiness is intimacy restored. Heaven is not simply reward; it is relationship without interruption. We will live face to face with the One we once knew by faith. No veil, no distance, no shadow, only endless light.

John wrote, *"His servants shall see His face, and His name shall be on their foreheads."* That name speaks of nature. The name of God etched on your being means you have become like Him. Glory will no longer come upon you; it will be you.

We will not reflect His glory temporarily; we will embody it eternally.

Glory's Final Harmony

When honor has done its work, glory takes its seat.
Honor builds the structure; glory fills it.
Honor disciplines sons; glory crowns them.
Honor prepares the bride; glory adorns her.

The final harmony of Heaven is not merely worship, it is oneness. Every sound, every being, every breath will echo with divine resonance. The kingdoms of this world will have become the Kingdom of our Lord and of His Christ. No pride, no pain, no night, only light.

In that day, the story of redemption will be complete,
and all of creation will exhale the same word: Glory.

Final Reflection: Living Toward Glory

Until that day, our assignment is simple but sacred: To honor the King in every sphere of life, so His glory may rest upon us now and be revealed in fullness later. When we honor rightly, Heaven leans near. When we live humbly, glory lingers. And when we love wholly, the weight of His presence becomes visible again on earth.

The destiny of glory is not distant, it is dawning.
The sons are rising.
The earth is awakening.
The King is being revealed.
And the cry of creation is being answered:

"Holy, holy, holy is the Lord of hosts; the whole earth is full of His glory."

Chapter 16 Review & Reflection

The Honor of Glory: The Weight of Divine Recognition

Core Revelation

Glory is the fruit of sustained honor. It is Heaven's acknowledgment that a vessel has been proven faithful, humble, and pure. Honor is what builds a life; glory is what fills it. When God finds a life, family, or community that reverences His presence, He rests His weight there.

Glory is not light to be admired, it is nature to be shared. It is the visible expression of the invisible God through sons and daughters who have been refined by honor. It is not achieved by ambition but entrusted through alignment.

The journey of honor ends where it began, in God's likeness. He made man in His image, lost in dishonor, redeemed through Christ, and restored to glory. To honor is to return to that image, to live as living mirrors of His nature until *"the earth is filled with the knowledge of the glory of the Lord."*

Kingdom Principle

Honor prepares the vessel; glory fills it. The weight of glory can only rest where humility has built a foundation.

Scripture Focus

- Psalm 8:5 – *"You have crowned him with glory and honor."*
- John 17:22 – *"The glory You have given Me, I have given them."*
- 2 Corinthians 3:18 – *"We all, with unveiled face, beholding as in a mirror the glory of the Lord, are transformed into the same image from glory to glory."*

- Habakkuk 2:14 – *"The earth shall be filled with the knowledge of the glory of the Lord as the waters cover the sea."*
- Romans 8:21 – *"Creation itself will be delivered from corruption into the glorious liberty of the children of God."*
- Revelation 21:23 – *"The glory of God gives it light, and the Lamb is its lamp."*
- Isaiah 60:1–3 – *"Arise, shine; for your light has come, and the glory of the Lord is risen upon you."*

Truths to Remember

1. Glory is Heaven's recognition of maturity. God places His weight on those who have been proven in humility.
2. Honor is the path; glory is the prize. The heart that continually yields will inevitably shine.
3. Glory is not for display but demonstration. It reveals Christ, not self.
4. The anointing empowers function; glory reveals nature.
5. Brokenness is the gateway to glory. God fills what He first empties.
6. Glory is sustained through fear of the Lord, gratitude, and continual surrender.
7. Love is the highest atmosphere of glory.
8. Creation itself responds to glory, it heals, aligns, and flourishes under its weight.
9. Glory is the destiny of every son. We were not created to visit His presence but to host it.
10. The story of redemption ends in radiance: Christ in you, the hope of glory.

Application

- **Personally**: Walk in daily awareness that God has trusted you to carry His presence.
- Protect your inner life, purity keeps glory stable.
- Practice gratitude and humility even in moments of recognition.

- Let every gift, platform, and opportunity become a mirror reflecting the Giver.
- **Relationally**: Treat others as carriers of glory; never dishonor the image of God in another person.
- Refuse jealousy, glory is not scarce; it multiplies through honor.
- Encourage others to mature through correction and humility so they too can shine.
- **Corporately:** Build atmospheres of reverence in your gatherings, avoid entertainment; pursue presence.
- Keep worship Christ-centered and Word-anchored.
- Celebrate transformation, not performance.
- Remember: a church that honors well, becomes a resting place for glory.

Reflection Questions

1. Do I desire glory for display or for transformation?
2. Have I created daily rhythms that sustain awareness of His presence?
3. What weights (distractions, offenses, ambitions) might be hindering the flow of glory in my life?
4. Am I living as a vessel or a mirror?
5. How can I help my church or community become a habitation for His glory rather than a stage for our gifts?
6. When God recognizes me publicly, do I reflect the honor back to Him privately?
7. What would it look like for *"the knowledge of His glory"* to fill my sphere of influence?

Declaration

"Father of Glory, I honor Your presence above all else.
I receive Your weight, not to be seen, but to reveal You.
Let my life become a mirror of Your majesty, a dwelling place where Heaven feels at home. I renounce pride, ambition, and familiarity and choose the posture of humility and wonder.

Christopher K. Turney

Fill me, refine me, and sustain me, until my words, my work, and my walk all shine with Your likeness. May the knowledge of Your glory fill the earth through me, until every breath echoes the anthem:

"To You be honor and glory forever.""

CHAPTER 17
HONOR: THE ANTIDOTE TO SHAME AND THE GATEWAY TO GLORY

As I look back through the journey of this book, I see a divine thread weaving through every page, honor leading to glory. But between honor and glory stands something ancient and stubborn: ***shame.***

Shame has been humanity's oldest shadow since Eden, whispering to us that we are unworthy of God's presence. It isolates, it hides, and it convinces the heart that glory is for someone else. Yet honor, true, Kingdom honor, is Heaven's antidote. Honor restores what shame strips away. It re-clothes the soul with dignity, identity, and divine worth.

Honor does not deny failure, it redeems it. It does not ignore nakedness; it covers it with covenant. And wherever honor reigns, shame loses its vocabulary, and glory returns.

Section 1 – The Fall: From Glory to Shame

Before man sinned, he was clothed in glory. That radiance was not external light; it was internal likeness, the very image of God reflected through innocence and fellowship. Genesis 2:25 says, *"The man and his wife were both naked, and they felt no shame."* There was no self-consciousness because there was no separation.

When Adam and Eve disobeyed, the first consequence was not physical death but awareness of shame. They hid among the trees, sewing fig leaves together, attempting to cover what had been lost. The covering of glory had lifted.

Shame is the emotional echo of spiritual nakedness. It is the inward proof that honor has been violated. Where honor once clothed them, now fear exposed them.

From that moment, humanity has lived between two conditions: covered by honor or concealed by shame. And every redemptive act of God since the garden has been a movement from shame back into glory.

Principle: Shame strips, honor covers, and glory clothes.

Section 2 – *David and Mephibosheth: The Restoration of Honor*

Centuries later, we find a crippled man hiding in a barren place, a picture of humanity's condition apart from grace. His name was Mephibosheth, the grandson of King Saul, living in Lo-debar, which means *"no pasture."* His royal lineage had been forgotten, his dignity stolen by circumstance. He was the descendant of a fallen house, and in his mind, he carried that shame like a chain.

Then one day, the voice of the king broke through the silence of exile. David remembered covenant and asked, *"Is there anyone left of the house of Saul, that I may show kindness for Jonathan's sake?"* (2 Samuel 9:1). When Mephibosheth was brought before him, trembling and unsure, David said, *"Do not fear… you shall eat at my table continually."*

In that moment, honor found shame and lifted it. David didn't just pardon him, he restored him. He gave him back his inheritance, his seat, and his name.

This is the gospel hidden in plain sight. The King calls the crippled, the hidden, the unworthy, and seats them among sons. Honor reaches where shame hides. Grace does what guilt cannot, it restores the crown of dignity.

Principle: Honor finds the forgotten, remembers covenant, and restores identity.

Mephibosheth entered David's house limping but left living in honor. And every time he sat at the royal table, his legs, those reminders of his weakness, were covered by the tablecloth of grace.

Section 3 – Noah, Ham, and Canaan: The Violation of Honor

Contrast this with one of Scripture's most sobering pictures of dishonor. After the flood, Noah planted a vineyard, became drunk, and lay uncovered in his tent. Ham, his son, saw his father's nakedness and exposed it to his brothers. Shem and Japheth, however, took a garment, walked backward, and covered their father without looking upon his shame (Genesis 9:22-23).

The difference was not in what they saw but in how they responded. Ham publicized; Shem and Japheth protected. Honor covers what love is willing to heal. Dishonor magnifies what pride wants to mock.

Ham's response birthed a curse; his brothers' response preserved a blessing. Dishonor always reproduces after its kind. What Ham sowed into his father's nakedness was reaped by his descendants, Canaan became a symbol of servitude and shame.

This passage is not about excusing sin; it's about stewarding sight. Honor doesn't deny wrongdoing; it handles it with redemptive discretion. To *"cover"* in Scripture is not to conceal evil but to restore dignity while pursuing truth.

Principle: Dishonor exposes weakness; honor restores worth.

In a culture obsessed with exposure, Heaven still calls for Shem and Japheth hearts, those who walk backward with a garment of grace.

Section 4 – The Pattern of Restoration

From Genesis to Revelation, God continually moves His people from shame to glory through honor.
- Adam and Eve were covered by God Himself with garments of skin, a foreshadowing of the Lamb.
- Israel was covered by covenant and atonement, so His presence could dwell among them again.
- The Prodigal Son returned home clothed with the best robe, ring, and sandals, the Father's public reversal of shame.
- Jesus bore our shame on the cross, stripped and mocked, so that we could be robed in righteousness.

Every story sings the same refrain: what shame removes, honor restores, and glory completes. Jesus did not just cancel sin; He re-crowned humanity. Hebrews 12:2 says He *"endured the cross, despising the shame,"* and now sits at the right hand of glory.

Principle: The cross is where honor and shame collided, and glory triumphed.

Section 5 – Honor as Glory's Gateway

Shame whispers, *"Hide, you're not enough."*
Honor declares, *"Come, you are chosen."*
Glory responds, *"Now reflect My image."*

The pathway to glory always passes through honor. You cannot live shamed and shine simultaneously. Agreement with shame keeps you beneath the weight of guilt; agreement with honor lifts you into likeness.

Honor re-teaches the soul to agree with Heaven's assessment: *"You are My beloved."* When you receive that verdict, glory begins to return to your countenance. Your perspective, your language, your posture change. Honor reconciles you to yourself so you can rightly reveal Him.

Principle: You cannot carry glory while still believing shame's lies.

Glory is not earned; it's inherited. But honor is the heart posture that proves you can bear the inheritance without breaking under it.

Section 6 – Living Covered Again

To live in honor is to live covered, not by concealment but by covenant. God's covering is not fabric, it is favor. He robes us in righteousness and wraps us in mercy. When you honor His covering, you remain radiant. When you dishonor it through pride or exposure, the light dims again.

The call of the Kingdom is to live covered but not hidden. Covered in grace, open in truth. Free from the accusation of shame, walking in the awareness of glory. This is the maturity of sons: not performing for acceptance but living from divine approval.

"Put on the Lord Jesus Christ." (Romans 13:14)
To wear Him is to wear glory again.

The story that began with fig leaves ends with fine linen, *"the righteousness of the saints."* Humanity's nakedness has been swallowed up by divine covering. Honor has triumphed over shame, and glory has returned to man.

Closing Declaration

"Father, thank You for restoring what shame removed.
You covered my nakedness with mercy and called me by name when I hid in fear. Teach me to walk as one clothed in honor and crowned with glory. Help me to cover others as You covered me, to restore, not expose; to redeem, not ridicule. Let my words carry healing, my presence carry safety, and my life reflect the radiance of Your Son. From shame to honor, from honor to glory, let this be the anthem of my life and the legacy of Your Kingdom."

Chapter 17 Review & Reflection

Honor: The Antidote to Shame and the Gateway to Glory

Core Revelation

Shame is the echo of lost glory; honor is the invitation to recover it. Every act of dishonor leads humanity back into hiding, but every act of honor re-clothes creation in dignity.

From Adam's fig leaves to Christ's righteousness, the story of redemption is one long movement: from shame → honor → glory. The same God who covered Adam, remembered Mephibosheth, and defended Noah's dignity still calls His sons and daughters to walk covered, not concealed in fear, but clothed in favor.

Honor doesn't ignore weakness; it restores worth. It is Heaven's medicine for the oldest wound of man. And where honor is restored, glory returns.

Kingdom Principle

Shame strips; honor covers; glory clothes. To receive honor is to recover your place. to give honor is to release another into theirs.

Scripture Focus

- Genesis 3:21 – *"The Lord God made garments of skin for Adam and his wife and clothed them."*
- 2 Samuel 9:7 – *"Do not fear... you shall eat at my table continually."*
- Genesis 9:23 – *"Shem and Japheth took a garment... and covered their father."*
- Hebrews 12:2 – *"He endured the cross, despising the shame."*
- Romans 10:11 – *"Whoever believes in Him will not be put to shame."*

- Isaiah 61:7 – *"Instead of your shame you shall have double honor."*
- Romans 13:14 – *"Put on the Lord Jesus Christ."*

Truths to Remember

1. Shame is not emotion only, it is evidence of lost honor.
2. Honor restores dignity before it restores position.
3. Covering others in love is an act of royal priesthood.
4. Dishonor exposes weakness; honor heals it.
5. True honor doesn't condone sin, it redeems sinners.
6. Jesus bore shame so His people could bear glory.
7. You can't reflect what you're still hiding from.
8. Honor re-teaches the soul how Heaven sees.
9. Glory rests where covenant love covers.
10. Every time you choose honor, you reintroduce glory into the world.

Application

- **Personally:** Identify areas where shame still shapes your responses; invite the Holy Spirit to re-clothe you with truth.
- Replace self-criticism with gratitude for redemption.
- Remember: forgiveness cleanses sin; honor restores dignity.
- **Relationally:** When you see another's weakness, respond like Shem and Japheth, walk backward with grace.
- Restore confidence to those who feel disqualified.
- Speak life where shame has silenced identity.
- **Corporately:** Create communities where confession meets covering, not condemnation.
- Preach honor as culture, not etiquette.
- Celebrate restoration stories publicly so shame loses its hold on your house.

Reflection Questions

1. In what ways have I allowed shame to shape my view of God or myself?
2. How can I cover others' faults without excusing sin?
3. Have I been more like Ham, exposing, or like Shem and Japheth, restoring?
4. Who around me is living in Lo-debar, needing to be invited to the table of honor?
5. Do I believe that glory can rest again on my life, home, and ministry?

Declaration

"Father of Mercy, thank You for clothing me again with honor. Where shame once ruled, Your grace now reigns. Teach me to walk backward with a garment of love, to restore the fallen and remember covenant. Let my life declare that You have covered me with Christ and may the radiance of Your glory rest on everything I touch. From shame to honor, from honor to glory, I am covered, I am called, I am crowned."

CHAPTER 18

HONOR: THE REMEDY FOR GLOBAL CHAOS

Introduction - *When Honor Departs, Order Collapses*

"Why do the heathen rage, and the people imagine a vain thing?"
Psalm 2:1 NKJV

The question David asked is not merely rhetorical, it is diagnostic. What causes the heathen to rage and nations to fracture under the weight of their own instability? The answer is not political, economic, or ideological. It is relational and foundational: Dishonor breeds rage. Rage is the voice of a world that has lost its alignment.

This chapter brings the revelation of honor from personal and relational levels into the global arena, showing that the same dishonor that fractures a home also fractures nations. Honor is not only interpersonal, it is intergovernmental, intergenerational, and intercultural. True apostolic reform cannot remain within the walls of the Church; it must address the breakdown in society at every level.

When honor returns, governance is restored. When honor is lost, chaos is inevitable.

Section 1 – *Dishonor: The Hidden Root of Global Collapse*

Dishonor is not an attitude, it is a breach in order. In Genesis 1–2, God established an ecosystem governed through honor: man, honored God, woman honored man, creation responded to man's honor-based dominion. The fall began with dishonor toward God's word, leading to dishonor between man and woman, and ultimately the Earth producing thorns and chaos.

What began in Eden now manifests globally

Dishonor dethrones principle and makes personality the governing force. When honor evaporates, restraint collapses, and *"every man does what is right in his own eyes"* (Judg. 21:25). This is not a governmental crisis, it is a fatherhood crisis.

Transition

To heal nations, we must trace the flow of order, not the symptoms of disorder. Reform attempts that do not deal with dishonor will produce alternate systems of dishonor. Therefore, true Kingdom reform cannot begin at the legislative desk, it must begin at the table of sonship.

Section 2 – Authority Without Honor Becomes Control

Authority was meant to be relational before it was governmental. Before Adam governed the earth, he walked with God. The first system of authority was not legal, it was filial (relating to sons). When authority is grounded in honor, it carries grace.

When authority is exercised without honor, it requires enforcement.

This is why cultural resistance grows toward:
- Law enforcement
- Parental authority ("children disobedient to parents" – 2 Tim. 3:2)
- Spiritual leadership ("having itching ears" – 2 Tim. 4:3)

It is not authority they reject, it is the absence of honor through authority.

Section 3 – *Honor Restores Alignment and Therefore Order*

Honor repositions authority from control to alignment.

Honor:
1. Reconciles relationship before reinforcing regulation
2. Restores equity without diminishing structure
3. Resurrects identity before expecting responsibility

Honor does not absolve men from supporting pregnant partners, it calls them back to design. It does not protect corruption, it re-centers truth. Honor brings both justice and restoration.

"Honor all people. Love the brotherhood. Fear God. Honor the king." 1 Peter 2:17 NKJV

Peter presents a four-tier system of Kingdom order:
- All people receive dignity (honor shared)
- The brotherhood receives love (honor extended)
- God receives reverence (honor exalted)
- Leaders receive honor (honor established)

Break the sequence, and society fractures.

Transition

Honor is not sentiment. It is the administrative protocol of the Kingdom. It is how Christ governs. It is how apostles build. It is how sons reveal the Father. Therefore, honor is not one of many virtues, it is the framework through which heaven administers culture.

Section 4 – *Honor: The Apostolic Cure for Cultural Crisis*

- Apostles do not establish structures; they establish foundations.

- Honor is not a trait, it is the foundational order of heaven.
- Reformation without honor rearranges dysfunction.
- Transformation with honor restores design.

Sonship is the language of honor. The orphan spirit is the language of dishonor. Orphan cultures produce rebellion, competition, territorialism, and abandonment. Honor cultures produce legacy, continuity, and government.

"When the prodigal returned, the father restored honor before responsibility. And honor repositioned him as a son before assigning him the work."

Final Chapter Transition

This brings Chapter 18 to its close. The next chapter will move from the global implications of honor to its most foundational expression, within marriage, family, and generational legacy. If dishonor has fractured nations, it is because it first fractured homes. Honor cannot truly heal the global unless it is first restored in the local.

Before honor can transform government, society, and culture, it must return to the first government God ever established: the family. Chapter 19, "Honor in Marriage, Family, and Generations", will explore how honor strengthens covenant, preserves legacy, and becomes the lifeline of generational transfer.

Chapter 18 – Review & Reflection

Honor: The Remedy for Global Chaos

Core Revelation

Dishonor is not merely a relational breakdown, it is the foundational fracture behind global instability. Where honor is absent, order collapses, governance weakens, and rage becomes the language of the culture. Honor is not sentimental; it is structural, governmental, and Kingdom administrative protocol.

The same dishonor that fractures a home, fractures nations. Honor is not only interpersonal, but is intergovernmental, intergenerational, and inter-cultural. True reform cannot happen legislatively without first being restored relationally, at the table of sonship. Honor restores alignment, and alignment restores order. What begins in the heart of a son becomes the framework of a nation.

The Kingdom does not advance through power structures but through relational order. Apostolic change begins in the order of honor before it ever reaches the systems of men.

Kingdom Principle

Honor restores divine order, first internally, then relationally, then culturally. Dishonor dethrones principle and establishes personality as the highest authority. Authority without honor becomes control. But when honor is restored, authority regains grace, and governance functions as service rather than enforcement.

Scripture Focus

- Psalm 2:1 – *"Why do the heathen rage...?"*
- Judges 21:25 – *"Every man did what was right in his own eyes."*

- 1 Peter 2:17 – *"Honor all. Love the brotherhood. Fear God. Honor the king."*
- 2 Timothy 3:2 – *"Children disobedient to parents…"*
- 2 Timothy 4:3 – *"Having itching ears…"*
- Malachi 4:6 – *"He will turn the hearts of fathers to children…"* (restoration through honor)
- Luke 15:22 – The father restores honor before responsibility to the prodigal son.

Truths to Remember

1. Dishonor is the seed of societal collapse.
2. Authority without honor becomes oppression.
3. Honor is not emotional, it is governmental.
4. Sonship establishes what structure alone cannot sustain.
5. Dishonor dethrones principle; honor reinstates purpose.
6. You cannot reform culture without first reforming relationship.
7. Rage is the sound of a world out of alignment. Honor is the sound of restoration.
8. Legacies are sustained through honor, rebellion ends them.
9. Honor reconciles before it regulates.
10. Honor constructs what revival ignites.

Application

- Practice relational order before organizational reform.
- Restore honor in the home, before attempting to restore honor in society.
- Respond to authority with humility, not suspicion.
- Treat honor as a governance principle, not a social gesture.
- Refuse to let personality override principle in leadership and decision making.
- Honor across generations, receive from fathers, empower sons.
- Lead through identity before assignment or obligation.
- Do not attempt correction before reconnection.

- View cultural resistance not as rebellion alone, but as evidence of fatherlessness.
- Build atmospheres of honor and watch alignment manifest in governance.

Reflection Questions

1. Do I honor people based on preference, or based on Kingdom order?
2. Is my leadership rooted in relational alignment or positional authority?
3. Where have I allowed dishonor (silently or openly) to disconnect me from the source of grace?
4. Do I treat cultural problems as structural, or do I look for relational causes?
5. How can I model honor in leadership to counter societal distrust and disorder?
6. In what ways have I attempted to reform behavior without restoring identity first?
7. What practical expressions of honor can I demonstrate toward fathers, leaders, and those I lead?

Declaration

"Father, I take my place in Your divine order. I renounce every alignment with dishonor, disorder, and rebellion. I receive the grace to lead with honor, to govern through humility, and to build culture upon principle, not personality. I declare that honor will be my posture, alignment my foundation, and sonship my identity. May my life become an answer to the chaos around me. Let honor restore what disorder attempted to destroy. Let Your Kingdom come, through honor."

CHAPTER 19

HONOR IN MARRIAGE, FAMILY, AND GENERATIONS STRENGTHENING COVENANT, SUSTAINING LEGACY

Honor must be more than a social remedy; it must be a relational restoration. Global chaos is not birthed in boardrooms, courtrooms, war rooms, or political offices, but in broken homes. The fractures we see in nations are often amplified expressions of unresolved dysfunction within families. If honor can realign nations, it must first reconcile households. Honor is the lifeline of covenant, and the first covenant God ever instituted was not with a city or a nation, but with a husband and wife.

Marriage is Heaven's prototype for governance, and family is the first incubator of culture. What is not honored at home will eventually be misrepresented in the world. Therefore, to heal generational dysfunction and secure lasting legacy, honor must be restored where God laid the original blueprint, marriage, family, and generational continuation.

Introduction – *When Love Isn't Enough*

Marriage is commonly built upon love, compatibility, and chemistry. But love alone is never what sustains covenant. Jesus commanded *"Love your enemies"* (Matthew 5:44), proving that love is universal. We can love widely, but honor determines who we value correctly.

Many relationships fail not from the absence of love, but from the absence of honor. Love may kindle connection, but honor sustains it. Love is partly emotional; honor is always intentional.

Love is God's commanded response; honor is God's commanded initiative. Love reacts to what has happened to me; honor acts based on what God has revealed about the other. Love expresses emotion; honor assigns worth. Honor is the highest and most mature expression of love, it is a predetermined decision to value, regardless of circumstance.

When love is required where honor has not yet been established, it becomes torturous, because love feels demanded without justification. This is why the Apostle Peter instructs, *"Honor all men."* Honor assigns enough God-given value to people that the command to love no longer contradicts the soul.

We are called to love even our enemies (Matthew 5:44). Without honor, that requires emotional expression toward someone we do not esteem. But when honor is present, value has already been revealed, therefore, love is no longer strained, but sustained.

Honor reveals value, and that revelation makes the object of our love worthy of it.

Honor gives love its foundation. Love obeys, but honor initiates. Love reacts; honor leads. Love expresses what I feel; honor declares what I believe. Honor conditions the heart to value before or after treatment. Love may reach for reconciliation, but honor carries the revelation that makes reconciliation possible.

For many struggling marriages, the issue is not love, but the absence of honor. When honor is missing, value is unrecognized, and love feels unreasonable in the midst of difference. Honor doesn't ignore behavior, it anchors identity. It sees beyond frustration and remembers purpose.

When spouses do not feel honored, their hearts cannot properly process love. Emotional expression without internal affirmation creates exhaustion, not intimacy. Many couples are not void of love, they are void of value.

Where honor is restored, love becomes possible again. What once felt forced becomes natural. When value is recognized, affection is rekindled. Honor doesn't remove difference, but it restores dignity within difference, and that is where covenant thrives.

We cannot honor what we're too offended to value.

When our focus shifts to how we've been treated rather than who the person is by design, honor gets obstructed, and love becomes strained. The problem is not that honor isn't available, it's that access to it is blocked by injury.

"For many struggling marriages, the issue is not love, but the absence of honor."

The road to honor is often blocked when our spouse's value is hidden beneath our focus on how they have treated us. Hurt clouds perception. Offense buries identity. When I fixate on behavior, I lose sight of design.

Honor begins the moment I choose to look beyond treatment and rediscover worth. If God created my spouse, and He did, then their differences are not defects but elements of divine design. **Honor reappraises difference**. What once felt irreconcilable becomes a place of compatibility when seen through value. Their wants, desires, and preferences, though different from mine emotionally, physically, financially, or relationally, can become part of the richness of my life when I recognize the treasure within the earthen vessel.

"Honor begins when value is seen before behavior is corrected."

Offense buries identity. Honor excavates it. Maybe what I have been demanding from them was never theirs to give, it was God's to supply.

When I shift from *"how they've treated me"* to *"who God designed them to be,"* honor finds its path again.

"Love inspires connection. Honor sustains covenant."

Section 1 – Love Feels, Honor Sees

Love responds to emotion. Honor responds to divine revelation.
- Love focuses on how someone makes me feel.
- Honor recognizes who God has called them to be.
- Love fluctuates with emotion.
- Honor stabilizes through purpose.

"Honor all men." —1 Peter 2:17

We extend honor to all because all bear God's image. However, in covenant relationships, such as marriage and spiritual fatherhood, honor must become deeper, more intentional, and covenant-protecting.

Section 2 – Valuing Differences: Design Over Defect

Genesis 2:18 records ʿēzer kenegdo, *"a helper corresponding to him."* It doesn't mean identical, but complementary. Marriage was designed around difference, not uniformity. Differences are not dysfunction, they are divine design.

"The difference you once celebrated may become the difficulty you later resist. Honor returns you to celebration."

Honor matures the marriage past compatibility of personality into compatibility of purpose.

Section 3 – Compatibility of Purpose, Not Just Personality

Compatibility based on personality can create peace, but compatibility based on purpose creates power.

Marriage was never meant to settle two people, it was meant to send them.
- Without purpose, marriages become maintenance-oriented.

- With purpose, marriages become mission-driven.

"And the two shall become one flesh." (Genesis 2:24)

Oneness is not sameness, it is alignment to assignment.

Section 4 – Covenant Means to Cut: The Honor of Commitment

The Hebrew word berith (בְּרִית), meaning *"to cut,"* reveals that covenant does not begin in comfort, it begins in commitment. Every true covenant is sealed with sacrifice. That is why Adam's covenant began with God opening his side, and Christ's covenant with the Church was established the same way. Covenant is costly because it creates capacity.

In marriage, the *"cut"* is not the wounding of one another, but the cutting away of what threatens union. Honor embraces the removal of selfishness, pride, fear, independence, and immaturity not as relational loss, but as prophetic preparation. What God joins together must also be refined together.

- Love pulls me closer.
- Honor keeps me aligned when closeness becomes uncomfortable.

"Love draws me near; honor keeps me there when nearness confronts me."

The test of honor in covenant is not in the moments of mutual delight, but in the moments where differences demand surrender. Honor recognizes that the cutting of flesh creates the joining of spirit.

That is why many marriages survive attraction but collapse under alignment. Attraction is emotional. Alignment is covenantal. When honor is present, challenge becomes development, not detachment.

"Before God multiplies influence, He purifies intent."

The apostle Paul echoed this marital mystery when he wrote, *"Husbands, love your wives, just as Christ also loved the church and gave Himself for her"* (Ephesians 5:25). Notice, He did not simply feel for her. He gave Himself for her. This is covenant love. Love expressed through sacrifice. Honor expressed through surrender.

When covenant is honored through sacrifice, identity becomes safe to impart. That is why honor must precede inheritance, which brings us to parenting and generational transfer.

Section 5 – Honor in Family & Parenting: Identity Transmission

"Honor your father and mother… so that your days may be long." Exodus 20:12

"The glory of children are their fathers." Proverbs 17:6

Honor is the first commandment connected to longevity and continuation, not merely in years lived, but in legacy sustained. This principle cannot be fully understood without recognizing the role of life sources.

A life source is someone or something without which we, or what we are called to, would not exist. They are not simply influencers; they are origins. Their contribution is foundational, not optional. To honor a life source is to acknowledge origin, assignment, and divine intentionality.

Just as God used our biological parents as the vessel through which we entered the earth, He also uses spiritual fathers, founding apostles, and prophetic initiators as vessels through which purpose enters identity. In either case, natural or spiritual, honor is not based on behavior but on origin.

Even if parental roles were imperfect, they were still essential. We may not be able to celebrate how they handled us, but we must honor that they were chosen by God to bring us here. We cannot dishonor the gate and expect blessed arrival.

Where dishonor is present, origin is questioned. And when origin is questioned, we subtly imply that God mishandled our formation and becomes suspect of injustice. This is where identity begins to fracture. When we dishonor the source, we came from, we begin to unconsciously accuse God of failing in His sovereign intellect.

In a healthy covenantal home:
- The father imparts identity.
- The mother establishes emotional foundation.
- Honor preserves that impartation for the next generation.

When honor is absent, inheritance becomes unstable. When honor is present, legacy becomes secure.

Our parents are life sources and life sources don't just precede us, they enable us. Honor keeps us connected to what enabled us."

Paul expressed this when he wrote, *"For though you have ten thousand instructors in Christ, yet have ye not many fathers…"* (1 Corinthians 4:15). Teachers influence. Fathers initiate. Instructors shape performance. Fathers release purpose.

Honor recognizes where things began so that what began can be sustained. You may grow beyond their strength, but you must never grow out of their voice."

Transition

When life sources are honored, inheritance becomes identity, and legacy moves forward rather than restarting. This leads to the next reality, that honor creates generational continuity and momentum.

We may not celebrate how a life source handled us, but we must honor that they were chosen to bring us. You may surpass what they've done, but you must never dismiss what they began. Honor does not excuse imperfection, it acknowledges origin. I cannot dishonor the platform I stand upon and expect to build anything of substance on it.

Section 6 – *Generational Continuity: Legacy Through Honor*

"A good man leaves an inheritance to his children's children." Proverbs 13:22

Inheritance in the Kingdom is far broader than finances. True inheritance is revelation, patterns, values, access, identity, and spiritual momentum. Wealth can be depleted in a single generation, but revelation continues to multiply long after we are gone. Honor is what determines whether a person receives just resources or whether they inherit responsibility.

Generational continuity is never accidental, it is intentional and always rooted in honor. Where dishonor enters, generational flow fractures. Sons become detached from fathers, and each generation must start over. But where honor is active, each generation doesn't begin at zero, it begins at overflow.

Dishonor forces descendants to recover what should have been received. Honor enables them to build on what has been entrusted.

"Love creates memories. Honor creates legacy."

Legacy is not what lives in people, it is what lives through them. Honor ensures that what God placed in one generation is not merely admired but multiplied. Every mantle is transferable, but only honor makes it receivable.

Consider Abraham, Isaac, and Jacob. God repeatedly introduced Himself as *"the God of Abraham, Isaac, and Jacob"* not because each man discovered God independently, but because each one continued what the previous one stewarded. That is not succession, that is honor in motion.

Honor does not create clones. It creates continuers.

This is why Paul longed for Timothy to hold to what was imparted: *"The things which you have heard from me... commit these to faithful men, who will be able to teach others also"* (2 Timothy 2:2).

That is not generational repetition, that is generational expansion. Where there are teachers, there may be replication. Where there are fathers, there will be reproduction. But where there is honor, there will be continuation.

Honor moves inheritance from being a resource to being a responsibility, the responsibility to build further than the generation that came before. Without honor, children only manage what they've received. With honor, they multiply it.

Generational dishonor forces people to live as survivors of what they should have inherited. Honor positions them as stewards of what they were meant to fulfill.

Transition to Conclusion

When honor is present, sons don't just remember their fathers, they extend them. Legacy stops becoming a memory and becomes a motion. And this brings us into the concluding revelation, honor is not a courtesy; it is the lifeline of covenant and the pathway to generational relevance.

Legacy is not what you leave behind; it is what you send forward. Without honor, inheritance becomes information. With honor, inheritance becomes identity. Honor does not create duplicates, it unlocks continuation.

Dishonor forces a generation to recover what they should have received. Honor allows them to multiply it.

Conclusion – Honor Is the Lifeline of Covenant

Love is the doorway of marriage.
Honor is the foundation.
Love builds a home.
Honor builds a lineage.

When honor becomes the relational culture, marriages stabilize, families strengthen, and generations receive momentum rather than recovery.

"If honor can heal a nation, it must first heal a family."

Chapter 19 – Review & Reflection

Honor in Marriage, Family, and Generations

Core Revelation

Love may connect, but honor sustains. Love is God's commanded response; honor is His commanded initiative. Without honor, love becomes strained under emotional pressure. Honor assigns value before or after treatment, reappraises differences as design rather than dysfunction, recognizes life sources, and safeguards generational continuity. What begins in love is only preserved through honor.

Kingdom Principle

Honor is the highest and most mature expression of love. It does not merely react to behavior; it recognizes divine design. Honor precedes reconciliation, justifies the expression of love, and sustains covenant through sacrifice. In marriage and family, honor restores identity and secures legacy. In generations, honor turns inheritance into momentum.

Scripture Focus

- Matthew 5:44 — Love your enemies
- 1 Peter 2:17 — Honor all men
- Genesis 2:18 — ʽēzer kenegdo (divine complement)
- Ephesians 5:25 — Christ gave Himself for the Church
- Exodus 20:12 — Honor your father and mother
- 1 Corinthians 4:15 — Many instructors, not many fathers
- Proverbs 13:22 — Inheritance to children's children

Truths to Remember

1. Love reacts; honor initiates.

2. Honor reveals value, making the object of our love worthy of it.
3. When love is required where honor has not been established, it becomes torturous.
4. Difference is not dysfunction, honor reappraises it as design.
5. Covenant requires cutting; honor endures the cost.
6. Life sources must be honored, regardless of performance, because they carry origin.
7. Dishonor forces recovery; honor releases continuation.
8. Without honor, inheritance is managed. With honor, legacy is multiplied.

Application

- Shift your focus from how you've been treated to who God designed the other to be.
- Reassess your spouse not by emotional impact, but by divine intention.
- Identify life sources (parents, spiritual fathers, founding leaders) and practice intentional honor toward them.
- Allow God to show you where offense has blocked perception of value.
- Reframe relational differences as strategic, not problematic, and ask God how to honor them.
- Make a decision to preserve not just connection, but purpose, through covenant honor.

Reflection Questions

1. Have I been trying to love where I have not first chosen to honor?
2. Where have I allowed treatment to override identity in my perception of others?
3. Which life sources have I neglected to honor due to their imperfection?
4. Where has dishonor caused me or my children to recover rather than advance?

5. What differences in my spouse or family frustrate me, and how would honor reinterpret them?
6. Am I demanding from relationships what only God was meant to fulfill?

Declaration

"I choose the posture of honor. I no longer allow emotional reactions to determine how I love or lead. I honor those God has placed in my life, not based on performance, but on divine design. Honor reveals value, and I align my love with that revelation. Where honor is restored, love is renewed. I choose legacy over preference, covenant over convenience, and identity over injury. What God joins, I will not fracture. I honor to preserve what love initiates. In Jesus' name, amen."

FINAL BENEDICTION OF THE BOOK TOPIC

Honor is the seed. Glory is the bloom. When you honor God, you cultivate a life weighty with His presence. When you honor others, you participate in Heaven's language of love. And when you honor the process, you become a vessel that shines with the very light of the Lamb.

"Arise, shine, for your light has come."

This is the destiny of sons, to walk in honor, to live in glory, and to reveal the Father in the earth.

AFTERWORD

FROM HONOR TO GLORY, THE JOURNEY CONTINUES

Honor was never meant to end with understanding; it begins with application. It is the posture of every son, the language of every kingdom, and the proof of every disciple who has seen the Father. Wherever honor rises, Heaven responds. Wherever dishonor lingers, glory withdraws.

As I finish these pages, I'm reminded that honor is not a performance, it's a **temperament**. It is how Heaven breathes through humanity. It's found in the patience you show to a stranger, the gratitude you express to a leader, and the forgiveness you extend to one who hurt you. Each act of honor builds a bridge for glory to travel.

We were never called merely to speak of honor but to embody it, to walk covered, to lead gently, to restore what shame stole, and to carry glory well. If this book has stirred anything in you, let it be this prayer:

"Lord, make me a vessel of honor who reflects Your likeness on the earth, and teach me the language of honor".

May the days ahead reveal sons and daughters who live by Heaven's etiquette, a people of weight, humility, and light, so that when others encounter us, they encounter the very culture of the King.

The language of sons is honor,
and the sound of honor is glory.

Christopher Turney

ABOUT THE AUTHOR

Apostle Christopher K. Turney is a revelatory teacher, apostolic father, and founder of Kingdom Reign Ministries, a Kingdom-centered ministry established to raise sons and daughters who transform culture through identity rather than performance.

Known for his ability to reveal timeless truth through prophetic clarity and doctrinal depth, Apostle Turney carries a mandate to restore the foundational principles of the Kingdom of God, reestablish divine order in the Church, and call believers into mature sonship. His ministry is marked by a rare balance of revelation and relational integrity, speaking not only to what people do but to who they are called to become.

A survivor of early childhood trauma and the absence of fatherhood, he encountered the transforming love of the Father that shifted him from striving orphan to secure son. This redemptive journey ignited a passion to help others break cycles of shame, identity distortion, and spiritual performance, leading them into wholeness through the revelation of sonship and Kingdom truth. Today, he serves as a spiritual father to leaders and believers across the United States and abroad, developing apostolic centers, training teachers, and mobilizing Kingdom voices.

A prolific author and theological architect, he has written impactful works such as 'We Wrestle Not', 'A Call to Sonship', 'They Shall Be Saved', 'Tithing: Law or Liberty', and 'The Ekklesia: Heaven's Embassy on Earth', each carrying foundational revelation intended to shift paradigms and build legacy. 'Honor: The Language of Sons' continues this assignment, calling the Body of Christ back to Heaven's culture of value, identity, and relational order.

He resides in Florida and leads Kingdom Reign Ministries with his wife, Jill, alongside a growing family of sons and daughters. His life is dedicated to awakening the Church to its original blueprint, one where presence replaces performance, sonship replaces servanthood, and honor restores what dishonor has broken.

For speaking invitations or ministry inquiries:
- Email: chris@krmchurch.com
- Mailing: 4550 NE Palmetto Dr.
  Jensen Beach, Florida 34957
- Web: www.chrisandjillturney.com

www.ingramcontent.com/pod-product-compliance
Lightning Source LLC
Chambersburg PA
CBHW060348250426
43667CB00051B/2497